# THE
# CONFUSED LAWYER'S
## FIELD GUIDE TO
## THE COURTHOUSE

by

LAWRENCE B. FOX

All rights reserved under International and other applicable Copyright Conventions. Published in the United States by Fox Publications, Inc. No quotations or other portions of this book may be reproduced in any form without written permission from the author.

This book is a work of fiction. Names, characters, places and incidents are the products of the author's imagination or are used fictitiously. Any resemblance to actual events, locales or persons, living or dead, is entirely coincidental.

Copyright 2007 by Lawrence B. Fox. Registered with the Writers Guild of America, East.

ISBN 09724891-6-2

## Table Of Contents

Preface ................................................................. i

Dedication ............................................................ iii

Illustrations ......................................................... v

A Note of Appreciation ........................................ vi

**Chapter One**
Get The Hook ............................................... 1

**Chapter Two**
Polka Dots ................................................... 12

**Chapter Three**
Tea Leaves .................................................. 22

**Chapter Four**
Enclosures ................................................... 35

**Chapter Five**
The Odyssey Of The Three Prodigal Pussycats ... 42

**Chapter Six**
The Velvet Elvis .......................................... 53

**Chapter Seven**
The Novena ................................................. 65

**Chapter Eight**
The Wedgie ................................................. 71

**Chapter Nine**
The Confession ............................................ 77

**Chapter Ten**
The Stress Test ............................................ 84

**Chapter Eleven**
The Ladder ................................................................. 93

**Chapter Twelve**
The Tiffany Lamp ..................................................... 98

**Chapter Thirteen**
It's A Gamble ........................................................... 106

**Chapter Fourteen**
Sic Transit Gloria .................................................... 117

**Chapter Fifteen**
The Heat's On ......................................................... 125

**Chapter Sixteen**
Congratulations ....................................................... 130

**Chapter Seventeen**
Big ............................................................................ 138

**Chapter Eighteen**
The Midnight Star .................................................. 145

**Chapter Nineteen**
The Lost Thought ................................................... 152

**Chapter Twenty**
But They're Already Dead .................................... 155

**Chapter Twenty-One**
The Proposition ...................................................... 162

**Chapter Twenty-Two**
The Valley Of The Weedwackers ....................... 169

**Chapter Twenty-Three**
The Helpful Grandnephew ................................. 173

**Chapter Twenty-Four**
The Security Clearance ....................................... 188

**Chapter Twenty-Five**
The Guilty Party ................................................. 197

**Chapter Twenty-Six**
The Outsourcing ................................................. 204

**Chapter Twenty-Seven**
The Copper Caper ............................................... 212

**Chapter Twenty-Eight**
Please Take A Number ....................................... 217

**Chapter Twenty-Nine**
What's Your Sign? .............................................. 223

**Chapter Thirty**
The Trail Of Evidence ........................................ 230

**Chapter Thirty-One**
Two Races Well Run .......................................... 237

**Chapter Thirty-Two**
Fish ..................................................................... 248

**Chapter Thirty-Three**
Bullshit Bullshit ...................................................... 258

**Chapter Thirty-Four**
She Might Squawk ................................................ 264

**Chapter Thirty-Five**
The Annual Exemption ......................................... 269

**Chapter Thirty-Six**
The Engagement Ring............................................ 276

**Chapter Thirty-Seven**
The Foghorn........................................................... 280

**Chapter Thirty-Eight**
The Unsatisfied Mortgage..................................... 286

**Chapter Thirty-Nine**
Enemies No More ................................................. 293

**Chapter Forty**
Calling Cards......................................................... 300

**Chapter Forty-One**
Irving Wiggleman ................................................. 305

**Chapter Forty-Two**
I'll Be Right There ................................................ 314

**Chapter Forty-Three**
The Monogrammed Towel.................................... 318

# PREFACE

This collection of 43 short stories constitutes my fourth humorous book and focuses upon the ironies that arise in the private practice of law. The comedic narratives found within these pages will, I trust, be enjoyed both by members of the legal profession and by non-lawyers. All of the stories are true, except where I have lied a little.

Each chapter contains an independent story that can be read separately and out of order from any other chapter. The common element running throughout these sagas is the noble pursuit of Justice. Unfortunately, finding Justice sometimes proves to be elusive, since most of the Justice that might once have existed in the courtrooms you are about to visit has already been extracted, and plans to re-stock some more of it may have been delayed. As any lawyer will confirm, Justice occurs only when the lawyer's client wins. Injustice occurs when the lawyer's client loses. It therefore follows that if there is more than one litigant, and only one party prevails, Justice and Injustice will probably occur simultaneously in the same courtroom before the same confused judge.

A word about my concept of humor. Humor related to the practice of law emerges in its purest form when the narrator shares a novel perspective regarding institutions or concepts, resulting in a re-evaluation of what might have hitherto been considered quite normal or acceptable. Humor naturally arises in the practice of law, since certain essential comedic elements simultaneously exist: confused and irrational clients who seek Justice within a courtroom setting. Simply stated, rational people never seek redress in a courtroom. Rational people are rational because they resolve their differences without third party intervention. Only an irrational person would chance his or her future happiness by paying some lawyer to appear before some agitated judge who may have spent the previous night living with an irrational spouse.  Only irrational people believe in the tooth fairy or believe that Justice can be found lurking somewhere in a courtroom.  It's a wonder that Lady Justice ever finds her way into a courtroom in the first place, given the fact she's blindfolded.

Inappropriate language has been used sparingly by the author, and only when the story required it.  Disparaging remarks, or topics that shock rather than clarify or enlighten will not be found in these pages.

You are about to meet some characters who decided to test the legal system, litigants who wondered if any juris or any prudence was left for them to claim as their very own.  These folks all have something in common - I told them not to go to trial.  As a result, if they won, they weren't inclined to pay me, since I hadn't sufficiently believed in their case and Justice probably prevailed in spite of my lackluster efforts.  If they lost, they weren't inclined to pay me, because I was an inept lawyer.  There is so much Injustice skulking about out there.

If you enjoy reading these misadventures, please let me know.  I can be reached at lbfox@fwmpc.com.  My other humorous books await your perusal: *There's No Justice - Just Court Costs* (1999); *Has My Lawyer Called Yet?* (2002); and *No Noose Is Good Noose* (2004).

At Bethlehem, Pennsylvania  2007

## DEDICATION

This book is dedicated to all the aspiring writers who have not yet published their first book. Here is a short story of encouragement just for you.

A few years ago, I wrote a humorous manuscript, or so I thought. For reasons that still remain unclear, no agent or publisher shared the same enthusiasm for my masterpiece. So I contacted one of those print-on-demand places, forked over $87.38, and instantly became the proud author-owner of 10 books sporting glossy covers. William Shakespeare should have had it so easy.

Rumor had it that amazon.com sold books, so I sent "them" one of my treatises, representing a tenth of my entire first-run inventory. Five days later I received an unsigned e-mail acknowledging that my book had arrived and that it was now listed for sale, along with Amazon's other five million book titles. I was given a sales popularity number reflecting that I was five millionth on Amazon's bestseller list. This humbling fact was also conspicuously posted on the Internet site that advertised my book.

Three months went by. There was an unexpected unsigned e-mail from Amazon. Good news: my book had been purchased by someone in Wisconsin. I could expect a check for 50 percent of the net sales price, less certain deductions, sometime during the next 60 days. This was unquestionably one of the more important days of my life. What a metamorphosis! Not only was I acknowledged as a published author - my work was now selling nationally.

Amazon e-mailed me to request another book. I was in demand and developing a readership. Best of all, my standing among all published authors had experienced a meteoric rise. My revised sales popularity number now stood near 2,500,000. *Mirabile dictu*, with the exception of just two and a half million other writers, I was the most widely read author on the planet.

The best was yet to come. Two months later, I received a check for $11.25. I fondled my first royalty payment for about 10 minutes, debating whether I should simply laminate it or have it framed. Now let's see, each book had cost $8.74 to print. The postage to Amazon ran $2.00, for a total of $10.74. What was $11.25 minus $10.74? I had made a net profit of 51 cents! That was more than Ford and General Motors had earned during the same fiscal year.

My second book sold before the onset of winter. My sales performance number shot up again. Since one-fifth of my entire inventory was depleted, I decided I better have some more books handy to keep pace with demand. The words "Second Printing" appeared on the inside cover of the next 10 books I ordered.

Being a responsible citizen, I completed the requisite sales tax form Q37-B and sent it to the state treasurer with the appropriate remittance. Apparently these sales records were accessible to the public. Soon I began to receive offers from around the country to appear at writers' seminars to divulge the secrets of profitable authorship.

I found myself smiling in the mirror. The agents and publishers who rejected my manuscript probably learned an important lesson. I had, in less than one year, netted 65 cents after payment of sales tax, and I didn't have to give those arrogant fools 10 percent.

# ILLUSTRATIONS

Illustrations by Louis J. Mattioli III, Esquire:

Get the Hook
Tea Leaves
The Odyssey of the Three Prodigal Pussycats
The Velvet Elvis
The Wedgie
The Confession
The Tiffany Lamp
Sic Transit Gloria
Big
The Midnight Star
The Lost Thought
The Proposition
The Valley of the Weedwackers
The Security Clearance
The Outsourcing
Please Take a Number
The Trail of Evidence
Two Races Well Run
Fish
Bullshit Bullshit
She Might Squawk
The Annual Exemption
The Foghorn
I'll Be Right There

Illustrations by Dana Smith-Mansell:

The Novena
The Stress Test
But They're Already Dead
The Copper Caper

## A Note of Appreciation

This book arises from the culmination of effort of several talented friends whose assistance was essential in order to achieve the elusive goal of publication.

Susan Tobey, Esquire and Dianne Pelaggi provided their insightful editing skills.

Richard and Joyce Harwick assisted with the cover photographs.

Laura Savercool and Tammi Gross patiently typed the manuscript.

Laura M. Mattioli, Esquire assisted with coordination of production and design.

Carl B. Williamson, Esquire, aided with technical support.

Thank you for your boundless energy and dedication to this project.

Larry

# CHAPTER ONE

## Get The Hook

The practice of law is encumbered with burdensome and inefficient rules and procedures that serve only to delay and frustrate the timely pursuit of justice. Such was not always the case. There was a time when, if a criminal did something wrong, within the span of 24 hours, he was tortured, he confessed, had a hand chopped off, or perhaps he was hung. Today, we carry on conversations half way around the world by speaking into one-ounce telephones hidden in an ear, and yet our system of jurisprudence crawls at a snail's pace.

Stanley Fribble owned a small, aging apartment building on Sixth Street near an abandoned cigar factory. He rented its four units to low-income tenants, some of whom received government-subsidized housing assistance. Every so often, a tenant would get behind in the payment of rent. That's when Stanley would show up at my door.

"The new guy in the second-floor west apartment is two months late again. I knew he was trouble the first day I met him. But I felt sorry for the bum, what with his limp and all. You know what I mean? So I let him sign the lease."

"Yes," I replied, "a limp."

"So now I'm out $450 plus another $450, and there's a late fee of $20. That's $920, and I just had a new load of heating oil delivered that I have to pay for. Everybody thinks it's easy being a landlord. Well, it ain't. School taxes are up and I don't even got any kids. Some of the tenants do. You know what I mean."

"Yes, school taxes," I replied.

"So I want you to evict him and get my back rent. Nobody ever let me live for free. Why, when I was just 16, I got my first job down at the corner ... "

"Excuse me, Mr. Fribble ... "
" ... drugstore jerking sodas ... "
" ... Mr. Fribble ... "
"What?"

"If you go to the magistrate's office and fill out the eviction forms by yourself, you'll save over an hour of my legal fees. Just let me know when the hearing date is scheduled and I'll be there to represent you."

That made fiscal sense to Fribble. Our initial office conference had already taken 20 minutes.

The next morning, Fribble made his way to the magistrate's office. He stood in line at the receptionist's plate-glass window and was finally given the proper form to commence eviction proceedings.

"Fill this out in triplicate," the secretary standing behind the bulletproof window instructed. "It's best if you use a typewriter, since the third copy goes to the constable for service on the defendant, and so it must be legible. Attach a copy of the executed lease, complete the 30 questions on the back, including the defendant's Social Security number, telephone number, and names of all co-tenants, and any dogs with vicious tendencies. A check for $65 must accompany the form with a separate check to the constable based on mileage from this office to location of service. Only certified checks or bank teller checks will be accepted. Make sure your attorney's identification number is stated in answer 17B. If you have a claim for rent due, the computation may include legal interest compounded daily at a rate not to exceed ..."

"Excuse me," Stanley interjected, "I'll have my lawyer get in touch with you."

The next day, Stanley brought over the form. My paralegal typed the answers, made copies of the lease and obtained two bank checks. Stanley signed the form.

This assistance took another 30 hours of billable time.

- - -

My receptionist, secretary, paralegal and junior associate each expect a paycheck every Friday. They just delivered more heating fuel to my office because my staff is composed entirely of females. It's October, and these women begin to turn bluish if the office ambient temperature dips below 72 degrees. It costs $150 per hour to operate my office. When I charge a client $200 per hour, I gross $50 per hour. The Uncle Sam and other governmental entities take half of the remaining $50. Yesterday my plumber charged me $60 an hour to fix the office toilet again. And that didn't include travel time.

- - -

I wrote the mandatory fee agreement letter to Stanley to advise him of the cost of my services.

"What? $200 an hour! That's highway robbery! Five hours from now I'll owe you more than the disputed $920!" he fumed.

Quite possibly. My office had already expended the better part of an hour in services and advanced nearly $100 in costs to the magistrate. The letter and this conversation added another 30 minutes.

"Can I sue my tenant for your fees?" an astute Stanley inquired.

"Yes, but if he has nothing, you'll collect nothing," I opined.

"That's not fair," Stanley protested.

Things aren't always *fair*. On Friday, I signed four paychecks even though no one had bothered to pay *me* for over a week.

The constable served the tenant, Fabus Tarpey, with the eviction notice, and that prompted the magistrate to schedule a hearing three weeks after the date of service. This was the first open hearing date available. Twenty-four hours before the hearing was to take place, I received a telephone call from Tarpey's legal counsel, Elmer Bernbaum, Esquire.

"I don't think we've ever met," I began.

"Probably not. I'm a legal aid attorney in Philadelphia specializing in disputed evictions of indigent and needy tenants."

Oh no! I was now doing battle with an attorney who paid no overhead, whose office was subsidized by my taxes, and who could take this case to the U.S. Supreme Court without charging his client a dime. Correspondence usually arrived on recycled paper inside an envelope sporting insufficient postage.

As a side note, it had been my past experience that such crusaders have one notable common characteristic: no sense of humor. I decided to find out.

"Counselor?"

"What?"

"Do you know why you never see a skunk in church?"

"No. Why?"

"They don't want to sit in their own pew."

Crickets and dead silence.

"Listen," Bernbaum replied, "I've sent my client, Mr. Tarpey, to the Consumer Counseling Crisis Center to review his budgetary needs. I have asked the magistrate for a 30-day continuance to evaluate Tarpey's finances. If you don't agree to this request, we'll file for immediate bankruptcy protection and obtain an automatic indefinite stay. In the meantime, I've drafted my first set of interrogatories addressed to your landlord, inquiring how he intends to bring this uninhabitable leasehold up to minimum housing code standards. I'm filing a formal complaint with the city housing inspector and demanding a hearing within 45 days. The other tenants in the building may be joining in that suit."

"Uninhabitable! He's been living there rent-free for two months without a single complaint," I responded.

"The paint on his windowsill is peeling, the hall light doesn't work and the hot water temperature fluctuates. He has shown amazing restraint living under such desperate conditions."

"Does this mean he's not going to pay the rent?" I innocently inquired.

Bernbaum burst out laughing.

And here I mistakenly thought he was humorless.

- - -

It had been a tough week. I needed to relax. I loaded my golf clubs into my car and drove to the municipal driving range. Nothing like a bucket of balls to clear the old noggin.

I sent two errant slices into the woods on the left. Consistency is a good trait.

"Fox. Is that you?"

Startled, I looked up in mid-swing. It was Joe Kenna, the insurance agent. He was a pleasant fellow and a pretty good golfer. I lowered my three wood and walked out of my protective cubicle to shake his hand.

"This is fortuitous," he observed. "We're looking for a fourth player. Interested in a quick round on the short nine-hole course? It'll be a foursome."

"Who's playing?" I asked.

"Barry and Earl Sage. They dabble in real estate. They've been clients of mine for years. They rarely break a hundred. You'll fit right in."

I handed my bucket of balls to an overjoyed kid and accompanied Joe to the nine-hole course.

Soon Barry, Earl and I were hitting slices into the woods, the pond, the marsh, other fairways or into little Bermuda Triangle-like places where the ball, once dispatched there, was never to be seen again. We began to bond as only truly inept golfers do. We had time to talk after launching a couple of balls into another thicket of brambles.

"I don't see them. Do you?"

"No. Watch out for the hornet's nest!"

"There's nothing like a round of golf to take your mind off things."

At the end of nine holes, we had encountered and survived several dangers. We had lost a total of 12 balls. We sat down in the clubhouse to review our exploits and savor the experience over mile-high sandwiches. Ultimately the conversation transitioned to the inevitable - what we did for a living.

Barry and Earl owned a mobile home park, the big one just past Ferndale. They were "hands on" proprietors. They personally installed each residential unit, connected it to utility services, wrote up the leases and collected the rent. They had been running this business for 20 years.

"There have been some bumps in the road," Barry confided, as he wiped his red face and bald head with a handkerchief. Earl projected the same image: a self-confident, hard working man who got things done.

"I'm a lawyer," I explained as I waited for the usual lawyer jokes. They didn't come.

"Do you like what you do?" Earl asked.

I pondered for a moment. "Most of the time," I told my new friends, "but there are times when the nonsense can be overwhelming."

"Give me an example," Barry suggested.

I didn't have to think for long. "This week some taxpayer-subsidized charlatan ripped off my client for two months of rent with some cute delay tactics. His client, the tenant, will never pay a dime and will probably keep himself holed up in the apartment another six months. It'll cost the landlord a couple thousand dollars for me to blast the scoundrel out. The worst part is my client will blame me for the delays, and the other tenants will have to pay for the nonsense, since their rents will go up. It's just like the jokers who drive without car insurance. We all pay for their free ride."

My new golfing buddies raised their eyebrows at each other. Then they turned to me.

"We've got 300 rental units and not one delinquent tenant," Barry boasted.

"We've never had anyone stiff us for the rent," Earl confirmed. "Not in 20 years."

I was astonished. "What's your secret?" I asked.

"You really want to know?" Earl inquired.

"You bet," I assured him.

"Okay. Tomorrow begins the first of the week and a new month. The rent is due. I've got the feeling one or two new renters may come up with excuses. Drop by around five at the end of the business day, and we'll show you why we don't need lawyers to collect our fees," Earl proposed.

"You're not going to hurt anyone, are you?" I questioned.

"Of course not," Earl promised. "We prefer to prevail through diplomatic reasoning and understanding."

*Reasoning and understanding.* Perhaps those were the concepts I should have utilized all along. Filing a formal complaint was probably too intimidating and served only to alienate the poor tenant.

"I'll be there," I assured them. I couldn't wait to learn the secret of their success.

- - -

Peaceful Valley Trailer Park lay secluded at the end of a quarter-mile gravel road. Farmland and rolling hills surrounded the 300 lots serving as home sites to various prefabricated metal and vinyl residences, all of which were rolled, towed or somehow transported there. Fifty years ago, the original units were referred to as "trailers," and many still sat on wheels, as if their inhabitants, similar to a turtle, planned to move their living quarters at a moment's notice. With time, the term "mobile home" caught on as the newer dwellings took on a more upscale nature. Half a century ago, the Spartan utilities at each site consisted only of a rubber hose for water and an outdoor propane tank. The single community telephone sat outside the shared bathrooms.

When Earl and Barry took possession of the place, improvements were undertaken. They dug underground utilities to each lot. Water, gas, telephone and cable were offered. Residents could flush their own toilets in their own homes. As each new residence arrived, Earl and Barry would personally connect the underground utility services. There was ample room to crawl underneath each unit to reach exposed pipes and cable connections engineered at the factory.

These partners were hands-on landlords. They knew how to operate the backhoe, the tractor and the pickup truck. They corrected electrical, plumbing and other utility problems. They were conversant with the office computers, they paid the bills and collected rents. They both resided at the park and, as a result, offered around-the-clock emergency services. With no need for a costly outside maintenance team, these owners were able to keep the lot rents stable and moderate. There was very little homeowner turnover.

I drove into the mobile home community about five p.m. and parked near the one-room office, a log cabin that appeared to be the only structure permanently affixed to the earth. My hosts were standing next to a large yellow tractor. Barry was loading a dented toolbox into the rear of the machine. This tractor was so big that it possessed a front bench seat upon which the operator and two passengers could sit.

Earl stuck out a friendly hand in my direction. "Have any trouble finding the place?"

"No," I confirmed, as I shook his hand. "The directions were great."

Barry joined us.

"Well, just as we suspected, one of the new tenants hasn't paid her rent, and it was due today. We need to remind her of her obligation to the community. When one person fails to pay, it puts a strain on the budget to the detriment of everyone else."

So very true, I thought to myself. With the diplomatic reasoning and understanding I was about to witness, hopefully the tardy tenant would acknowledge the need for timely compliance.

"Well, let's all get onboard the tractor and see if Ms. Evans is home," Earl suggested.

He and Barry hoisted a bucket with a thick metal chain inside into the tractor and motioned for me to take a seat.

A tractor? Wouldn't an initial phone call to the tenant have sufficed?

Barry brought the 400-horsepower diesel engine to life and grabbed the steering wheel with both hands. It was only then that I realized I had never before ridden on a tractor. It seemed as if everything was vibrating: the tractor, my teeth, Barry, Earl, the toolbox and the bucket containing the chain.

We headed up a slight hill and around another as we bounced up and down on the gravel road. Mobile homes and trailers of every color, configuration and age passed by on both sides of the roadway. Once in a while a resident would give us a thumbs up, and the two partners would wave back. I began to get the impression that the tenants who greeted us in this fashion had sent a silent acknowledgment in our direction that they understood what we were doing, and approved of it.

We turned to the right and stopped on a side street where a modest grey mobile home about 24 feet in length reposed. There were no bushes or shrubs, nor any protective metal skirt surrounding the bottom of the residence. As a result, one could see that this home rested on several stacks of exposed cinder blocks. The water line and other utilities were visible from the bottom of the home. Obviously the structure had only recently been transported to this location.

Earl dismounted from the vibrating tractor and walked up the dirt path leading to three cement blocks serving as temporary steps ascending to the front door. He knocked, waited and then he knocked again. A lady, perhaps 40 years old, opened the door and they began to engage in a conversation. I could not hear this discussion over the roar of the diesel engine, but I did note the body language of both landlord and tenant. He shook his head; she shrugged her shoulders. Neither appeared to be pleased. Finally Earl turned and proceeded back to the tractor. Ms. Evans slowly closed her door.

Earl made his report. "She says she doesn't have the rent, that she just got laid off and that maybe next month things'll be better."

"That's unfortunate," Barry noted, as he reached for his toolbox.

"Unfortunate," Earl repeated, as he strained to lift the bucket containing the heavy metal chain.

The two men apparently had no need to discuss strategy or their options. Barry crawled under the mobile home and disconnected the water line, the sewer hookup and the electrical cable. As he did so, Earl ran the one-inch-thick chain from the tractor to the home's rear hitch, a fixture used by the manufacturer to pull the structure along the highway.

Earl gave the "all clear" sign, so Barry put the tractor in gear and slowly moved forward until the 70-foot chain became taut, dangling above the ground. Barry inched the machine ahead and, as he did so, Ms. Evans' ensnared mobile home made a screeching sound as it began to take leave of its cinderblock foundation. Not unexpectedly, Ms. Evans made a hasty appearance at her front door. The tractor engine was racing, but this time I could hear what she said.

"WHAT THE HELL ARE YOU PEOPLE DOING!"

"Getting the lot ready for a paying tenant," Barry explained. "We're moving you over to the non-paying area."

"You can't do that!"

"Watch us."

"Wait a minute. Wait just a minute!" Ms. Evans disappeared into her very *mobile* home and quickly emerged with a fistful of cash, which she thrust in Barry's direction. Barry counted out what was due and handed the remaining bills back to the startled woman. Then he crawled under the home and reconnected the hoses and pipes as Earl disconnected the chain from the hitch. We returned to the office in less than 15 minutes.

"Would you have pulled her home off its cinder blocks?" I asked my two mentors.

"Hard to tell," Barry responded. "Never had anyone fail to pay us. A little reasoning and understanding. That's all it takes."

# CHAPTER TWO

## Polka Dots

There is a reason I have never sought to become a judge: I wouldn't be very good at the job. Judges must at all times display a judicial temperament creating an illusion of impartial, unemotional neutrality. When a defendant who has just murdered 16 people in front of a dozen witnesses enters the courtroom, a learned and seasoned judge will refrain from displaying his or her true feelings, and will effortlessly refer to the accused as "sir" or "the defendant." The judge will assure the perpetrator that he has all sorts of rights and that for the moment he is presumed to be innocent.

When a baseball hero hits an historic record-breaking, game-winning home run, thousands of spectators at the ballpark display their emotions with abandon. But there's one exception: the umpire standing closest to the action at home plate. His adrenalin may be flowing too, but he must hide his feelings. He's the only person who can't jump up and down.

Judges are umpires who never get to swing a bat or cheer. They can neither laugh nor cry at the comedic tragedy unfolding before them.

Furman Dingelacher and his wife, Sylvia, had run out of luck, not that they had much to begin with. Two months ago, Furman lost his job packing cans of horsemeat on night shift at the dog food plant. His lack of formal education limited his search for new employment. But his four small children needed to eat, as did Sylvia, who suffered from life-threatening ulcers in her intestinal tract, a condition that had occasioned multiple surgeries, with more possibly to follow. They no longer had health insurance.

"How are you folks?" I asked, still unaware of their problems.

Sylvia picked up an infant who was stirring in a beat-up stroller. She gently rocked the baby as Furman did the talking.

"The sheriff served these papers on us," he explained as he pushed a thick legal-size document across the table in my direction.

The title in bold print at the top of the formal complaint left no doubt regarding the severity of the problem:

*IN THE COURT OF COMMON PLEAS OF
NORTHAMPTON COUNTY, PENNSYLVANIA
CIVIL DIVISION - LAW*

| | | |
|---|---|---|
| *FEDERATED UNITED BANK,* | : | *ACTION IN MORTGAGE* |
| | : | *FORECLOSURE* |
| *Plaintiff,* | : | |
| *vs* | : | *NUMBER 20053 OF 2007* |
| | : | |
| *FURMAN DINGELACHER,* | : | |
| | : | |
| *and* | : | |
| | : | |
| *SYLVIA DINGELACHER,* | : | |
| | : | |
| *Defendants.* | : | |

"I've been late payin' the bank," Furman admitted. "Lost my job. With her in and out of the hospital and no insurance, things have been tight."

I paged through the complaint. They were seven months delinquent on a mortgage secured by a row home located directly across and downwind from the city dump. They had purchased this shack three years ago for $18,000 by paying $1,000 down and taking out a $17,000 mortgage. With interest, back payments, penalties and bank legal fees added on, they now owed $21,709 on a hovel worth about $20,000, if the prevailing winds were to blow the other way.

"We don't know what to do. I got two toddlers and two pre-schoolers and no place to go. Can they throw us out of our home?" Furman asked.

"Can you pay anything toward the debt?"

"Not right now I can't. Maybe when I find a job."

I decided it wasn't the time to ask if they could afford a lawyer. Another *pro bono* case.

That afternoon I telephoned Dalrymple, Kresge, Forrester and Sheetz, a mega-lawyer Philadelphia law firm representing the bank. One of the junior associates in their mortgage foreclosure department took my call. Cranston Summerfield, Esquire, and I exchanged the usual pleasantries. But when I asked him if he might delay throwing my clients into the street, his voice took on a degree of formality.

"No can do, counselor," he responded. "They already got a seven-month free bite at the mortgage apple. I have a responsibility to the bank whose loans are federally insured by public taxpayer monies, so my obligation also extends to you and the other fine citizens of this great country."

"But Mrs. Dingelacher is sick and there are four young children," I interjected.

"Federated United isn't a charity, Fox. It's an internationally traded institution. If you were in my place, would you counsel the bank to look the other way? Suppose the bank gave your clients more time? Wouldn't such a dangerous precedent become a valid defense for every other debtor who made a late payment? We can't just discriminate in favor of your clients, now can we?"

What a glamorous, self-righteous, and advantageous position being legal counsel to a bank. The client's got money - lots of it. That meant this guy Summerfield would probably get paid, no matter what. Perhaps some day, I might be lucky enough to foreclose on some procrastinating debtors, throw them and their worthless dog into the street, all the while knowing in my heart of hearts that I have done the right thing by protecting the rights of countless stockholders and the good citizens of this fine country.

Three weeks later, Attorney Summerfield sent me notice he was beginning eviction proceedings. That afternoon I got a call from luckless Furman. Some constable had just nailed a sign on his front door scheduling a judicial sale of the home.

"Can't you do something?" he pleaded. "We've got nowhere to go."

"Are you absolutely sure you're unable to pay anything toward the delinquent mortgage?" I inquired.

"Nothing at all right now," he confirmed.

I pushed 10 files belonging to paying clients toward the corner of my desk and began to draft a "Petition For Emergency Relief."

I had, once upon a time, taken a creative writing course in college, and since there was no theory in law I knew of to rescue my clients, I hoped the muse of originality might enter my brain and help me formulate something helpful to assist Mr. and Mrs. Dingelacher.

I wrote that the Dingelachers were nice people and that they had every intention of paying their mortgage, just as soon as Furman found a job. I noted that Mrs. Dingelacher wasn't feeling well and that they had four young children. I explained that since the bank had lots of money, it didn't need the paltry sum allegedly owed by the defendants. I concluded the petition by reminding the court that my clients had a dog that, similar to the Dingelachers, had no place to go.

I filed my creative petition at the courthouse, sent Attorney Summerfield a copy, and listed the matter for an emergency hearing on the following Monday, just two days before the scheduled judicial sale. I told the Dingelachers to be present in Courtroom Number One at nine a.m. sharp.

"We'll be there," she assured me in her soft voice. "And don't you worry. We have faith that everything will be okay."

I didn't sleep Sunday night, knowing that while faith works fine in church, we wouldn't be talking to a priest on

Monday. In 24 hours, the Dingelachers would probably be homeless.

The next morning I climbed the familiar worn marble steps leading to Courtroom Number One. As usual, this great chamber was rapidly filling with scores of people, all of whom sought relief in one form or another. There were young parents hoping to adopt an infant, criminals trying to make bail, property owners arguing over disputed boundary lines, parties to a condemnation proceeding, applicants for protection from domestic abuse, beneficiaries seeking distribution from an estate, parties pursuing a divorce or spousal support, applicants attempting to schedule an arbitration, police officers waiting to be called as witnesses, and assistant district attorneys objecting to attempts by public defenders to suppress evidence. And there were Mrs. Dingelacher, Attorney Summerfield and me, convening to consider whether a judicial sale would take place, thereby dumping my clients and their gaggle of offspring into the street.

"Where is your husband?" I inquired. "He must be present as well."

"Downstairs in the lobby with the children. I didn't want them running around getting into mischief. When the hearing starts, I'll get Furman and the kids."

I introduced myself to Summerfield. He was what I expected. About 27, just out of law school, wearing the requisite big city, nondescript tweed three-piece *I'm a go-getter new associate in a large Philly firm* suit. He had probably set his alarm clock for five a.m. so he could commute the 60 miles through heavy traffic to arrive on time here in the hinterlands. Stupid. We shook hands.

"This is my first time in Northampton County," he admitted as he surveyed the ceremonial chamber and the throngs of litigants and attorneys milling about. "How do we get assigned to a judge and a courtroom?"

"The president judge will ascend the bench in a few minutes and will call each case listed for today to determine if the parties are ready to proceed. There are usually five

I now had a perspective on how Garbonne conducted hearings. He had seen it all before, thousands of times. No emotion, no fanfare, just pay what's due, or ba-da-bing ba-da-boom.

The Dingelachers sat in a back pew, accompanied by their four girls. Each child was about one inch shorter than the next older sister. They were all attired in the same red-and-white polka dot dresses that Mrs. Dingelacher had acquired at the dollar store.

"Federated United Bank versus Dingelacher," the tipstaff called out.

We were up to bat. I made my way to the bench, accompanied by Attorney Summerfield. Garbonne didn't bother to look up. His grim, all-business face was studying my emergency petition for special relief - the petition that didn't contain a single valid legal argument - the petition based upon mushy sentimentality for my clients who last tendered a mortgage payment the previous winter.

The judged rubbed what was left of his hair. "Who's who here?"

"Cranston Summerfield for the bank, Your Honor."

I looked at this kid standing next to me, full of himself and his new diploma. Had I ever been 27? Had I ever been so completely self-assured, yet so blind?

"Lawrence Fox for the defendants, Your Honor," I announced.

The judge stared at me as if his x-ray vision were studying the inner workings of what was left of my brain.

"Interesting petition, Fox. Still, I didn't come across any citations to case law or any statutory language."

"That's true, Your Honor. Sometimes such things aren't very helpful. Sometimes I just let the facts speak for themselves."

"Are your clients present, Mr. Fox?"

"Yes, they are."

"Why not have them join us here at the bench?"

"Certainly, Your Honor." I turned and motioned for Mr. and Mrs. Dingelacher to come forward. They did as requested, accompanied by their bashful daughters. The oldest, who only came up to her father's waist, led her sisters in a chain of little hands. The girls, resplendent among a multitude of red-and-white polka dots, now fidgeted before the court. The judge adjusted his glasses as he bent over the bench to get a better view.

"Mortgage foreclosure," he mumbled to himself. "You've scheduled a sale of the house?" Garbonne inquired of Summerfield.

"Tomorrow," the three-piece-suit responded.

"And your clients haven't been able to pay the bank for seven months?" the judge questioned.

I thought about the bum His Honor had just locked up for nonpayment of child support. I pondered what the proper answer might be. I wondered what I was doing here, with this stupid expression on my face. Suddenly, there came a tiny voice out of nowhere.

"Daddy says we'll be living in our car, unless the judge is wise and good. Mommy cries at night."

It was the tallest of the small fries.

"What's your name?" the judge asked.

"Rebecca, but everyone at school calls me Becky," she responded politely, as her siblings hid behind her.

"Rebecca," the judge echoed, gazing out over the courtroom. He was suddenly a thousand miles away recalling another Rebecca he once knew. Was that a tear glistening in his eye? Then just as fast, he snapped his gaze on Summerfield.

"You plan on putting these polka dots in the street?" he demanded of the neophyte lawyer, who still thought he was attending a legal proceeding.

"You see, Judge, the bank has shareholders who do not expect to subsidize charities. And by failing to take action, a dangerous precedent may be set ... "

It did not appear that Garbonne, who was lost among the polka dots, was listening to this well-reasoned argument.

"The bank has been very patient in this matter," cold-blooded Summerfield continued. "The case law is clear that where a default in payment occurs - "

I decided to step in. "Hey, pal," I whispered to the boy genius, "I'd give it a rest. You don't want to upset the judge, do you?"

I, too, was in a vulnerable emotional state. All those client interviews, the petition full of nonsense and now this difficult hearing, and yet I hadn't been paid a dime. Probably never would be. A tear of self-pity began to form in my eye as well.

"We'll take a five-minute recess," Garbonne proclaimed as he stood up, blew his nose and exited the bench. A few minutes later, the tipstaff approached Summerfield and asked him to join the judge in chambers alone for a little chat.

I never became privy to what was discussed behind those closed doors. Actually, I never saw Summerfield again. He simply disappeared, as did his action in mortgage foreclosure.

Not long ago the Dingelachers sent me a Christmas card. They reported that the bank's foreclosure notice blew away during the last snowstorm, and that Furman recently found a job working night shift at the varnish factory. There was a five-dollar bill tucked inside the envelope. Paying clients.

# CHAPTER THREE

## Tea Leaves

Somebody may have killed Agnes Fitch. At least that's what the police theorized. After all, the classic indications that a homicide had occurred were present. A large quantity of blood on her living room rug. Her sudden and unexplained disappearance. Her dog abandoned and unfed for three days. Her mail and newspapers uncollected. Evidence of a vicious struggle, including a broken lamp and shattered TV screen. They even found a quantity of hair, possibly hers, pulled out by the roots. But what the cops couldn't seem to locate was a body, or for that matter, a motive behind the crime.

Admittedly, there were reasons someone might have done away with old Agnes. She was obnoxious and had no real friends. She seemed to go out of her way to antagonize anyone who crossed her path. Seipstown was such a small village that everyone knew everyone, and everyone knew to keep clear of the widow Fitch. Even her dog appeared to lack the basic social graces.

Agnes lived alone in a forlorn mobile home set back in the woods. Her only source of income came from Social Security. She had nothing of value. Whoever killed her didn't remove anything from the trailer, because there was nothing of value to steal.

The Seipstown police force was composed of three cops, a chief and two part-timers. There had never been a murder in this tiny municipality, and so this was their first murder investigation. Chief Fitzgibbons struggled to do the best he could, but any modest progress in the case seemed imperceptible. After a few weeks, he reluctantly called upon the state police for assistance, but by then the crime scene had been compromised, and there was little that these experts could accomplish.

With each passing day, the townsfolk grew more uneasy. Doors and windows were locked for the first time in memory. What had actually happened to the widow, and if it was murder, who was the murderer living among them? Some of the citizenry now looked upon the chief and his part-timers as incompetents unable to protect the tight-knit community. The chief sensed this loss of confidence and dedicated all of his energy to chasing down every lead or shred of evidence, but without success.

One of the part-time patrol officers, Harold Portley, had a novel suggestion. "Chief ... I've been thinkin'... "

"About what?"

"The Fitch case. We've run plum out of leads. Maybe it's time you consulted Madame LaRue for some new clues."

"The fake fortuneteller at the end of Main Street! Are you out of your mind, Portley? You want me to ask some crystal ball gazer to assist with our murder investigation?"

"I wouldn't be too quick writing her off, Chief. She's been known to have answers when other sources of information have failed."

"How in heaven's name did you reach that hairbrained conclusion?"

"I'll admit it. I've used her services on a couple of occasions. She's given me helpful answers to things nobody else could have possibly known."

"You paid good money for some charlatan to peer into a crystal ball and ... "

"She ain't just some run-of-the-mill charlatan. She's a recognized para-abnormal or something. She has an advanced degree in studying the past and future just like one of them stockbrokers, or a meteorologist on the weather channel."

"Have you lost all your marbles?"

"What can it hurt, Chief? All we've done is chase after dead-end leads. Why just last month Madame LaRue told me my grandmother was going to pass away."

"Your grandmother was 97."

"Yes, but a *young* 97. There were times Grammy didn't even use her wheelchair. All I'm sayin' is it might not hurt to have a brief consultation. What have you got to lose?"

The next day a clueless Chief Fitzgibbons drove to the edge of town and knocked on Miss LaRue's door. It was already ajar.

"Pleez enterre my inner sanctum, Chief Fitzgibbons," the inviting voice with the exotic, unrecognizable accent sang out. "I've been expecting you."

The incredulous chief waded through a forest of glass beads suspended on hanging ropes and inched his way into a dimly lit room. He found Miss LaRue sitting at a tapestry-covered table gazing into an illuminated crystal ball. He didn't notice any wires, so he concluded it was probably operated by battery.

"Pleez seet down, Chief."

*What am I doing here?* the chief thought to himself, as he obediently took a seat. Was that his heart pumping in time to the new age background music?

"How did you know it was me at your door, Madame LaRue?"

"Pleez, Chief, vhat a ridiculous qvestion. Madame LaRue knows every-ting."

"She does?"

"Vhat do you take me for, an amateur? De Agnes Fitch murderrr. Is dat not so? Now place your hands on de table ... Good ... I see dat you need help ... I might be able to assist ... if you put aside your obvious doubts ... I don't vork vell vid non-believers."

"What's your fee? I've got to see how much is in the department's petty cash box."

"I don't vant your money, Chief. I'm after some-ting better. Eef I help you find de body, you must give me credit in de newspapers. Some people tink dat I am a fraud. I vish to be recognized for de truly awesome powers dat I possess."

"You think you can find the corpse of Agnes Fitch?"

"Eef you stop doubting me. From dis moment on, trow avay your doubts about my supernatural powers. Only den vill de spirits tell us vhere to find de body."

"What spirits? Are they here?"

LaRue extended a left hand decorated with rings on each finger and thumb and grabbed a large porcelain jar on the shelf behind her. She gingerly transported the antique container to the table and placed it next to the crystal ball. She lifted the lid and brought forth five brown tea leaves, tenderly spreading them before her.

*Shouldn't they be placed in boiling water?* the chief thought to himself.

"No," LaRue corrected him out loud. "Only amateurs boil leeffs."

He was beginning to believe in her unusual talents.

"Now repeat after me: Naboo Sabam Kereff."

The chief did as instructed. "Naboo Sabam Kereff."

LaRue continued with her mysterious chant. "Hhelibebcnof-nenam-galsipscl." She nodded to the chief to again join with her.

"Hehili Bobcanof Monsansi Miscap-bull," he mimicked.

"No! No!" the sorceress corrected. "Eet's 'galsipscl.'"

"Galsipscl," her chastised student whispered.

LaRue continued with her tutorial lesson. "De tea leeffs never lie. Vhen interpreted simultaneously vit de tarot cards and de images from de crystal ball, secrets thought to be hidden are brought to light." The fortuneteller raised her hands upward, calling out for assistance: "Spirits of de crystal ball, eet is time to tell us all. Agnes Fitch must be found, even if she's underground."

"Do you see anything in your crystal ball?" the chief questioned as he inched closer in his seat.

"Quiet. I'm trying to concentrate. Yes, de image is becoming clearer ... I see a cornfield."

"You do?"

"Vit newly planted corn. Fitch is buried in a nearby cornfield."

"Can you take me there?" the excited chief asked.

"Eet's not quite dat dimple. First ve must valk up and down de cornfields vhile I extend my magical divining rod."

"Divining rod?"

"And vhen de divining rod points downvard, dat is de spot vhere you vill dig."

"Maybe I better bring a shovel."

"And a lantern. De spirits only come to life after midnight. Meet me here at de stroke of tvelve. Den ve vill valk de cornfields. Now go. De spirits have retired for de afternoon."

No one else had offered to produce a body, so the chief decided to take mysterious LaRue up on her invitation.

At the stroke of midnight, he reported as ordered. LaRue met him at her door. She carried a small tree branch similar in shape to a wishbone.

"Now what?" he asked.

"Ve drive in vhatever direction you prefer, and vhen ve come to a suspicious cornfield I vill employ de sacred divining rod."

"Okay, I know of a field near where the victim lived. We'll start there," the chief reasoned.

Ten minutes later, the strange duo trespassed onto the old Ruckenberg farm, armed with a shovel, a lantern and a divining rod. They walked silently shoulder to shoulder along a row of three-foot-high cornstalks. LaRue held two branches of the divining rod in her hands, as the third branch pointed ahead.

"Eef I feel a tremor and de rod moves downvard, we vill dig dere," she explained.

They walked up and down 50 rows of whispering cornstalks. The divining rod never came to life.

"Maybe eet's time to pick another cornfield," LaRue suggested.

They drove to another unsuspecting field and began the process anew. After three hours of labor, they still had found nothing.

"De sun vill be coming up soon. De spirits cease der vibrations at dawn. Ve can try again at midnight," LaRue suggested.

And so it went during six consecutive nightly tours. The chief's footprints appeared aside LaRue's dainty imprint among hundreds of rows of young corn. Just before daybreak, they entered unannounced upon the Minnich farm's lower 40 acres. As they progressed in a southeasterly direction, the inanimate divining rod began to take on a life of its own. It vibrated and trembled, and suddenly pointed unmistakably toward the earth.

"Dig heer," LaRue instructed in her strange accent as she took possession of the sooty lantern, since the chief would need both hands for the labors he was about to perform.

And dig he did, in the pre-dawn moonless night. It was a macabre scene witnessed only by a flying bat or two and LaRue. The perspiring civil servant dug down about three feet, similar to a World War I infantryman, creating a trench and a large mound of dirt. When he came upon the decomposing body, it was as if he almost expected to find it. It was Fitch, a fact confirmed within the week by the coroner, who also determined that the victim had died from blunt force trauma.

Admittedly the chief came from a hick town with a population of less than 800 souls and admittedly this was his first and perhaps only murder investigation. But Fitzgibbons was not an amateur and he wasn't a fool. LaRue had located the victim's body in the middle of an isolated field. Perhaps she knew more about this murder than what might simply have been gleaned from a few tea leaves and a crystal ball. Maybe her ego and lust for favorable publicity as a psychic renowned for locating corpses had ensnared her. Was she the murderess?

"Miss LaRue ... " Chief Fitzgibbons began just before the press conference to announce the coroner's findings.

"I know vhat you're going to ask me," the psychic interrupted.

"You do?"

"Can I account for my vhereabouts de veek of de murderrr."

"It's just a formality, you understand."

"Of course. I vent to visit my sister in Kansas City, Missouri, tree days before old lady Fitch vent missing, and I stayed an entire veek."

"You drove there alone?"

"Yes."

"Where did you stay?"

"De Kingston Hotel at Fifth and Center Streets."

"Thank you, Miss LaRue. We don't want to be late for the coroner's press conference."

- - -

The chief was in actuality a dedicated and energetic professional. He ordered a videotape for the week in question from every interstate tollbooth existing in a direct line from Seipstown to Kansas City. Then he contacted the Kingston Hotel and ordered a similar videotape of the lobby area for the same seven-day period. He also requisitioned the credit card signature receipts allegedly utilized by Miss LaRue when she checked into her room. She was in fact telling the truth. She had been out of the state the week the victim was killed and buried, and the videos and receipts confirmed it.

Good to his word, Fitzgibbons ultimately called his own press conference to answer the multitude of questions regarding how the body had been found. He gave credit where credit was due.

"It was Miss LaRue, our local psychic, who located the body. Without her assistance the victim's remains would never have been found."

"Do you have any suspects?" a reporter from the *Sentinel* yelled out.

"We're working on that," the chief confirmed. "We're continuing to study the shallow grave and the evidence found near the corpse."

---

Confirmation by the chief that it was Miss LaRue's psychic powers that had located the body brought about the result sought by the fortuneteller. People rushed from across the country to seek her advice and assistance. There was a four-week waiting period to schedule an appointment and an hour's consultation now cost more than a New York City tax lawyer. National television networks clamored for her appearance. She was becoming wealthy, and the pressure of this traumatic change in her life was beginning to take its toll. It was time to get rid of her shiftless unemployed husband, Frank. He didn't deserve to share in her hard-earned bonanza.

---

"I want a divorce, and I want it now," Miss LaRue advised me from the other side of my conference room table. "And the bum gets nothing," she emphasized in perfect English devoid of any accent. "We've got no kids and until last month all we owned was a crystal ball, a jar full of used tea leaves, and a delinquent lease. He isn't to share in anything. Got it?"

She had made her position quite clear, so I contacted Frank's attorney, Roland Seltzer, to arrange a meeting at my office. Three evenings later, at seven, we all sat down together to resolve the equitable distribution of the marital estate.

"She's worth over three million as of today," Seltzer calculated. "After the *People* magazine interview next week, she'll be worth more."

"You'll get nothing, and be thankful for it," Miss LaRue corrected opposing counsel.

Apparently Seltzer had failed to hear her. "Half right now, or we'll seek half of her future income as well," Seltzer interjected.

"Listen, Seltzer," Miss LaRue snarled, " I'm a psychic with unusual powers. Your client, my useless husband, knows that. It's best not to upset me."

"That's true," the worthless bum chimed in. "She can be very persuasive."

"What's that supposed to mean?" Seltzer inquired.

"It means you better agree to a speedy divorce with no cash settlement, or I'll cast a gypsy spell to show you I'm not fooling around."

"A gypsy what?" disbelieving Seltzer laughed out loud.

"You shouldn't laugh at her," worthless Frank pleaded. "She can turn this building upside down if she wants to."

"You're both nuts," Seltzer responded.

"You asked for it," Miss LaRue proclaimed. "Beelsey cabooboo," she chanted with hands raised high. And with those words, all the electrical power in my law office went out: the lights, the computer, the air conditioning, the security system - everything instantly ceased. We sat in the dark for about 10 seconds, although it seemed an eternity.

"Now if you do as I say, I'll lift this minor curse," LaRue proposed. "Boorah saleem," she chanted. Then the electrical power returned and we all rubbed our eyes.

"Is this some sort of a joke?" the disbelieving Seltzer bellowed. "Well, I'm not amused."

"Maybe you'd prefer that I make your cars disappear into thin air," LaRue offered.

"No, not again," her worthless husband conceded. He turned to his lawyer. "Look, Seltzer, maybe you and I better talk alone. I don't need the money that badly. Some curses can follow you around for years. You don't want to grow a second nose, do you?"

The doubting Seltzer apparently conducted business under the slogan "the customer is always right." He put Frank's file in his briefcase and they scurried out the door before the lights went out again. I was left with Miss LaRue and her strange smile.

"What just happened?" I asked.

"What do you mean?"

"You know what I mean. How did you cut my electrical power?"

For a moment, LaRue thought about handing me some nonsensical response about her psychic talents. But then the realization spread across her face that I could best serve her if I had a grasp of the true facts.

"Are you my attorney?"

"Of course," I confirmed.

"So anything I tell you is subject to the attorney-client privilege?"

"I can't repeat what is said in confidence."

"Fair enough, counselor. I've got something to tell you."

I put down my pencil and sat back in my chair. LaRue had my undivided attention.

"Ever hear of Harry Houdini?"

"The magician? Sure."

"He could escape from anything."

"That's what they say."

"It was an illusion - just a trick. Oh sure, they wrapped him in chains and locks, but he had a simple ploy. His worried wife would appear on stage at the last minute and kiss him good-bye as if they were parting forever. During the kiss she would pass a key from her mouth to his. Then they would put Houdini in a trunk or box outside the view of the audience. He was a talented contortionist and well-trained athlete. He was able to unlock the first shackle on his chest with the key in his teeth, and work down to his feet. It was all just a simple trick. Well, in a way the same can be said about me, too."

"What happened to the office electrical power?" I repeated.

"I knew when our evening meeting was scheduled. The night before, I instructed my friend Bob, the electrician, to find the source of your building's power and to rig a temporary breaker to turn it off. At just the proper moment during our conference, I pushed a button on the cell phone in my purse and text messaged him to cut the power. Then I signaled him when to turn it back on."

"Dare I ask about the corpse you located in the cornfield? Was that an illusion as well?"

"I suppose confession is good for the soul," LaRue thought out loud. "And you're the only person on the face of the earth who can't take this story beyond these four walls. Well, here goes: I had been struggling for years as a fortuneteller. There are only a limited number of suckers who will fall for the hanging beads, cards, crystal ball and tea leaves schtick. Fewer still will actually pay 20 bucks for a half-hour consultation. My drunk husband couldn't hold a job and the rent was always late. So I realized I had to create a demand for my services, or get a real day job. After old lady Fitch was taken care of, I told that part-time idiot cop, Harold Portley, who assists Chief Fitzgibbons, that my psychic powers might be able to locate the body. Well, the cops were desperate for any help they could get, even from a tea leaf reader. I knew if I found the body, I'd become an overnight sensation and a financial success."

"But you were cleared from any involvement in the crime. How did you know where to find the body?"

"I'm not admitting that this scenario actually happened, counselor, but suppose, just suppose for a moment that I had a sister in Kansas City, a sister who looks like me, drive my car from here to Kansas and back. Suppose I outfitted her with a wig, glasses and dresses just like mine so that we might be mistaken for each other. Suppose she practiced for a month to replicate my signature on credit card receipts. Suppose I agreed to split any money I made with her instead of wasting it on my fool husband. The plan was so simple. All I had to do was come up with a body. Nobody would miss obnoxious old Agnes Fitch, and nobody else would get hurt. The cops will never make an arrest, so no innocent bystander has had to pay the price."

I looked directly into this murderess's unemotional eyes. "You mean to tell me ... "

"Listen, counselor, the suckers are lining up 10 deep at my door clamoring to pay me $500 an hour to look at tea leaves and to tell them what they want to hear. 'Yes, your Aunt Freda will die and leave you a million bucks.' 'Yes, you will soon find the love of your life.' Lately, all I've had to do to earn a week's vacation in Paris is look at re-usable tea leaves I pull out of a jar, and replace the crystal ball battery once a month. *America is truly the land of opportunity.*"

# Chapter Four

## Enclosures

No spouse is worth murdering. Why risk being incarcerated for the rest of one's life in an eight by ten-foot cell with a new roommate with whom you might have less in common than the decedent?

Why would any man murder his wife? It's so much easier to write a check and walk away. Or get a divorce. Or rent a room at the YMCA. Dante Fiore thought otherwise. When he caught his wife in bed with another man, he became upset and decided to take matters into his own hands. Even though she moved out the next day to an apartment of her own, he felt the need to tie up some loose ends. A week after the separation, he bought some rope, barged unannounced into her new residence and overpowered her. He wrapped the rope around her neck and strangled her to death.

I represented Dante at his trial. The jury came back with a unanimous finding of first-degree murder. The judge sentenced my client to life in prison without the possibility of parole. Dante was just 24 years old.

They took him away to his new home at Graterford Prison, about 30 miles down the road. He sent me a letter on coarse prison stationery, advising that he was now Number 827443 and that he wanted me to file an appeal. He ended his note by explaining that he had no telephone privileges, but he needed to talk to me. This would be my first trip to Graterford.

I drove down Route 100, past the cows and farms and antique shops. Graterford was located out in the country. I turned the last corner past an endless meadow of clover, and there in the middle of this pastoral setting stood an edifice with an appearance similar to the Great Wall of China. An empty feeling of sadness and loss of hope washed over me, despite the fact that a large herd of deer stood at the base of the 60-foot-high barricade, as if posing for some serene Norman Rockwell painting. Human beings, perhaps thousands, actually lived on the other side, yet not one soul was visible.

I drove up the lane to the guard shack with the riot-proof, one-way-mirror windows. Apparently some hidden authority figure could see me even if I couldn't see him. I told the weather-beaten speaker box why I was there. It was like ordering a fish sandwich at a drive-in window. A gravelly voice instructed me to proceed to parking area "G," as a foreboding red gate began to rise. I had begun my descent into hell.

I followed the signs marked "Visitors" situated along a paved pedestrian pathway. They led to three ascending cement steps and a sliding door that sensed my presence, since it opened just as I began to search for its handle. On the other side lay chaos.

The waiting room into which I entered was the size of a tennis court. Yet it was overpopulated well beyond the limitations of the "Maximum Capacity 80 Persons" notice posted on the wall. There were unsupervised kids running in all directions and scores of mothers who didn't seem to care. There were babies crying and grandmothers trying to sleep in prison-made wooden chairs not designed for those in need of rest. There were girlfriends, lovers, fiancées and sisters. And there were two men, the only two males. One appeared to be a minister.

A guard sat behind a wire-mesh screen fidgeting with a pencil. I instinctively looked in his direction while attempting to avoid stepping on a half-dressed toddler squirming on the floor. A lady stood at the partition as she engaged in conversation.

"Is they bringin' my *man* out for visitation?"

"Uh huh." Then the bovine guard began to chew on something again.

"Well, do I gotta wait some more?"

"Uh huh."

"If I get my half-hour with him, will they still feed him his lunch?"

"Uh huh."

This wealth of information seemed to appease her, so like a penguin nesting on a frozen island, she went off to search for any offspring who resembled those with which she arrived.

I stepped up to the batter's box. Mr. "Uh huh" looked me up and down.

"Waz up, Pops?"

*Pops?*

"Yes. I would like to see Mr. Dante Fiore, number 827443."

"Ain't no *Misters* on the other side, just cons," the guard responded with a laugh as he surveyed my tweed suit. "You his mouthpiece?"

"Yes, sir."

"Uh huh" entered the numbers into the keyboard of his computer. As he did so, a beach ball bounced off the back of my head. Some rug rat retrieved the ball and ran back toward the 30-yard line and field goal position.

"Your client's in 'C' wing. It could be a while. I'll call you when they bring him down."

"How long? I have an appointment back at the office at two."

The guard began to laugh again. "Listen, pal, Graterford is the end of the line. The only thing they got enough of here is time. Fiore - he'll be with us another 60 or 70 years, whether you're in a rush or not. First they gots ta strip-search him, and then shackle his legs, and that means he can only walk six inches at a step. 'C' wing is 15 minutes away if you're an Olympic track star and all the gates open with no delays. So, friend ... did you pack a lunch?"

It was becoming painfully clear why so many people were milling about in the waiting area. I could have secured an interview with the President at the White House with less difficulty. The scores of prison movies depicting the inmate talking with his lawyer? What a load of crap. I don't recall a single prime-time law drama scene in which legal counsel sat stewing for an hour in a romper room turned hellhole.

Once in a while, Mr. "Uh huh" called out a name, and the lucky participant was then permitted to enter the imposing electronically controlled door to the left.

I looked at my watch, as I imagined Fiore walking a mile in six-inch shackle steps. It was time to get an update on my client's progress, so I approached the wire-mesh window.

"Do you know if number 827443 is on his way?"

"Uh huh."

I sat back down, pleased with the updated information.

Once in a while, "Uh huh" would buzz open the door to the left, call out a name, and a lucky soul would enter the conference area.

An hour and a half slipped by. My spinal column had begun to take on the curvature of the poorly designed chair. "Fox ... Lawyer Fox!" "Uh huh" called out.

I was ushered into the adjoining room. There were eight riot-proof, two-inch-thick windows, each equipped with a telephone receiver hanging at each viewing area. A guard sat along the back wall, monitoring the activity in the room. Seven women sat at seven seats, some with children in their laps, as they talked into telephones to inmates a riot window-width away. Various emotions could be observed on both sides of the glass: anger, joy, depression, desperation, compassion, confusion.

"Stick out your hand," the menacing guard in the dark corner ordered as I entered the room.

"I beg your pardon?"

"You've got to be stamped in," he instructed as he reached for his rubber marker and ink pad.

I held out my arm. He imprinted the back of my right wrist with cold wet ink. Surprisingly, nothing appeared visible to the eye where I had just been tattooed. I looked up, confused.

"The ink don't show up, except under special ultraviolet lights," the guard explained.

"Then why do it?"

"If there's a riot and they try to change into your clothes, we'll still know who the bad guys are."

"Oh."

I sat down at the eighth window and faced Fiore, who had just arrived. He looked tired in his ill-fitting orange prison jumpsuit. I was looking at a man who might never again touch green grass or kiss a woman. A man who probably might never walk 30 feet without turning a corner or waiting at a gate. He was locked in his cell 23 hours a day. He had a radio, but had not yet gained television privileges. He alone had chosen this lifestyle, living in an eight by ten-foot box. Given the option, I would have rented a room at the YMCA.

- - -

I got a call from Freeman Dinbocowitz, the attorney in Easton. Freeman was a well-respected senior member of the bar who had been a sole practitioner for 57 years. At age 80, he was still going strong, although he now sought to avoid the stress and aggravation of court appearances. So he contacted me to assist him in a complex real estate boundary dispute. His clients agreed that I would appear on their behalf at time of trial.

Freeman had opened his office over half a century ago in the Commonwealth Building and never moved to another location. He had been paying rent on the same four-room office suite through the administrations of nine different presidents. Everything about Freeman spoke to unwaivering constancy. He appeared at his eighth-floor office Monday through Friday precisely at nine a.m. He departed for lunch precisely at noon. He returned precisely at one p.m. He closed his office precisely at five p.m. He never worked evenings or weekends.

"Working crazy hours is a sign of inefficiency," he once told me.

The Commonwealth Building was constructed in 1910, similar in style to New York City's Chrysler Building. *Art Deco*. This proud skyscraper possessed 10 floors and an elevator considered at the time to be the eighth wonder of the world. Perhaps it still was, for it continued to operate utilizing its original hydraulic water design. A huge underground pit, perhaps 10 feet deep, existed below the elevator, and through an intricate system of hydraulic pumps and lifts, the elevator ascended and descended, using the vast unseen tank of water to cushion its ride.

Church organs employing air pumps and bellows have a distinctive sound superior to their modern electronic counterpart. This ancient elevator maintained the most gentle, subtle ride. A passenger would be hard-pressed, indeed, to tell when the elevator came to rest at any given floor. But this cushioned ride came at a price. It took no less than two and one-half minutes, a full 150 seconds, to ascend from the first-floor lobby up to Freeman's eighth-floor suite, if there were no stops along the way. The descent took slightly longer. Nonetheless, if a passenger were to hold a martini glass filled to the brim, the contents would remain undisturbed as the lift moved in either direction.

Freeman was used to the elevator ride and didn't find anything unusual about it. I, on the other hand, expected to progress from lobby to eighth floor in no more than 20 seconds. I didn't need to float like a delicate bubble between floors. One night I did some calculations. Now let's see:

Freeman goes up in the morning, down for lunch, up after lunch and down at day's end. That's 600 seconds or 10 minutes per day multiplied by 250 working days per year or 2,500 minutes or 41.6 hours per year multiplied by 57 years. Freeman had been stuck in the damned elevator for 3 months 8 days 19 hours and 12 minutes! Columbus discovered America in less time.

Does everyone live in a box they've involuntarily fashioned for themselves?

Uh huh.

Prison cells, one-way-mirror guard shanties, seats behind wire-mesh screens, and elevators. All things being equal, I'd probably still choose a room at the YMCA.

## Chapter Five

The Odyssey Of The Three
Prodigal Pussycats

The transportation of house pets sometimes creates unforeseen legal issues that are not easily remedied. That's because the law continues to struggle with the concept of whether a dog or cat is to be regarded as a piece of personal property that has no greater status during shipment than a chair, or whether furry creatures, as members of one's family, enjoy the rights and privileges associated with humans.

The Pennsylvania Bar Association recently published a scholarly treatise regarding the legal status of domestic animals. The paper notes that certain connotations are changing as societal attitudes continue to be reshaped. The term "pet" is being replaced by the phrase "companion animal," and "pet owners" by the more personal "pet guardians." In the matter of *Desanctis v. Pritchard*, 803 A.2d 230 (Pa. Super. 2002), the Superior Court of Pennsylvania was called upon to review the possible shared custody and visitation arrangements applicable to Barney, a family dog. Should he, for example, be transported with a properly fitting seatbelt?

The relocation of animals from one jurisdiction to another has, on occasion, given rise to formal litigation. In *Commonwealth of Pennsylvania, Appellee v. Barbara Gosselin, Appellant*, 861 A.2d 996 (Pa. Super. 2004), the Pennsylvania Superior Court was called upon to adjudicate the fate of an adopted squirrel. Learned Judge Hudock, writing for a unanimous court, began with a short biographical sketch of the animal in question.

*This appeal revolves around the life and times of Nutkin the squirrel. Nutkin's early life was spent in the state of* ferrae naturae, *in the state of South Carolina and, as far as we can tell, in a state of contentment. She apparently had plenty of nuts to eat and trees to climb, and her male friends, while not particularly handsome, did have nice personalities. Life was good. Then one day tragedy struck: Nutkin fell from her tree nest! But fate was kind. Nutkin was found and adopted by Appellant and her husband who, at that time, were residents of South Carolina. Appellant lovingly nursed Nutkin back to health, and Nutkin became the family pet. A large room-sized enclosure was built so Nutkin had plenty of room to run and climb. Life was good again.*

*Nutkin's captivity and domestication were perfectly legal in South Carolina, possibly a reflection of that state's long tradition of hospitality to all.*

*In 1994, Appellant and her husband moved to Pennsylvania and brought Nutkin with them. Life was full of promise.*

*Dark clouds began to gather, however, in November, 2002, when ... (a Pennsylvania) Game Officer ... spotted Nutkin in her room-sized enclosure, (and) advised Appellant that it was a violation of the law to keep Nutkin in this manner. The Game Officer acknowledged that the squirrel was too old and too tame to be released to the wild. (A situation akin to that of an old appellate judge, like the undersigned, attempting to return to the boiling cauldron of the trial court after being tamed by years of peace and quiet above the fray. Chances of survival of both species are poor.) He offered to forgo citing Appellant if she would relinquish Nutkin to his control. Appellant and her husband refused.*

*The reasons for this refusal are not apparent of record, but familial ties no doubt played a part in the decision. (At oral argument, our esteemed colleague, Judge Klein, alluded to the possibility of "squirrel stew," but there is insufficient evidence to support this horrific supposition.)*

*Nutkin would then learn the shocking truth that the cheery Pennsylvania slogan "You've got a friend in Pennsylvania" did not apply to four-legged critters like*

*Nutkin. On December 2, 2002, the Wildlife Conservation Officer issued a citation ... entitled "Unlawful taking or possession of game or wildlife."*

The reader will be pleased to learn that wise Judge Hudock reversed the lower court's judgment of sentence, dismissed the citation and ordered that fines and costs be returned to Appellant Gosselin. As a result, Nutkin's domestic bliss and her faith in the law were both restored.

- - -

I finished doing some laps at the club and located an empty pool-side table for lunch. A young couple sat at the next table. Soon we struck up a conversation, and I learned that they were new club members enjoying the sunshine and quiet surroundings. It was one of those unplanned happy moments in life when new friends unexpectedly find each other.

Jim taught high school math and Madelyn was a nurse. They were expecting their first child in five months, so they had recently purchased a larger home on three acres in an upscale subdivision near Orefield. The topic turned to outdoor maintenance.

"The backyard is rather large, so we had to buy a riding mower just to keep up with the grass," Jim noted.

"And that required that we construct a two-bay storage shed for the mower and Jim's beat-up blue VW Beetle," Madelyn explained.

"You want to hear something amazing?" Jim asked.

I nodded.

"About two weeks after we constructed the shed, would you believe this cat finds a way to sneak in and sets up house. I figured it might catch a mouse or two, so I started giving it milk. Word about the free lunch spread throughout the feline community. A week goes by, and a second cat takes up residence as well. Soon a third calls the place home. Well, I didn't bargain for a menagerie, and these cats were feral. I couldn't get near them, so I decided they had to go.

"I bought one of those no-kill traps and the next day I bagged the first one. A black cat with a white left rear paw."

"And half the right ear was white, too," Madelyn recalled.

"That's right," Jim confirmed. "So I fired up the old VW, put my caged quarry in the back and set out to find a new home for the cat. I drove a good five miles into the agricultural hinterlands and finally spotted an expansive farm with several outbuildings and a large barn situated a couple hundred yards from the road. I knew Blackie would quickly become acclimated there and would be able to make a good living tracking down mice. I released him in the field and headed back home.

"The next day I caught the orange cat with one green eye and one blue eye."

"She was the most tame," Madelyn volunteered.

"Same story. Just before sunset, I drove her over to the farm, let her go and returned home.

"The third day I snagged the calico with a pink nose and black facial patches surrounding both eyes."

"We actually named her 'Cal', " Madelyn said.

"So I put Cal in the VW, drove out to the farm and released her in the field as well. I felt good about what I had done. The cats weren't hurt, got a good home and would benefit the farmer. It was a win-win situation.

"About three weeks go by," Jim calculated.

"It was last Thursday," Madelyn reminded him.

"I went out to the shed to mow the lawn. You're not going to believe what I'm about to tell you ... "

*Not the Lassie come home story*! I thought to myself.

Jim sensed my disbelief. He raised his right hand. "As God is my witness, the three cats were back, as if they had merely been gone for an afternoon walk."

"Maybe it was just three different ... "

Jim interrupted my ridiculous suggestion. "The black cat had a white left rear paw. The orange cat had a green eye and a blue eye. The calico had two black eye patches."

"I gave them milk that night. They were the same cats," Madelyn assured me.

Jim continued on with the astonished enthusiasm of a Cub Scout at his first cookout. "These cats loved us so much that together they journeyed five miles over a period of three weeks to return home, guided only by their instinctive navigational skills. They had to cross over the Lehigh River Bridge, survive the dangers inherent in traversing six lanes of Interstate I-78, not to mention all the traffic, predators and barriers along the way. They may have gone for days with no food or water, just to seek out our meager shelter and a bowl of milk."

"Who knew," Madelyn said shaking her head. "Obviously, we have decided to keep the cats. Do you have any cats?"

"No," I admitted.

"You should," Madelyn suggested. "I was never a cat person, but they are truly amazing creatures."

- - -

The next day, Monday, started the workweek anew. My secretary had scheduled the first appointment for nine a.m., bright and early. I didn't want to be late. Harold Kleinschmidt, a long-time client, had something on his mind. He owned the largest dairy farm in the county. With 500 head of cattle tended by 12 employees, legal issues arose on a regular basis. He took a seat across the conference room table.

"I want your opinion on something," he began. "It ain't easy running a 300-acre spread. You know that. Deer eat about 10 percent of the corn before the harvest. I can't shoot the deer. The game commissioner would throw me in jail. If I use insecticide, the environmentalists crawl up my backside. What the bugs don't eat, the ground hogs do. Then there are the kids with their damn ATVs. There are trespassers, hunters and the curious. It never ends.

"A couple of weeks ago, this beat-up blue Volkswagen pulls off the side of the road down by the glen where the creek enters. The driver stops a couple hundred feet from my house, but I got my spotting scope and I watched him through the 200-power lens. He's got a trap in his hands, and he dumps something on my pasture. Then he takes off like nothing happened. These clowns always come back, so the next evening at sunset I was ready when he appeared again. I copied down his license number. In three consecutive days, he drops off three cats without so much as a thank you.

"I contacted the Department of Motor Vehicles and with some doing I got his name and address. It took a couple of weeks for the information to arrive. I gathered up the damn cats and dumped them back at his house where they belong. Can I sue the bum for my time and trouble?"

- - -

My neighbor Mrs. Altmyer took her teenage kids to the local cinema to see this tear-jerking movie about a family that goes on vacation cross-country to a remote mountainous national park. They take the family dog, a big, goofy golden retriever, and proceed to hike for miles into the wilderness along some desolate trail. After several hours slogging through uncharted canyons and arboreal dells, it finally dawns on this family of idiots that Casey, the dog, is missing. Panic and hysteria ensue as the family searches in vain for their lost mutt. For three days they retrace their steps, fending off mountain lions, venomous snakes and voracious mosquitoes, but to no avail. The dog is gone, probably eaten by a coyote. Grief-stricken, mom, dad and the three children drive back to their home in far-off Connecticut. They all require professional grief counseling and erect a granite and marble font in the backyard in memory of Casey.

The movie jumps forward a month. Then, with just 10 minutes left before the production credits start to roll, Casey limps up to the family's backdoor and falls in a heap, filthy and exhausted. He has survived a 2,000-mile arduous journey, compelled by raw courage so that he might return to the family who loves him.

This film apparently had an impact upon Mrs. Altmyer's two impressionable children, Randy, age 17, and Susan, age 13. They wondered if their golden retriever, Marmaduke, possessed navigational skills and doggone determination similar to that of the canine hero in the movie. And so these budding animal psychologists devised a little experiment to see if their pooch might display the same traits of tenacity and loyalty exhibited by the dog on the big silver screen.

Randy located a red bandana while his sister found some string. Then they invited Marmaduke to join them for a ride in the family's Ford van. Like all golden retrievers, Marmaduke was loving and trusting, and enjoyed unscheduled motor vehicle excursions, even if the itinerary and estimated time of arrival were unknown. The naïve dog jumped into the van without hesitation.

Randy created a blindfold by fixing the bandana around Marmaduke's head, tying a knot behind the pet's floppy ears. As he did so, Susan secured the victim's front paws together so that Marmaduke could not remove the blindfold.

The two sibling dognappers were now prepared to drive Marmaduke to an unknown location. They intended to release their prey, return home, and wait to see if the dog could find her way back home.

Marmaduke took her usual right front seat, her tail wagging, her paws bound, her eyes blindfolded. She was a typical golden retriever: eternally optimistic, dumb, trusting and ready for adventure, even if she could no longer see a thing.

"I've got an idea," Randy announced as he fumbled to find the van key. "Let's drive to Grandma's house in Easton and drop Marmaduke there. If Marmaduke doesn't feel like returning, at least she'll be safe until we go get her."

Conservative Susan wasn't quite so sure. "That's 10 miles away! You've never driven that far on your junior license, and Dad told you not to leave Bethlehem without permission."

"Look, Susan, Mom and Dad won't be back for another three or four hours. They'll never know, 'cause we'll return in just 30 minutes," Randy assured his sister. "I can find Grandma's house in my sleep."

And so the trio departed for Easton, a mere 10 miles away. Blindfolded, hog-tied Marmaduke, sitting upright, looked to passersby like a condemned prisoner being transported to the pound to be shot by a firing squad. She didn't seem to care, though. After all, she was with her two best friends and was getting out of the house.

This was only the third time that Randy had driven the family van unchaperoned, and the very first time that he had left the city limits of Bethlehem, Pennsylvania. Despite his lack of experience, he found his grandmother's house without incident and parked in her driveway. He untied Marmaduke's blindfold as Susan removed the restrictive string. Then the quizzical junior scientists invited their dog out of the van and led Marmaduke to Grandma's front porch.

"Okay, Marm, I want you to find your way home. Understand?" Randy instructed.

"Bark," the dog responded, as her tail wagged back and forth.

Randy and Susan returned to the van and drove away, leaving the abandoned Marmaduke to fend for herself.

Three hours later, Marmaduke reappeared at the family residence in Bethlehem, just in time for dinner. Unfortunately, the same could not be said of Randy, Susan, or the missing van. So when their parents returned home, they called the cops in frantic desperation. It didn't take long for the New Jersey State Police to respond. Apparently inexperienced Randy had taken a left instead of a right, and crossed over the Delaware River Bridge into New Jersey. The cops stopped him near Trenton. He probably should have taken the dog with him as a front-seat navigator.

- - -

Of course, the smartest dog in these here parts was Gypsie, The Wonder Dog! She arrived at our house on Christmas day, a surprise gift from Santa. The toy terrier and I instantly bonded because we had a great deal in common: We were both thrilled that she was there. She was six weeks old and I was six years old. She liked to play and so did I.

Gypsie spent Christmas night in a cardboard box in our finished basement. She cried because she was lonely, but Dad said Gypsie had to learn to "go to the bathroom" outside before she could gain access to the rest of the house. This didn't make a lot of sense to Gypsie or to me, since there was no bathroom outside, just frozen lawn.

I asked Dad how he planned to teach Gypsie this rule of etiquette. Did he speak dog language?

"It's easy, son," he explained. "When Gypsie has an 'accident' you say 'no, no, no' in a stern voice, pick her up, carry her outside, and tell her 'this is where we go.' If she does her business outside, lavish praise on her and give her a doggie treat."

The next morning, Gypsie pooped on the basement floor. Dad said that Gypsie had an 'accident.' I wasn't quite so convinced. It seemed to me that Gypsie knew exactly what she was doing.

Dad pointed at the small pile on the floor and said "no, no, no." It was at this point in time that I learned that dogs apparently understand English. Then Dad picked up my dog and took the puppy outside and put her on the frozen lawn. She stood there and shook, but didn't do much else. Fifteen minutes passed, so we took her back into the house so we could all thaw out. After Gypsie warmed up, she pooped on the floor.

"No, No, No," Dad explained.

This scenario continued for several weeks. Poop on floor. "No, No, No." Dog and owners outside shivering. Back inside. Poop on floor. "No, No, No."

Dad was beginning to lose patience. "There's only one thing left to do," he concluded.

The next time Gypsie pooped on the floor, Dad said "No, No, No," then picked up my dog, and stuck her nose in the little pile of excrement. This exercise continued for two or three days. Poop on the floor, "No, No, No," nose in poop. I sure was glad I was, for the most part, housebroken. And then one day, Gypsie the Wonder Dog figured it out all by herself. She pooped on the floor, and before Dad could say a word, she stuck her nose in it.

- - -

A well-to-do lady who spent each winter at her Florida villa made arrangements with an airline to have her orange pussycat shipped down to her. The cat was sent at significant expense and care from New York City's LaGuardia Airport to Miami International. At the end of the flight, the luggage handlers opened the pet travel box and looked in. Wouldn't you know it - the poor cat was dead. The head luggage handler got a bright idea. He turned to his assistant.

"Here's five bucks," he said. "Go down to the corner pet store and buy another orange pussycat. The old lady will never know the difference."

His subordinate did as ordered. They threw the dead cat in the garbage and placed the new furry impostor in the carrier box.

The old lady showed up for her cat. She gazed into the box. The cat looked up and said, "Meow." That caught her attention.

"That's not my cat," she announced.

The luggage handler strongly disagreed. "Of course it is, lady. The manifest says you shipped one orange pussycat, and that's what we got here."

"Perhaps," she said. "But my cat is dead. I shipped him here for his funeral."

## CHAPTER SIX

### The Velvet Elvis

It didn't take me very long as a kid to figure that things at my house were "different." Those things included me. All my kindergarten classmates, including the boys, boasted nice straight hair that could move in the wind. When they nonchalantly tossed their heads to one side or another, their stylish bangs would fall back beautifully into place, like the shiny mane on a well-groomed horse. I had stupid curly hair, just like my mother and father and brother. When I shook my head, nothing happened. When my ridiculous hair grew, it grew up. Everyone else combed their hair, and instantly become even more beautiful. I tried to comb my hair once. The comb broke.

Most of my five-year-old schoolmates maintained well-developed loyalties toward "the Yankees" or "the Phillies" or teams that only wore red socks. I could not join in their animated discussions, since we did not watch sporting events at home. That is not to suggest that we did not engage in family-oriented activities. On the contrary, during lighthearted moments, Dad would produce one of his favorite books, *A Dictionary of Musical Themes*, and we would gather 'round to see if we could stump him. The 658-page book, copyrighted 1948, listed all of the major Western composers in alphabetical order. Depicted under each name were the musical scores of the first four measures of each movement of each composition scored by the artist. The identification of each line of rambling sixteenth, eighth, quarter, half and whole notes by master work, opus, number, movement and theme followed. As an example, 𝄞 ♫ ♪ was identified as "Grieg, Sonata in G, Opus 13, Number 2, 1st Movement, 1st Theme."

# GRIEG

## NOTATION INDEX

| | | |
|---|---|---|
| A A A A A A A A | S1554 | A B A B C D | T304 |
| A A A A A A A G | J125 | A B A B G C | H740 |
| A A A A A Ab | W144 | A B A D C B | D33 |
| A A A A A B | D70 | A B A E A G# | D203 |
| A A A A A G | R371 | A B A E G A | D18 |
| A A A A B A | P91 | A B A G A C | S69 |
| A A A A B C B | H544 | A B A G F E | D85 |
| A A A A B C C | S182 | A B A G# A B | H486 |
| A A A A B C D | S1579 | A B B A C C | S1506 |
| A A A A G A | C73 | A B B C D E | R428 |
| A A A A G G E | M166 | A B B C G A | Z11 |
| A A A A G G F | G67 | A B B E E E | D61 |
| A A A A G# A | B434 | A B C A B C | C587 |
| A A A B A G | S1497 | A B C A C Bb | F221 |
| A A A B B B | S1349 | A B C B A C | L195 |
| A A A B G G | K83 | A B C B A E | T221 |
| A A A G F E | S654 | A B C B A G | W2 |
| A A A G G G | B1646 | A B C B C B | B505 |
| A A B A B C A | A69 | A B C Bb Ab G | B1332 |
| A A B A B C D | D106 | A B C C D C | W86 |
| A A B B B A | R425 | A B C C# D D# | G282 |
| A A C A G F | S1098 | A B C D B C | C397 |
| A A C Ab Ab Eb | H791 | A B C D C B | S1092 |
| A A D A B G | S832 | A B C D E E | B454g |
| A A E A Ab Ab | L227 | A B C D E F G A | S1074 |
| A A E E F G | D216 | A B C D E F G F | R219 |
| A A F F B D | S596 | A B C D E F G G | S462 |
| A A G A G E | D237 | A B C D Eb D | R5 |
| A A G E D E | D420 | A B C E F G | S779 |
| A A G F E D C B | B1312 | A B C G A E | B488 |
| A A G F E D C D | M906 | A B C G F G | S678 |
| A A G G E E G | K221 | A B D C C B | M761 |
| A Ab B Ab G A# | I36 | A B D G F G | B1117h |
| A Ab G B A G | S694 | A B E B A B | T296 |
| A B A B A B A | R137 | A B E G D G | R278 |
| A B A B A B D | L256 | A B F B A Ab | H809 |
| A B A B A B F# | S1597 | A B F G A B C | B1740 |
| A B A B B A | B37 | A B F G A B D | L253 |

527

## NOTATION INDEX

| | | |
|---|---|---|
| A B F♯ A A♭ G | G352 | A D E F G G♯ | S700 |
| A B G A B B | B1185 | A D E G A E | D34 |
| A B G A D C | S1578 | A D F♯ C D D♯ | S924 |
| A B G B A B | H804 | A D G F E D | H742 |
| A B G C A F | E10 | A D G F♯ F♯ E | C469 |
| A B G C F E | T159 | A D♯ E G A A♯ | D206 |
| A B G E F D | A21 | A E A E E E | E41 |
| A B G G♯ A A | P280 | A E A G C D | S1094 |
| A B♭ A A D F | H560 | A E C D C D | S1491 |
| A B♭ C E♭ G C | S901 | A E D B G C | T241 |
| A C A C A E | R409 | A E D E C A | M125 |
| A C B A C B | H847 | A E D G A E | R140 |
| A C B A G C | B1094 | A E F B♭ A E | D66 |
| A C B C D E | K99 | A E G C A D | S1527 |
| A C B G A C | D161 | A E G C D G | S1173 |
| A C C A G F | G27 | A E G D F C | W66 |
| A C C D C D | M392 | A E G D F E | N16 |
| A C D E E C | D223b | A E G F C F | W89 |
| A C D E F G | T305 | A F A B A G | C352 |
| A C D E G F♯ | I 57 | A F A F A F | T3 |
| A C E F G A | E53 | A F C D E A | S833 |
| A C F A C D | D15 | A F C♯ D E F | S1496 |
| A C F D♯ G♯ E | P212 | A F E D D C | M274 |
| A C G A C G | D242 | A F E D E F | B599 |
| A C G C F A | H817 | A G A A C A | B1711L |
| A C G E G F | S1110 | A G A B C C | B613 |
| A D A B C♯ D | S679 | A G A B C D | C360 |
| A D A D A D♯ | R207 | A G A C A G | C415 |
| A D A D B E | B1294 | A G A C D C | G365 |
| A D A D G C | S1276 | A G A G A G C | S789 |
| A D A G E F | T98 | A G A G A G E | C342 |
| A D A G F E | D356 | A G A G C D | S995 |
| A D B G C A | B635 | A G A G C F | S1005 |
| A D C D C B | B1291 | A G A G E A | R191 |
| A D C D E D | L247 | A G A G F E C♯ | R124 |
| A D D A D D | B786 | A G A G F E D | C105 |
| A D D C♯ D E | W278 | A G A G F E F | S1581 |
| A D D E A G | G200 | A G A G G F | P213 |
| A D E C♯ D A | T41 | A G B A D G | C290 |
| A D E E D A | H808 | A G B C B A | B1597 |
| A D E F D G- | L153 | A G B D F F | S1322 |
| A D E F E F | S18 | A G B G B A | M128 |

57

The precious out-of-print book's second section was jammed with countless combinations of letters in ascending alphabetical order, starting with

AAAAAAA

and concluding 30 pages later with

G # F # E D C C

These hieroglyphics appeared similar to some undeciphered World War II spy code. Actually, the rows of letters comprised listings of the first notes of every major classical musical composition.
"Okay," Dad relented, "I'm ready!"
I ran my finger down a column of meaningless letters. "B flat C D E flat D C sharp D," I offered.
Dad bounced the letters around in his head for a moment. He was no idiot savant who had memorized the book's contents. Rather, as he listened to the letters circling about in his brain, he assigned to each the correct timing and emphasis.
"Mendelssohn, E Flat Octet, 1st movement, $2^{nd}$ theme, Opus 20."
He was, of course, correct.
Why had I been born into such an odd family? Why did Dad put both salt and pepper on his cantaloupe slices? Why did he eat uncooked kohlrabi at night?
Why was it that he saw things no one else noticed? At age five I witnessed my first solar eclipse. We were taught in kindergarten how to construct a pin-hole camera so we could study this natural phenomenon without looking directly at the sun. Dad had a better idea.
"Come with me to the back yard," he said.
We stood together under the expansive silverleaf maple tree. Hundreds of golden droplets of sunlight, originating 93 million miles away, passed through the leaves of the trees, ending their journey as they danced upon the ground.

"Look at the grass next to your feet," Dad said. "What do you see?"

"Little spots of sunlight," I responded.

"Look closer," he suggested.

The tree's leaves acted as countless tiny pinhole cameras, permitting narrow beams of sunlight to filter to the ground. Every golden spot that shimmered near my feet took the shape of a crescent, giving silent testimony to the existence of the distant solar eclipse. No one else at school would become privy to this celestial display.

It soon became obvious to me that my kindergarten buddies were only too willing to accept explanations rooted in nonsense. Miss McKenzie began reading to us about Peter Pan, a kid in Never-Never Land who didn't want to grow up. There was Tinkerbell, too, a fairy who dispensed pixie dust at will, and Captain Hook, whose hand had been eaten by a crocodile. The captain now sported a metal hook in place of his lost appendage. Suspicious at best.

"And so they lived happily ever after." She closed the book and exhaled a contented sigh. I did not share the same feeling, so I raised my hand in the air.

"Yes, Larry. You have a question?"

"What was Captain Hook's name before he lost his hand?"

McKenzie thought for a moment. "Captain Hand," she confirmed.

*Captain Hand?* In an instant her credibility had become suspect. *Falsus in uno - falsus in omnibus.* Was it possible she had fabricated the entire story? Did she actually expect me to believe that commissioned naval officers names reflected the body part most recently replaced? In her opinion, how many Captain Baldies had initially passed through officer candidate school as Ensign Hair?

- - -

Dad said it was time to vote, so he loaded our strange family into the Buick for the two-mile ride to the Hanover Township Volunteer Fire Company Social Hall.

"Who are you voting for?" I innocently asked. I might as well have sought the elusive combination to the wall safe, had we possessed one.

"That's a private matter," Dad scolded. "It's a secret."

Dad never discussed his political inclinations. One day, 30 years later, he and Mom discovered that for three decades they had consistently canceled out each other's vote.

We arrived at the polling place and scrambled out of the Buick. A rather unusual Buick. Dad had read in *Mechanics Illustrated* that for better traction in the snow, the answer was simple: kitty litter effortlessly dispensed by a motorized conveyor belt hidden in the car's trunk. The magazine's colorful illustrations depicted how just about anyone could install this important safety feature that had obviously been overlooked when the improperly designed vehicle first rolled off the assembly line.

Dad meticulously followed the instructions. Soon he had inserted aluminum tubes through holes he had drilled in the trunk floor, about two inches in front of the rear tires. A 50-gallon garbage can, secured on its side, held 125 pounds of brand named absorbent kitty litter. Miniature conveyor belts ran in opposite directions from the garbage can to the aluminum tubes. If Dad needed traction on ice or snow, he'd be ready, especially since the rear of the car now hung about four inches lower than normal.

There was a small patch of ice in the polling place parking lot. This brought a smile to Dad's face. Like the Caped Crusader flipping on the Batmobile jet engine, Dad steered straight for the ice, and then grabbed the newly installed white handle next to the cigarette lighter. I could hear the little conveyor belts come to life as 10 pounds of litter surreptitiously exited from the bottom of the trunk.

Dad beamed. "You'll notice we didn't slip on that patch of ice," he announced. I looked out the rear window. Three square feet of dangerous ice were hidden from view. All that was left was a pile of kitty litter a foot and a half high.

We entered the polling place. The polling registrar, the polling inspector, the guy standing next to the curtain hiding the machines, his friend sitting on the bench, and the man near the exit door all had on denim farm overalls, boots and plaid shirts. Each one also had a huge lump in his cheek, as if, similar to a chipmunk, these fellows were storing food in their mouths for the long winter lying ahead. Once in a while, one or the other would spit orange-brown saliva into a bucket.

"What's wrong with those men?" I questioned as I tried to hide my fear.

"They have a disease, son. It's called an addiction. If you stay away from people like that, you won't catch it."

I took Dad's advice and have continued to do so to this very day. Sometimes it's not that important to conform with the crowd. And so my hair remained curly, and people who had slid off the side of the road would point at our bizarre Buick as it plowed effortlessly through the snow. Yet, come to think of it, the men at the polling place and the Buick did have one thing in common. They both left a unique brown trail behind wherever they went.

- - -

The widow Vandemeer called my office for an appointment. She needed a will. I had known Alice and her husband for years. Bentley died almost two decades earlier. They had raised four sons. She was 70. It was time for her to make her testamentary wishes known.

"Can you stop by?"

It was difficult for her to move about with the wheelchair.

We met the next Tuesday. Photographs of her husband and four sons hung in prominent positions above the fireplace. She rolled her chair into the kitchen and I followed. The small house was unpretentious and clean.

There were no notable works of art or fine furniture. Here was someone struggling to exist on Social Security.

"I want my four boys to share equally in my estate. The only asset is the house. Donald is the oldest, so he'll be the executor. Norm is next in line, so he'll be the alternate."

I jotted down notes as my client spoke. Simple will, four-way split, oldest son as executor. "I understand, Mrs. Vandemeer."

The backdoor opened without warning and in walked Donald and Norm.

"Got your will all wrote up, Mom?"

"Yes, Norm, just as we discussed."

The two men moved into the living room. "Them Yankees got the pennant sewn up," one declared.

"You're nuts! The Red Sox'll take it."

I thanked Alice for her time and made my way through the living room, past the photos on the wall. Everyone sported straight hair, same as Alice. Once outside, I didn't find any Buicks in the driveway disgorging kitty litter. This family probably ate cantaloupe without salt or pepper. Did they know how lucky they were to be normal?

Alice died a month later. Donald requested that I assist him with the administration of the estate. We scheduled a meeting at the house two days after the funeral. All four brothers were there. They couldn't agree on the Yankees or the Red Sox. They couldn't agree if the house should be sold, or at what price. They argued about having an appraisal done. They disagreed about distribution of the personal possessions in the house.

I looked about as we sat in the dining room. There was nothing of value. Nothing.

"I want the velvet Elvis painting hanging in the bedroom."

"Why should you get it?"

"Because I've always been a fan of classical musicians."

"We can sell it on the Internet. It might bring five or ten bucks."

The next day the prized canvas was missing from the house. Elvis had mysteriously left the building.

*One less thing to argue over*, I said to myself. *Thank you. Thankyouverymuch.*

## Chapter Seven

The Novena

Prayer is a means by which you can speak to God, or if one is patient, God speaks to you. It is a highly efficient form of communication, since it can occur almost any place at any time, without an appointment and without long-distance cost. As one of the most personal forms of clear thinking, it can serve to accomplish a multitude of different goals. It may be used to glorify God, or to thank God. It may be submitted to ask for forgiveness or guidance. It may be utilized to mark an important occasion, to obtain a particular grace, to seek comfort and protection for oneself or others, to offer up a special intention, or to remember those who have passed on.

A prayer can be offered for a special need or a seemingly hopeless cause. It can be proposed through an intermediary, such as a saint or a priest in the confessional. Prayer can take many forms, both scripted in the written word, or spontaneously uttered in original, unedited prose. It can be silent or spoken. The originator of prayer is free to choose the form and substance, for God is patient and attentive. No matter how many simultaneous prayers may be offered, God is never confused and always blesses the offeror with His undivided attention.

Bernard and Mary McKenna appeared at my office as scheduled to discuss the drafting of their last wills and testaments. There are those individuals who are justifiably proud of their heritage, and they strive in all that they do to assure that third parties are cognizant of such lineage. Upon meeting an orthodox Jew with angular hat and hair ringlets, for instance, there is no confusion in differentiating him from an Amish farmer, even though both wear black outer garments.

And so it was with the McKennas. They both wore imported Irish clothing, from sweaters, shoes and socks to pants, skirt and blouse. Their watches, tie clip, earrings, bracelets and glasses were from Ireland, as were their parents, grandparents and great-grandparents. They owned an Irish setter. At Christmas, their fireplace only burned imported peat from a thousand-year-old Irish bog. They preferred Irish soap, music, food, liquor and literature. They vacationed in Ireland with Irish friends. Their children took Irish step classes.

This was our first meeting, and yet an instant bond formed with this likeable, humorous, intelligent, handsome couple. It was as if we had been friends for years. The McKennas' infectious laughter, uninhibited smiles and obvious love for each other created an atmosphere of warmth and camaraderie.

We talked informally for a few minutes, to see what mutual interests and friends we might share. He was in the building trades. She was a stay-at-home mother. Their children were enrolled at St. Anne's. It was time to get down to business, so I reached for my pad of paper.

"Is this the first marriage for both of you?" I asked.

"And the last!" Bernard interjected. They both laughed again.

"Mrs. McKenna, what is your formal legal name - the name that will appear on your last will and testament?"

Mary thought for a moment. "That's a good question," she mused. "See, I was born Mary Grace O'Herlehey, but when I was baptized, I was given the name Mary Ann, in honor of the saint, and that's the name the nuns used throughout school. It stuck. I've been Mary Ann ever since, except on my birth certificate."

"Mary Grace McKenna, also known as Mary Ann McKenna," I wrote on my notepad.

"How many children do you have, Mary?"

"Eight."

I stopped writing.

"Eight!" I blurted out.

"Seven girls and one boy. He was the last arrival, just three years ago."

"Eight kids," I repeated, shaking my head. "Are any adopted?"

"Nope," Bernard assured me. "We created them all."

"Are you able to remember their names?"

"Most of the time," Mary assured me with a smile.

"Starting with the oldest, please give me the names and ages."

"Certainly," Mary, the proud mother, responded:

    Mary ...    17
    Teresa ...    15
    Catherine ...    13
    Ann ...    11
    Maureen ...    9
    Grace ...    7
    Erin ...    5
      and
    Murray ...    3

"What is the middle initial of each child's name?" I innocently inquired.

Mary paused again, similar to when I asked her for her formal name.

"Now that's interesting," Bernard interjected. "See, that's what we call the girls - Mary, Teresa, Catherine, Ann, Maureen, Grace and Erin - but for six of them, actually those *are* their middle names. Otherwise things would be confused."

I stopped writing again. "I'm not quite sure I follow you."

"See, there was a *novena*," Bernard informed me.

*They bought a car?* I thought to myself.

Mary noted my perplexed expression as she placed her delicate hand on Bernard's. "Perhaps I should explain."

I sat back and placed my pencil on my notepad.

"We'll be married 20 years this April. We entered into the sacrament of marriage so that we might be blessed with children, but after two years, we still awaited our first gift from God. And that's when Dr. Gross broke the news. I was infertile and could never have babies. I wept for a month."

"She didn't stop crying," Bernard agreed as he squeezed her hand.

"There was only one thing left to do," Mary assured me as she fidgeted with the gold cross dangling from her neck. "A novena," she whispered.

"A what?" I whispered back.

"I entered into private prayer for nine days. I directed my devotions to St. Jude, the Patron of Hopeless Causes, seeking his assistance. I prayed that he intercede on my behalf and that I receive the consolation and help of heaven in my hour of need, and that I be made fertile. In return, I promised that if I were ever blessed with a daughter, I would name her after the Virgin Mary," Mary explained.

"It worked. We started popping daughters out like Chiclets," Bernard confirmed.

"I never forgot my sacred promise," Mary assured me. "I named each daughter 'Mary,' but gave each one a different middle name so we could tell them apart:

Mary Jude
Mary Teresa
Mary Catherine
Mary Ann
Mary Maureen
Mary Grace
and
Mary Erin

"All your kids are named Mary?" I queried.

"Except for Murray," Bernard corrected.

"Is that legal?" I questioned.

"I dunno, you're the lawyer," he reminded me. "The nuns at St. Anne's don't seem to mind."

"Actually, it simplifies things," Mary opined. "When one of the girls misbehaves, I just yell out 'Mary, stop that!' without going through the whole list. Honestly, my mother could never get our names right."

Later that week I drafted their last wills and testaments. The documents provided that if the McKennas died simultaneously, their daughters, Mary, would receive seven-eighths of the estate in trust. Odd man out Murray would get the other eighth.

## CHAPTER EIGHT

### The Wedgie

My friend Wendell had made a comfortable living selling school textbooks. He'd load his car with a few samples of the newest biology, math or English grammar books, and make the rounds from school to school showing teachers what was hot off the press in educational publications. He liked his chosen profession, since he enjoyed imparting emerging knowledge and instructional techniques to staff members and pupils alike. Then one day, he abruptly quit his job. He told me why.

"Two things have changed my world," he explained. "The 9-11 attacks on the Twin Towers and the first kid to take a semi-automatic weapon into the classroom. I used to be able to enter a school unannounced, find a teacher on break, carry on a polite conversation and get a book order or two. And then, almost overnight, I was barred entry, and had to send in an approved written visitation schedule and be accompanied to a sterile, isolated visitor's area. They made me feel like some kind of a criminal, so I retired. Funny - the guy who took over my job never leaves his house. He sells books over the Internet to customers he's never met. The world's getting to be a lonely place. So much communication technology, and yet no one talks to anyone anymore."

Wendell was correct. Schools have dramatically changed, as have the students. A few months ago, my neighbor Martha made a comment in passing that saddened me as if I had just learned of the sudden death of a close friend. She teaches third grade at an elementary school located just 10 miles from our neighborhood.

"There are 30 children in my homeroom this year. Not one comes from a family with a mother and father living together."

Certainly there were problems when I attended school. Once a month we had to hide under our desks to practice for the moment when the Russians might drop a nuclear bomb on us. The emotional impact of those useless drills remains with me today. Why did the Russians dislike us third-graders so much? Would my desk actually have protected me when the big one was dropped?

I went through school without ever seeing a single policeman in the hallways. Nobody brought an AK-47 to class because no one had an automatic weapon or the need to brandish one. On occasion, a playground scuffle or two broke out, but such confrontations were usually quickly resolved by the combatants themselves without adult intervention. In truth, it was the adults who engaged in physical assaults in far greater numbers than did my fellow students. My parents spanked me, and on occasion, some teachers utilized modest corporal persuasion.

Today any bodily contact by either teacher or student may be perceived as a crime. It is considered more civilized for an instructor to engage in polite discourse in an endeavor to convince the child through logic and infinite patience of the wisdom bestowed in their direction. The inmates have finally taken over the asylum.

- - -

Mr. and Mrs. Ritter brought their nine-year-old son Timothy to my office. He was accused of assaulting another student. He had been sent home in disgrace to think about his criminal transgression, since the school maintained a zero tolerance policy regarding such alleged aggressive behavior.

Timothy's parents were legitimately concerned. The juvenile authorities had been called into the case, and they in turn had notified the district attorney's office, which scheduled a formal, accelerated hearing before a county judge. A finding of delinquency could adversely impact my young client's life for years to come, especially if down the road he were perceived as an habitual offender. It was not uncommon for forgotten juvenile records to resurrect themselves at the most inopportune time, precluding a teenager later in life from entering the college of his dreams or securing a military academy appointment.

"What exactly did Timothy do?" I inquired of his nervous parents.

"A wedgie," Mr. Ritter confessed. "He gave John Adamson a wedgie."

"Who is John Adamson?" I asked.

"He's in my class, and he wears weird glasses," Timothy answered.

Was it possible that "wedgie" meant the same to him as it did to me and my fellow third-graders 50 years ago?

"What's a wedgie?" I asked.

The little assailant told me. Apparently some things never change.

I did not venture to ask Master Timothy *why* he gave the wedgie. It would have been like asking a mountain climber why he ascends Mount Everest. Obviously, because it's there for the climbing. Obviously, poor John Adamson had a pair of underwear calling Timothy's name.

A week later, I accompanied my third-grade client and his nervous parents to the courthouse for a hearing before the juvenile court judge assigned to preside over such significant matters. Admittedly, from a sexist standpoint, had my prepubescent client inappropriately touched some female classmate, he would have faced dire consequences. But the victim here was some kid with thick glasses. He probably deserved what he got. But would His Honor agree? In attendance were the judge, the straight-arrow assistant district attorney, the tipstaff, stenographer and sheriff's deputy who was, at that very moment, struggling not to burst out laughing. What were the odds that not a single onlooker ever gave a fellow acquaintance a wedgie?

"My name is Judge Singleton."

The proceedings had begun. His Honor stared at the three-foot-tall defendant. "Are you Timothy Ritter?"

"Yes."

"You're charged with assaulting a classmate, John Adamson."

"It was just a wedgie, Judge, that's all," came the explanation.

"What is a wedgie, Master Ritter?"

"Huh?"

"Tell me for the record, son."

"It's when you yank someone's underpants up their butt crack. Know what I mean? Didn't you ever give anyone a wedgie, Judge?"

The judge thought back to a simpler time in his life and momentarily focused upon some unspoken fond memories. Then he returned to the matter at hand.

"That's the beauty of our system of jurisprudence, Master Timothy. Around here, I'm the only person who asks questions. You're the guy who gets to answer them. Okay?"

"Okay."

"Do you think your conduct was appropriate?"

"Well, it wasn't like I gave him a 'super wedgie' or an 'atomic wedgie'."

The court and, for that matter, I were caught off guard. I had never heard the term "wedgie" utilized in concert with the words "super" or "atomic."

"What is a super wedgie?" Judge Singleton innocently inquired.

"That's when you yank so hard, some of the underpants tears off and you get to keep a piece or two. On a good day, you get the whole thing."

The judge swallowed. "I have significant reservations, but it's my duty to ask: What, pray tell, is an atomic wedgie?"

"That's when the kid is wearing his dad's boxer shorts and his dad has an extra big rear end. Then you can pull the shorts all the way over his head. Usually, if his eyes are covered, he'll start running full speed and smack into a wall or something."

I studied the assistant district attorney for a moment. He had no sense of humor and no common sense. He was the one who had approved the charge of assault against the clueless Timothy. Now we were wasting precious time and resources talking about underwear. When had a wedgie - not a super wedgie or an atomic wedgie, just your run-of-the-mill wedgie - become the stuff of judicial proceedings?

The assistant district attorney had something in common with Adamson, the alleged victim. He deserved to be wedgied, and after this hearing was over, I'd be just the guy to do it.

## Chapter Nine

The Confession

The armed robbery at Mueller's Meat Market did not go off as planned. Apparently one of the Muellers made an unanticipated move and, in an instant, Mom, Pop and Junior Mueller lay dead on the floor of the small butcher shop from which the family had for the better part of 50 years struggled to make a living. The assailant got away with $48.

The cops came, gathered up shell casings and multiple bullet fragments lodged in the wall and in the victims' bodies, and began their search for the killer.

Just about everyone from the neighborhood showed up at the simultaneous trilogy of funerals. The shop never reopened. The realtor had a tough time trying to sell the place, since it was rumored there were three ghosts circling the butcher table at night. With no on-lot parking, the rundown, obsolete corner store sat vacant and would eventually be razed.

Several months later they arrested John Toth and charged him with three counts of first-degree murder, since the homicides had occurred during the commission of a felony. I was assigned to represent him, because everyone in this country has a right to a lawyer - even a vicious, antisocial creep.

John and I did not bond very well during our weekly interviews at the prison. He quickly caught on that he was not the type of fellow I would invite for Christmas dinner. Even Adolph Hitler petted his dog, had a lover, and occasionally said pleasant things about his mother. Toth, however, possessed no discernible commendable or benevolent attributes. It remains unclear to me why he had been placed on the face of the earth and what purpose he served.

He was devoid of any feelings, good or bad. He could as easily snuff out someone's life as step on a bug, and having done so, think nothing of it. It was as if this amoral automaton's soul had been plucked from his body and nothing had been inserted to replace the vacuum existing in the hollow of his being. He felt neither pity nor remorse for anyone, including himself. His most pressing issue was what the prison planned to serve for lunch. In five hours, the most pressing issue would be what they were serving for dinner.

Toth had from the outset insisted upon a trial. If he were guilty, the district attorney would have to prove it. The day had finally arrived to pick a jury, test the overburdened limits of the judicial system, and see whether Toth would walk free or face the hangman. A cluster of deputies brought him into the courtroom and removed the shackles from his legs and arms. He looked about his new surroundings as he sat next to me, and then he focused upon the guards.

"Any of you guys hear what they're dishing out for lunch?" he barked.

I knew all the courtroom players from previous trials. Judge Fordham was presiding. Assistant district attorney Angelo Mangello represented the Commonwealth of Pennsylvania. The usual cast of lesser but necessary characters was present as well, including the stenographer, bailiff, court clerk, tipstaff, sheriff's deputies, newspaper reporters, and the ever-present curious onlookers hoping to catch a glimpse of a real live murderer.

It was time to begin the tedious process of *voir dire,* a phrase derived from Latin roots and French usage, meaning "to see" and "to speak." This exercise in jury selection permitted the combatants to view and speak with potential members of the citizenry drafted both to hear this case and to decide Toth's fate. Unlike most criminal cases where the entire jury panel was assembled together for one time-saving questioning period, the court rules required that in capital cases each juror be brought into the courtroom separately for individual inquiry. Sometimes selection of a jury in this manner took weeks.

They escorted the first potential juror into the courtroom. She had that unmistakable look of panic in her eyes. Would she be drafted into a month-long trial, sequestered in some cheap hotel, separated from family and friends, unable to watch the evening news on TV? Had she, too, become another victim of this crime?

Toth tapped me on the shoulder as we sat together at the defense table. Thousands of other defendants and their counsel had, at various times, labored at this very same table for the better part of a century. The entire writing surface of this proud black cherry Chippendale was protected by half-inch-thick plate glass, weighing 40 pounds or more. How many closing arguments had been scribbled here? How many desperate clenched fists had banged upon this polished surface in an attempt to make a point now long forgotten?

"Hey, Fox," Toth snarled in my direction.

"What?"

"You gonna pick a jury?"

"Yes."

"You got an extra pen and pad of paper? I wanna take my own notes."

I was shocked. Toth actually maintained an interest in something other than the day's menu. His request was legitimate. I turned to the armed guard standing behind us.

"Officer, I'm about to give the prisoner a pen and some paper. Any objection?"

"Nope," he shrugged.

I reached into my briefcase and extracted a fresh notepad as I rummaged about in the leather container for another writing instrument. My fingers located an abandoned ballpoint pen among other debris. Toth studied both ends of the pen without thanks, without emotion, without a sound.

I turned to the unhappy potential juror. She faced long and arduous questioning regarding a multitude of bar examination topics. Did she believe the defendant was guilty merely because he had been charged with a crime? Did she believe police witnesses were always truthful? Did she believe in capital punishment? Did she agree the defendant had no obligation to take the witness stand in his own defense? Did she agree proof was required of guilt beyond a reasonable doubt? Had she read or heard about the case? Had she formulated an opinion of guilt or innocence? Would she keep an open mind throughout the entire trial?

After two hours of inquiry by both the defense and prosecution, they brought in the next juror, and we began the selection process anew. After the lunch break, a third poor soul underwent similar scrutiny, and at day's end a fourth was subjected to the same line of questioning.

During each examination, I often rose from the defense table to approach the potential juror. At such times, Toth remained seated behind me, pen in hand, presumably taking notes. The armed deputy who was guarding Toth apparently began to view things from a different perspective. He motioned to the assistant district attorney, and whispered in his ear as the officious guard pointed at the glass tabletop over which Toth sat hunched and sullen.

Without seeking the court's permission, the assistant district attorney suddenly shoved Toth's blank notepad to the side and peered closely at the glass tabletop. Then Mangello carefully removed his bifocal glasses, and lowered his pudgy nose and squinting eyes to within an inch of the glass surface.

"I see what you mean," he confirmed with the tattletale guard. Then he turned to Judge Fordham to awaken him from his glazed alien-being trance.

"Your Honor!"

"Say what?"

"Your Honor, a matter of grave importance has been brought to my attention. Will you please suspend *voir dire* and temporarily dismiss the potential juror while an issue of some urgency is discussed?"

They ushered confused juror #44, Marjorie Hudock, from the courtroom, and then the assistant district attorney motioned for me to join him at the bench.

"What's the problem?" I asked.

Mangello pointed a menacing finger at my poor client, the only person in the courtroom presumed to be innocent of everything, and with dramatic stage presence announced, "The defendant just confessed to the crime! I want his confession introduced at time of trial!"

I found this proclamation to be unusual. After all, Toth had never bothered to confess anything to me, and since I alone represented him, the assistant district attorney didn't have the right to pursue communications with my client. The judge was caught off guard as well.

"Could you be more specific, counselor?" Fordham asked.

The assistant district attorney was not to be dissuaded. "Your Honor, the deputy sheriff thinks he saw the defendant use a pen to scratch words of confession into the glass tabletop."

"What words?" Fordham asked incredulously.

"I KILL," Mangello stated.

"I KILL?" the judge repeated.

"Yes. I KILL," Mangello confirmed, his case having now been proven beyond a reasonable doubt.

"Wait a minute!" I interjected. "I kill ... what? Did he say he kills human beings?"

Mangello was not to be denied. "Your Honor, I demand that the glass tabletop be seized and taken into evidence as a trial exhibit, since it constitutes proof of the defendant's confession."

"You can't be serious, Angelo," I interjected. "Assume for the moment that Toth somehow was able to carve those words into the hard-as-rock glass with a 25-cent pen. If so, it was done at the defense table and represents a privileged communication between lawyer and client. And just how do you expect to prove those words were carved by my client? They may have been there for a century. Maybe Toth's cheap pen can't even scratch glass."

"We'll take a handwriting sample from the defendant!"

"The words weren't handwritten. It's an etching or engraving," I suggested.

"The defendant's fingerprints are all over it!"

"So are mine," I explained. "We both sat at the table at the same time."

"That's his pen!" the exasperated prosecutor shot back.

"Actually, it's mine," I confessed. "Maybe I'm the scratch-artist and the deputy only thought he saw Toth at work. I gave Toth a pad of paper this morning and he hasn't written a word. Maybe he's illiterate."

"It's a confession," the frustrated assistant district attorney screamed.

"To which murder?" I asked. "How do you know he's not confessing to some other episode of homicides? Hundreds of actual confessed murderers have sat at that very table. Maybe it's their handiwork."

Mangello's face turned beet-red. "This is the reason nobody likes smart-alecky defense attorneys. You're all full of crap!"

I walked back toward the glass tabletop, the object of new or possibly old graffiti carved into its surface. I sat down next to Toth and grabbed my misused pen from the hand that may have shot three innocent citizens.

"Don't you have any concept of proper courtroom decorum?" I angrily lectured.

As those words left my mouth, I began to laugh at the incredible stupidity of my question. Courtroom decorum? This guy was facing a lethal needle or perhaps three consecutive life sentences. Suppose the district attorney were to add the charge of defacing public property. Would Toth toss and turn at night if he received another 20 days in the slammer?

Our eyes met. I began to giggle despite my fits of anger.

"What grub they servin' for dinner?" he asked.

## Chapter Ten

### The Stress Test

My next door neighbor of 25 years, Horace Wildonger, has always lived alone. He's a nice guy, and over the years we have become good friends. He recently retired as a baker with the local bread company and now he keeps busy manicuring his very green, unblemished lawn and its accompanying flower beds. A few days ago as he dug among some petunias, he spotted me across the fence that separates our backyards.

"Hey, Larry!" he called out. "You got a minute?"

"Sure."

"Well, here's the thing. My doctor, he says I've got to go for a stress test, on account of my heartbeat. He's been talking about installing a pacemaker or something. I ain't exactly sure. Well, anyway, you're a lawyer ... "

"Yes ... I am."

"So I'm gonna need a living will authorizing someone to pull the plug, in case I go permanently comatose."

"Horace, you're not going to die from a stress test. They just put you on a treadmill for a few minutes to check your respiration and pulse."

"If you still got a pulse! Sometimes people go into the hospital vertical and come out horizontal. Anyway, I was wondering if you could write up one of them living wills and then drive me to the hospital. The doctor says he may need to medicate me, so I can't operate a car. And it'll be convenient. If someone has to pull the plug, you'll be right there."

I nodded a lawyerly nod, even though Horace wasn't quite done with his instructions.

"Now here's the thing. I hate hospitals, and I'm scared to death. Would you stay in the stress test room with me? It would mean a lot having a friendly face there."

"Of course, Horace, you bet."

A week later, I drove Horace to the local hospital. The caring, gentle admissions lady sensed that Horace was upset, and she did her best to assure him there was no need for concern.

"Now Mr. Wildonger, don't you worry. They just put little suction cups on your body and check your pulse. Nothing of an invasive or painful nature takes place."

Horace mopped some perspiration from his flushed brow, as he shook his head up and down in silent disbelief.

"Is it permissible for me to accompany Mr. Wildonger into the testing area?" I inquired.

"Yes, you may, if that is the patient's wish," the nice lady confirmed.

And so we began our journey together into the bowels of the hospital.

"Just follow the yellow dots on the floor," the nice lady instructed, without asking if we were both colorblind.

Now I knew how Dorothy felt as she entered the Land of Oz.

"Follow the yellow dots?"

"Yes, follow follow follow follow ... follow the yellow dots."

The purple dots trailed off to "short procedures." The green dots led their victims to "pre-admission surgery." The red dots to "internal medicine." Horace noted with some suspicion that there was no "external medicine" counterpart. Those in "ambulatory care" abandoned all hope when the black dots turned sharply to the left.

What, exactly, were we of the yellow dot road known as in medical lingo? The answer lay just ahead. The yellow dots stopped at the big door entitled "outpatient testing." As we approached, the doors automatically opened so that we might visit the Wizard without further delay.

An unseen intake person lurked behind the hidden cubicle she called home. In order to comply with medical privacy regulations, the partition wall separating her from the public only permitted exposure of her shoes and the shoes of some hidden poor soul facing her. However, their conversation was as clear as a bell.

"From here they will transport you on the gurney to the holding area where the intravenous needle will be inserted. Then the procedure will take place. Any questions?"

Weren't those instructions, word for word, the same explanation the warden gave my last client who had faced execution?

"Next," the concealed body attached to the exposed shoes called out.

Horace, the cowardly lion, motioned for me to accompany him. Two chairs faced the tiny intake lady, who struggled to peer over her computer. We sat down.

"Name?"

Horace told her.

"Date of birth?"

Horace told her.

"Your social?"

Apparently she had neither the energy nor the inclination to finish her question with the two missing words that would possibly have given the inquiry meaning.

Horace gave the inquisitor his "social." An artificial doorbell somewhere in the computer went "ding-dong," giving the lady's life renewed meaning and direction.

"So you're here for a stress test?" she observed.

"Yes," disheartened Horace acknowledged. All the fight was gone. He knew he was caught in the web. It was only a question of time until the life juices would be sucked out of him.

She pointed a finger at me. "Is this your significant other?"

I sensed that this question was also missing an important word or two, but Horace didn't seem to mind acting as our interpreter.

"Yes," he confirmed.

"Okay. He may go with."

I waited for the rest of the sentence, but it did not come. How exactly did she determine which words were unnecessary?

"You are number 64. Just wait in those seats right there until the stress test technician calls for you."

*Stress Test Technician* - what an unusual title. Of course, not quite as strange as that name given to the guy in charge of fruits and vegetables at my favorite supermarket - *The Perishable Manager*. Imagine trying to locate him. *I'm sorry. That's not possible. He dried up and died this morning. We're trying to find another, since the last seven we hired have all similarly taken on some mold and expired.*

Horace and I took seats next to the magazine rack. There were 20 or 30 different periodicals, including *Pregnancy Monthly*, *The Blood Pressure Journal*, and *Today's Hospital*. I was about to reach for the *Skin Graft Quarterly*, but there was no time.

"Number 64!" the voice announced, a voice that sounded remarkably similar to my old fun-loving boot camp gunnery sergeant. Perhaps he worked here now?

"Number 64," the impatient stress test technician called out again from behind the green door. Horace and I stood up and began to proceed to a fate unknown.

"Are you number 64?" The question came from a face that looked as if it had been chiseled from granite. It was cold and emotionless like the unfeeling portrait of Queen Victoria imprinted on an old English penny. Maybe the body standing in the crisp nurse's uniform was 40, or 50, or 60. It was hard to tell since all the joy had long been squeezed out of it.

"Yes," nervous Horace responded.

She looked me up and down to see if I was one of those troublemakers. "The significant other can come, too, if you wish," she barked as she opened wide the green door.

We entered the cramped inner sanctum. Her work area consisted of a desk, a chair, a computer, a hospital bed, a treadmill machine with handrails, and a complicated illuminated panel complete with blinking lights and document printer, similar to a lie detector machine. Nearby hung about three-dozen suction cups dangling from their individual sequentially numbered electrical lines.

Standing at the ready between the array of suction cups and the computer was a young assistant who instinctively knew to keep out of harm's way.

"I'm Stress Test Technician Hadley," our guide offered almost as an afterthought. Then she pointed. "And this is Stress Test Technician Apprentice Flowers. Now strip to your briefs, Number 64."

So much for introductions. I had represented prostitutes who at least extended the courtesy of lighting up a victim's cigarette before they removed his pants.

Hadley had all the mother love of a crocodile, and she wasn't quite done bestowing some more of it upon poor Horace, the unsure recipient of her heartfelt bedside manner.

"Now before you hop up on the treadmill, I've got to attach the suction cups in precise numerical order. This requires that Stress Test Technician Apprentice Flowers apply suction cup holding glue to each area of the torso to be tested. You're not one of those ticklish types, are you?"

Horace just stood there in pre-glue stunned silence.

"Okay. We'll start with the right and left carotid arteries. Now hop up on the treadmill."

Horace and his boxer shorts made their reluctant way onto the silent gaping apparatus, as Stress Test Technician Apprentice Flowers approached with what appeared to my untrained eye to be a plastic jug of glue with accompanying paintbrush. She applied an abundant amount of the swill from her makeshift slop bucket onto Horace's neck, whereupon Stress Test Technician Hadley raced up the treadmill uninvited and stuck suction cups one and two on Horace's neck, giving him a sophisticated Frankensteinian air.

Hadley would prove to be a dedicated and tireless mentor. She turned to her charge as she adroitly grasped two more suction cups.

"Now, Stress Test Technician Apprentice Flowers, tell me, where do numbers three and four go?"

I could think of a couple of places, but I probably would have been wrong.

"The right and left clavicular intercepts," bright Flowers replied.

"Correctimundo. You may apply more electrolytic solution."

Flowers painted Horace's upper chest with the slimy goop, followed closely by Hadley and suction cups three and four. And so it continued. The dynamic duo peppered dazed Horace with suction cups that descended to his non-existent belt line, and then they turned him over like a three-minute egg and began the ascent up his back with numbers 16 through 32. The whole process took about 10 minutes. All the while tutor Hadley demanded to know where the next set of suction cups were to be placed. Flowers always answered with flawless precision.

I was impressed. However, from the look on his face, greased pig Wildonger did not share my admiration for a job well done.

"We're ahead of schedule by two minutes," hyperactive Hadley panted as she stopped to regain her breath. Doctor will be pleased. You may buzz Doctor, Stress Test Technician Apprentice Flowers."

Stress Test Technician Apprentice Flowers did as instructed. She pushed a call button on the side wall.

"Doctor will be here momentarily, Number 64. When he arrives, I will activate the treadmill at an initial three mile per hour crawl. As you become acclimated, I will increase the speed in imperceptible increments to elevate your heartbeat. If at any time you feel faint or need to rest, simply raise one hand, both of which should at all times hold securely to the handrails. Do you have any questions?"

It appeared to me there was something on Horace's mind. He unclenched one sweat-soaked hand from the aluminum railing and turned his body toward Stress Test Technician Hadley. Thirty-six suction cups now accentuated his naked upper torso. Thirty-six sequentially numbered electrical lines led to 36 automated receptor graphs, each standing at the ready to record every nuance of every heartbeat and its resulting flow of blood, from the Adam's apple to the bellybutton. Horace looked like some celebrated general who didn't possess any other place on his body from which to hang yet another medal for valor.

"I need to go to the can," Number 64 stoically announced.

The significance of this statement did not initially register with overworked, preoccupied Stress Test Technician Hadley, who was, at that very moment, making final adjustments to her computer printout paper.

"I beg your pardon," she replied.

"The bathroom. I got to go to the bathroom," the condemned fly said to his spider captor.

"Number one or number two?" she inquired of Number 64. "I've got a little bottle here."

"Both."

"Both? That's not possible. You're all hooked up."

"Both. Real bad."

"But Doctor has already been buzzed. Do you expect me to unbuzz him and unsuction you? My perfect schedule! I'll be behind the rest of the day!"

It was as if someone had thrown a bucket of water on the Wicked Witch of the East. She was beginning to melt away before my very eyes. She turned to Stress Test Technician Apprentice Flowers.

"I'm feeling a little lightheaded," she whimpered. "Perhaps I'll lie down on this convenient hospital gurney for a moment."

Hadley was out cold before her head hit the pillow. Flowers pushed the lifeless body out the exit door with a combined speed and dexterity only possessed by 19-year-old stress test technician apprentices.

"Good morning," happy doctor sang out as he bounded through the same doors through which horizontal Hadley and vertical Flowers had so recently departed. "Are we all ready for your stress test?"

"I'm not sure," Horace confided as he realized his support staff had disappeared. "Do you think you could rustle up a bedpan?"

## Chapter Eleven

### The Ladder

State lotteries were created for those not conversant with the science of probability and statistics. Only once did I ever plunk down a hard-earned after-tax dollar and take a stab at the elusive numbers. I chose 12 random figures and that night I wasted precious time watching TV as dancing Ping-Pong balls shot through tubes. I had failed to pick a single qualifying number. However, somewhere out there somebody else was about to receive my dollar and several million others just like it, in preparation for early retirement.

- - -

Maynard Goshenhoppen and his wife, Elsie, lived in the mobile home park two miles past Kricksville. One night after finishing his shift as a welder at the fabrication plant, Maynard stopped in at the Save-A-Lot mini-mart and bought a carton of unfiltered cigarettes so that federal tobacco subsidies would remain stable. On a whim, he also purchased a lottery ticket. That night, as he reclined on his worn Barcalounger, he watched with lottery ticket in hand as the Ping-Pong balls began to shoot through the tubes.

He stopped sucking on an unfiltered butt dangling from his lips because what he was about to say was important. He called out to Elsie, who was in the kitchen feeding the cat.

"Hey, Ma!"

"What?"

"Come in here once, now."

"I'm feedin' the cat."

"Well forget about Fredo and get in here."

Maynard's voice had not contained such a sense of urgency since the Brooklyn Dodgers had decided to relocate to L.A. Elsie dropped the cat dish and rushed to the living room.

"I think you might have something here," Elsie muttered as she scanned the numbers on the TV screen and the numbers on the coffee-stained ticket cradled in her hand.

This was an understatement. In actuality, few people in the world possessed luck equal to Maynard's, luck that just earned him $128 million gross, or $74 million clear after taxes. He would now be able to pay off the $700 due on his shopper's club credit card.

- - -

"Mr. and Mrs. Goshenhoppen are here," my secretary announced.

I had offered to meet them at their mobile home, since I didn't wish to inconvenience people of such sudden new standing in the community, but they declined my offer.

"Actually," Maynard explained, "it's better here. Them photographers and TV people won't leave us alone. I don't think we'll be able to stay at the mobile home park much longer."

Another understatement.

"You've been our lawyer for some time now," Elsie explained. "You helped us when the car got smashed and when we needed a last will. We figure you can help us again."

"Glad to," I assured them, and that was an understatement, too. Before me sat the rarest of all human species - people who could pay a legal fee without wincing. I hoped they might stay and chat the entire afternoon.

"We'll need a couple of things," Elsie began. "We'll probably buy a new house, and we have to rewrite our wills. And we think it would be best if all the people who are hounding us for money contacted you instead as our representative. We had no idea we had so many impoverished relatives."

"Most important, we're thinkin' of buyin' a boat," Maynard explained. "So we'd like you to look over the sales contract before we sign on the dotted line." Maynard pulled a crumpled document from his pocket and handed it to me.

For a mere $25 million, he and Elsie could purchase a 95-foot mahogany yacht that once belonged to the Shah of Amur.

"It's a real bargain," Maynard beamed. "It was listed for $35 million, but the guy needs to unload it quick. Something about an uprising ... "

I studied the sales agreement and the detailed description of this floating palace. There were berthing facilities for 12, a galley capable of preparing four-star meals, onboard living quarters for a crew of five, and the standard royal accouterments including an anti-terrorism fail-safe system in case of attack on the high seas, and a state-of-the-art medical operating room in case of an ocean appendectomy. The helicopter landing pad was located midships for guests dropping in; the alabaster private bath was aft. The six-page schematic exhibit described each amenity in exquisite detail.

I tried to regain my composure. "Mr. Goshenhoppen," I began, "do you think it wise to spend a third of your assets on something you could possibly rent?"

"I'll still have $50 million left," my client reminded me. "Why not enjoy our good fortune while we can?"

In fact, Maynard had an answer for everything. He had several friends at the bowling alley who had been in the Navy, and they figured they could steer this barge in the correct direction. Their first voyage would be to Bermuda.

It was useless attempting to dissuade the Goshenhoppens. So we discussed the deposit of their remaining monies in insured accounts, and then I obtained the information for their last will and testament. A week later they purchased the shah's yacht for $25 million, and then they and several other bowlers set sail from New York Harbor. I received a fax from their onboard communication center as they ran parallel with the Florida coast. They were having the time of their lives.

- - -

My receptionist announced that the U.S. Coast Guard was calling. Since I was 25 years beyond the maximum age for recruitment, I figured the Goshenhoppens might have run into some trouble. That would prove to be an understatement.

"This is Lieutenant Meshaw, Station Miami, U.S. Coast Guard. Are you Lawrence Fox?"

"Yes," I tentatively responded, hoping my clients hadn't caused the Queen Mary to run aground.

"We found your name and number in the emergency log of the yacht named *Ping Pong Balls.*"

"Ping Pong Balls?"

"Registered to Maynard and Elsie Goshenhoppen. Do you know them?"

"Yes ... yes, I do. Are they okay?"

"Their yacht is in our custody for processing. Do you know who has authority to act on behalf of the Goshenhoppens?"

"Lieutenant, are they okay?" I demanded.

And so he told me the story. While on routine patrol 30 nautical miles off the southern coast of Florida in calm seas and favorable weather, a coast guard cutter spotted the yacht *Ping Pong Balls* adrift and unresponsive to radio or light signals. Upon approach and boarding, no passengers or crew were located.

"What initially caught our attention was the fact that the main mess, the dining area, was set for a formal dinner. Wine had been poured in each crystal glass. Several decanters and glasses were only partially filled. Lobsters and steaks remained heated in covered serving dishes. Salads and appetizers adorned eight plates."

"The Bermuda Triangle ... " I muttered.

"And we noticed something else. It appeared that all the dinner guests and crew had placed their clothing, from shoes to shirts, on their respective dining chairs."

"The Bermuda Triangle ... " I repeated.

"There were no signs of foul play. See, down here north of the Florida coast, many times pirates storm a vessel for drugs or loot. Then they blow it up to hide any evidence of the crime. But this yacht hadn't been vandalized. Everything was in its proper place, and besides, it has an anti-terrorism system that guards against such attacks."

"I don't quite follow, Lieutenant," I said.

"The sides of the yacht can't be scaled. Nothing like an exterior anchor chain or railing descends into the water, which lies eight feet below the main deck. There are electrical and other devices to preclude unwanted marauders from gaining access. And that's how we finally figured out what happened."

"Figured out what? Did you find the Goshenhoppens?" I persisted.

"Apparently everyone had a few drinks too many and decided to go skinny dipping. So they took off their clothes and everyone, passenger and crew alike, jumped into the water."

"What are you driving at, Lieutenant?"

"No one thought to bypass the anti-terrorism system. They didn't press the button that lowers the ladder from the deck into the water. There was no way to climb back on board, unless they were spiders with suction-cup legs. There was no one left on board to assist. They probably treaded water for an hour or so. What a way to go."

Another understatement.

# Chapter Twelve

## The Tiffany Lamp

Carmello Iaccobelli invented the concept of frugality. He lived for 65 years of his life as a bachelor in the row home he had purchased in Seipstown near the brass foundry. He walked to work, purchased two-for-one canned items at the grocery store, and his entire wardrobe came from the Salvation Army thrift shop.

"It saved on gas," he once observed.

He began his career at the foundry as a laborer. Forty-eight years later he retired as a laborer.

"I enjoyed smelting," he once said. Uncle Carmello was a man of few words.

Every time the steam forge at the brass foundry pounded out another brass billet, Uncle Carmello's house shook a little. Uncle Carmello didn't seem to mind.

"It's much worse inside the foundry," he once noted. He figured as long as his house occasionally vibrated, he still had a job. It was of little consequence that his dinner plates sometimes fell off the kitchen shelf.

An examination of the interior of his row home suggested that the residence was uninhabited. There was no air conditioner, no cable and no central heating system. No rugs, too. The lone upright coal stove in the living room met his needs. On cold nights he shoveled more coal in, similar to his job at the foundry. Actually, his home was rather cozy, even in the midst of winter. That's because he shared common walls with the neighbors on each side, and they were constrained to keep their dwellings warm because of the cold walls they shared with him.

Uncle Carmello drank only the water from a bottle he filled from the kitchen sink faucet.

"Tea bags cost too much," he once observed. One year on his birthday this regimen was temporarily interrupted when someone gave him a gift of 24 plastic bottles of Diet Pepsi. He had never indulged in such a luxury, so he made it last. Once or twice a week, he'd take a sip or two from a bottle as if it were the family heirloom scotch. Then he would add tap water to bring the precious contents back to its original level. In this manner, with care, a bottle lasted the better part of a month.

There wasn't much of value in the house. A burglar would have been disappointed. Upon looking about, the crook would probably have felt sorry for the occupant, and might have left a donation on the folding card table Uncle Carmello had, since the day he moved in, used as his combination kitchen-dining room suite. There were no newspapers or newspaper rack. No curtains accented the windows, just loose hanging fabric that upon closer examination appeared to be used potato sacks. The walls were unadorned, with the exception of an unframed black-and-white picture of Niagara Falls on the Canadian side.

There was one exception. A hanging lamp made of multiple pieces of cut colored glass hung over the card table. The lamp's design included the mosaic pattern of a bunch of grapes and two bananas. The fixture's one 60-watt bulb provided the only illumination in the kitchen. No one could recall when Uncle Carmello had acquired the lamp, or why it had caught his fancy, but he truly must have loved his "Tiffany lamp," since it was the only luxury he ever permitted himself.

Every Friday Uncle Carmello personally transported his foundry paycheck to the Seipstown National Bank and Trust. He deposited almost all of it into his savings account.

Carmello was *Uncle* Carmello because he had a niece and nephew, Angelina and Rocco, children of his deceased brother. They were his only living relatives. Rocco was frugal, a characteristic Uncle Carmello found endearing.

Uncle Carmello liked Angelina, too. She might not have been a prudent saver, but she did visit her uncle every single Sunday. She would make his favorite spaghetti dinner with black olives, sausage and fresh peppers at no cost to him. More than once Carmello told Angelina, a kind and good-natured young lady who sought nothing in return, that he planned to leave half his estate to Rocco and half to her.

Uncle Carmello didn't like lawyers. "They cost too much," he once explained. So to draft his one sentence Last Will, he did so in his own hand on a piece of scrap paper. His intentions may have been clear to himself. They weren't quite as evident to a court.

*I give my house to Angelina. I give my bank account and everything else to Rocco.*

Uncle Carmello wrote this will 30 years prior to his death, when the house and bank accounts were roughly of equal value.

One Sunday Angelina showed up with all the ingredients for a sumptuous spaghetti dinner. Carmello didn't answer the door. She found him lying face down near the surplus army cot he used as a bed.

Rocco flew in from California for the funeral. While rummaging through some boxes in Uncle Carmello's hall closet, he discovered the unwitnessed holographic will. He also uncovered a bank savings book reflecting a balance of about two million dollars. Rocco was about to become rich.

Uncle Carmello had failed in the will to name an executor of his estate, so Rocco and Angelina successfully petitioned the court to be named as the joint estate representatives. Thus empowered, the brother and sister contacted the funeral director in Seipstown, since Uncle Carmello had not made any funeral arrangements.

"We have a very handsome brass inlaid final resting encasement for $4,950. It's waterproof," Mr. Hundeldorn offered. "I understand the departed worked at one time in the brass foundry? How fitting."

Angelina ignored the awkward pun as her eyes scanned the full-color glossy catalog of gleaming coffins. There were so many models from which to choose.

"That's a bit pricey," the future multimillionaire nephew responded. "Do you have a pine box?"

Angelina began to picture Uncle Carmello's only two-piece suit taking on water with the first significant rain. "You can't be serious!" she stammered.

"Look, Angie, the old guy never spent a nickel on himself. If he were here in the room, he'd be asking about cardboard coffins," Rocco said.

The funeral director tried to intercede. "We have a nice simulated aluminum model on page eight."

Angelina quietly rose from the casket salesroom table. "I'll pay for the funeral," she announced with quite resolve. "This meeting is over."

So, too, for the foreseeable future, were polite conversations between brother and sister. Rocco retained Hermilda Schnalzer, Esquire, of Smith, Smith and Thornton to do his talking for him. Angelina sought my counsel when it became clear another unresolved issue required clarification.

Hermilda called me two hours after the funeral service. She was one of those in-your-face bulldog lawyers with the patience of a three-year-old. Her theory of negotiation was rather simple: *I want it! You got it! Give it to me now or I'll file something in court.*

My phone rang. "Fox? Are you Fox?"

"This is Lawrence Fox."

"Fox. This is Hermilda Schnalzer. I don't think we've ever met."

"It's nice to make your acquain ... "

"Whatever. Listen, I represent Rocco Iaccobelli. You represent his sister, Angelina."

"Yes, I have been contacted by ... "

"Listen. The dead uncle, what's-his-name ... "

"... Carmello ... "

"Yeah, Carmello, well, anyway, his will provides that the house goes to Angelina. The bank account and everything else go to my client Rocco."

"That's correct," I confirmed.

"So, I'm calling to tell you Rocco is taking the Tiffany lamp. He doesn't want anything else from the home. He'll be at the house tomorrow to remove the lamp."

This bulldog had caught me off guard. It took a moment to clear my mind. "Wait a minute, counselor," I responded, "the house belongs to my client and the lamp is part of the house."

"No, it isn't. It's just part of the furnishings, and the will doesn't give her the house contents, just the house."

"The lamp's a fixture. If it's removed, it will cause permanent damage to the house! Are you suggesting that whenever a house is sold, the seller can rip out all the lighting fixtures before turning over the key to the front door?"

"My client says the lamp is secured to the kitchen ceiling by just one screw. That doesn't sound like a permanent fixture to me," Ms. Bulldog barked back.

I told her I'd talk to my client to see if Angelina would relinquish control of the coveted lamp.

"Yeah, you do that, counselor. But I've got to have an answer by tomorrow. My client flies back home on Sunday, and he expects to take the lamp with him. I've been instructed to file an emergency petition with the court if necessary."

It was unclear to me just what "emergency" existed. The lamp had been hanging in the same location for decades. Perhaps my client didn't even want it.

"I certainly do," Angelina responded over the phone. "It's part of my house."

"Is the lamp worth anything?" I asked her.

"I dunno," she admitted. "Does it matter?"

"It would if I were you. If we end up in court, the legal fees may exceed the value of the lamp."

"What would you do?" she asked.

"Have the Tiffany appraised."

"Okay. Do it," she confirmed.

I called up my friend Joe at the antique store. He agreed to meet Angelina and me at the house. An hour later, we all gathered at Uncle Carmello's residence.

Joe stared at the object of all this contentiousness. Then he took his bifocals off and stepped even closer.

"This here is the thing youse guys is fightin' over?"

"Yes," I acknowledged. "Is it worth anything?"

"Yup"

"How much?" Angelina asked.

"Ten bucks, maybe less. Walmart's got 'em on sale right now. You just snap the plastic bananas and grapes together like a jigsaw puzzle."

I thanked Joe and returned to my office. Unfortunately, I had not jumped quite fast enough to suit Rocco's legal counsel. My fax machine was spitting out the last pages of her emergency petition seeking injunctive relief to gain possession of the Tiffany lamp. A hearing was set for the next morning. Assuming Hermilda had only spent an hour drafting such nonsense, the petition and the next day's hearing would probably cost Rocco a thousand dollars. I called my client and told her about the petition.

"Let's go to the hearing," Angelina suggested. "I want to see what the judge does."

- - -

Judge Hargrove was very busy. There were eight hearings pending before him, and each sought emergency relief. He reached our "urgent" case by mid-morning. Hermilda, Rocco, Angelina and I were summoned up to the bench as his honor read Hermilda's impressive petition. The judge lifted his nose above the packet of papers resting in his hands.

"A fight over a kitchen lamp? Is that why you're all here?" he inquired.

"Rocco can have it, Judge," Angelina offered, "but I'd like $300 so I can buy something similar and have an electrician install it."

The judge banged his gravel. "So ordered. Now get outta here."

Rocco took the lamp back to California. It cost him about $1,300. For that type of money, it's probably hanging somewhere nice.

## Chapter Thirteen

It's A Gamble

"What-cha doin'?" Stanley asked me over the phone.

I knew it was Stanley. No one else with a New Jersey accent had my private number, or used the phrase "What-cha." Stanley claimed he had no accent at all, and that it was difficult understanding everyone else's strange dialects.

Stanley and I had formed a lifelong bond starting with the first day of boot camp. We had nothing in common other than our military service, but that was enough. We had kept in close touch for more than 30 years.

Stanley was one of those guys who always seemed to have time on his hands. Although he worked a 40-hour week, he had seniority at the grocery store, so he chose steady night shift, stocking shelves 11 p.m. to seven a.m. He assured me that the benefits far outweighed the deficits.

"Night shift is da greatest," he once confided in a guarded whisper as we sat alone in my office. "Da big brass ain't der ta supervise ya, so ya can catch 40 winks reclining on one of dem large cases of tuna, and annudder great bonus is ya don't never see da wife. Ya live in da same house, but ya is two ships passing in da night, so ta speak."

Stanley was one of those people who never seemed to have a need for sleep. After he left the grocery store in the morning, he was ready for action until 11 in the evening. He thought it unusual that some people actually worked during the day and slept at night.

"Well, what-cha doin'?" he asked again.

"It's five-thirty, Stan," I explained. "I'm trying to wind things up after a tough day. I've been on the go since seven this morning."

"Me, too," Stanley commiserated. "Listen, Larr, I'm headin' over your way for some combined business and a little relaxation, and I want-cha ta join me. It's been a month since we went out."

"Where are we going?" I innocently asked.

"Da Downs."

The Downs, a 20,000 square-foot computerized, multi-screen, state-sanctioned horse betting parlor that simultaneously ran televised broadcasts of every major thoroughbred race in the country. Hundreds of greying and balding men chewing on cheap cigars found solace there, drawn to this windowless paradise so that they might blow their pension and Social Security checks as they chased yet another elusive trifecta. The allure of this better's mecca had always escaped me. I worked too hard for my money to spend it on some nag, and I disliked cigar smoke. I advised Stanley of my feelings.

"Listen, Larr, dis is gonna be fun. You'll have a blast. We'll just stay a coupla hours, dat's all."

Every time Stanley used that well-worn line, something I didn't quite expect invariably occurred. Like our first liberty together off the Coast Guard base. Stanley stumbled upon a tattoo parlor and some kid from Georgia who tagged along ended up getting the image of a third eyeball permanently stenciled into his forehead. This newest "eye," similar to the one on the back of a dollar bill, never blinked.

Stanley was persistent. "Larr, I'll be acrosst da free bridge in 15 minutes, and at da Downs in annudder 15. See ya der." The phone fell silent.

Stanley lived along Route 22 near Philipsburg (Stanley called it Pee-Burgh), New Jersey, and could have easily entered Pennsylvania by paying a one-dollar toll to cross over the interstate Delaware River Bridge. But that would have cost a dollar, which made no sense to Stanley, since travelers seeking to enter Pennsylvania had been doing so free of charge for over a century.

"Washington crossed da Delaware widout payin' no toll," he once explained.

I didn't have the heart to tell him Washington was trying to leave Pennsylvania.

So Stanley decided to take a slight 10-minute detour into downtown Philipsburg, cross over the narrow two-lane, century-old "free bridge" into the center of Easton, Pennsylvania, and find his way back onto Route 22 again. The fact that this circuitous exercise cost three dollars in gas did not seem to concern Stanley.

Only once before in my life had I briefly engaged in the misfortune of visiting the Downs. I had a female client who was married to some derelict who hung out there night and day. I walked in with a constable and identified the bum so the constable could serve him with a divorce complaint. The idiot didn't object to receiving the legal papers, but he was genuinely upset that we had disturbed his concentration as he sought to focus his attention on the third race at Aquaduct.

I drove over to the Downs to meet Stanley. I did so willingly and without hesitation, even though Stanley was a little strange, the Downs was depressing and I had no interest in gambling. I did so because old shipmates are hard to come by and Stanley was one of the oldest.

He met me at the sliding automated front door behind which the security guard lurked, looking diligently for those under 21 years of age attempting to sneak in. The rent-a-cop had just stopped a couple of kids and demanded to see their driver's licenses. They protested, but finally produced the necessary identification. I laughed to myself as I rubbed my grey hair. What a compliment it would be to have someone, anyone, question my age. Those kids should have cherished that fleeting moment.

Stanley and I shook hands, paid the guard a two-dollar admission fee, and passed through the turnstile into gambler's heaven. I appeared to be the only person embarrassed to be there. Didn't any of these people have a life or something legitimate to do?

*"FOUR MINUTES TO POST TIME,"* a stern voice announced over the public address system. Several of the living dead partially returned to life and shuffled off to waiting TV screens, their race receipts and betting

paraphernalia clutched securely in shaking, age-spotted hands.

"Let's get a copy of da daily wager magazine," Stanley suggested. "It lists who all da winners will be in each race." I was dumbstruck! How very convenient. Now I understood why everyone was here. If only there were a similar periodical published daily in the law business. I would simply pursue those trials I was guaranteed to win.

Stanley walked over to a guy holding a stack of magazines, gave him five dollars and returned with what appeared to be a large brochure with today's date printed in bold lettering on the front cover. It listed every racetrack in the country, every horse thinking of making an appearance and every jockey riding each charger. It described the horse's win-loss history, the jockey's win-loss history and the gross earnings of each. Once again I thought how such similar information might assist a client searching for just the right lawyer.

"Stanley, how come the guy selling the magazines isn't betting on the horses?" I questioned.

Apparently he didn't hear me. "Now here's da ting," Stanley shot back. "Ya gotta follow da jockeys, not da horses. If a jockey hasn't won in a while, da udder riders in da clubhouse will trow a race in his direction, sorta as professional courtesy, so he can make a buck."

If only other lawyers or a friendly judge or two felt the same way toward me, I thought to myself.

"Ut ... Oh ... look once!" Stanley pointed a pudgy finger at a column of names and figures. "Dis here jockey hasn't made a dime in a week. He's in da fourth race at Pimlico. And da book says da horse is guaranteed ta 'place.' I'm puttin' a sawbuck on dis nag ta win. See ya in a minute."

Stanley disappeared into the animated crowd of hopeful betters, only to return three minutes later. He proudly waved a piece of white paper in his hand.

"If dat horse comes in, I'll make maybe 25 ... maybe ... 30 bucks, depending on da odds," he explained. "Now let's find a table and a TV screen. It's only tree minutes ta post time."

- - -

I did not share Stanley's enthusiasm. That's because I had learned from prior personal experience that in horse racing, nothing is a sure bet. The raw memories of that fateful day 30 years past, still lingered fresh in my mind.
The public defenders' staff decided to take an all-day Saturday excursion to the horse track.
"You coming, Fox?" Rudy, the chief defender, asked.
"I'd prefer not. I don't enjoy gambling, and so I've never been to a horserace."
"Everyone's going - me, Bob, Steve and Gus. If you don't come, you'll be thought a snob. You want to be a team player, don't you?"
That Saturday we drove forever over the free bridge, through the desolate Pine Barrens and up the New Jersey coast to Monmouth Raceway, a track lying within eyeshot of the New York City skyline. There was quite a large crowd milling about, eager to witness the day's nine races. We sat down at a table in the upper level of the grandstand, ordered lunch and watched as they brought out the first group of three-year-olds for the initial race.
Rudy turned to Bob. "You know what I'm thinking?"
"What?"
"Fox here has never been to a race. He's bound to have beginner's luck, don't you think?"
I stopped munching on my sandwich, like a trespassing rabbit newly discovered in the lettuce patch. Everyone was staring at me, their heads bobbing up and down in lawyer-like synchronization.
"No doubt about it," Bob agreed. "Fox, this is our golden opportunity to make some real money. You pick the horse in the first race. We can't lose."
"I don't think that's a good idea," I protested. "I don't know the first thing about horses or racing."

"That's the beauty part," Gus assured me. "The pros - guys who have been around the track their entire lives - they strike out like everyone else. But the real amateur - I've seen some beginners hit it big."

Steve took over the crusade. "This is your one lifetime opportunity, Fox. It'll never come again. All we ask is you let us share in the wealth. Don't be a thoughtless sissy-la-la. After all, we're your friends. Just name the winner so we can buy you the biggest steak dinner in all of New Jersey."

I hoped the steak didn't have marks where the jockey hit it.

Four lawyers couldn't all be wrong, and I certainly didn't want to be a sissy-la-la. Actually, they "sorta" made sense. After all, I won my first trial with no knowledge of the law, no defense and no preparation. Since then I hadn't been able to convince a jury of anything. I tentatively began to study the racing form as the horses pranced by. Now let's see ... Cocoamuffin was a nice name, but one of his legs had a strange white spot. Haley's Rosegarden looked promising, but his jockey seemed preoccupied. Conchshell Queen had some bounce in her step, but I didn't like the color of her mane.

"Well, what's it gonna be, Fox? We've only got two minutes to place our bets," Gus pressured me.

I took a breath. "Drop-In-The-Bucket," I declared. "He's just about done taking a dump, so he'll be light on his feet," I reasoned, since that's how I always feel under similar circumstances.

The quartet of counsel each reached for their wallets. In an instant there were four 100-dollar bills reposing on the table.

"Aren't you in, Fox?" Rudy asked.

"I don't like to bet," I informed my friend.

"Suit yourself. We're going to make enough to retire."

Steve grabbed the money, more than I had seen in a month, and stood up. "Should I put it all on Drop-In-The-Bucket to win?"

There was an instant consensus. Steve took off toward the betting windows, the communal bets in hand.

*"ONE MINUTE TO POST TIME,"* the omnipotent Wizard of Oz voice announced.

Steve, winded as a racehorse, returned and flopped down in his seat.

"The bets are in," he assured our party of soon-to-be-rich attorneys. There was electricity in the air.

*"AND THEY'RE OFF!"* the voice announced.

Forty hooves pounded the turf as the steeds bolted from behind a gate now wide open. The crowd let out a primal roar.

*"And at the first turn, it's Hole-In-The-Wall, followed by 45 Calibre, Cheesecloth and Drop-In-The-Bucket."*

"Come on Drop-In-The-Bucket," Bob screamed.

I doubted the horse could hear him.

*"And into the second turn it's 45 Calibre, with Scary Dream closing fast, followed by Drop-In-The-Bucket and Cheesecloth."*

"He's gaining!" Steve yelled out.

How could anyone know what was happening? The horses were now far away near New York, and people were beginning to stand up, blocking our view.

*"Into the third turn, it's Drop-In-The-Bucket by a length, followed by Cheesecloth, 45 Calibre and Tie-The-Knot."*

That sounded promising. Perhaps I should have placed a bet.

*"And heading for the clubhouse, it's Drop-In-The-Bucket by three lengths, followed by ..."*

That's when a collective gasp rose from the assembled multitude that seemed to suck in the six-foot floor-to-ceiling tinted windows.

*"Ladies and gentlemen ... Ladies and gentlemen. A horse and rider are down. It's Drop-In-The-Bucket. The jockey doesn't appear to be injured."*

I sat in stunned silence as one by one my comrades slowly sank back into their seats. Five lawyers and not one could find a word to say.

Emergency personnel flooded the track to attend to poor Drop-In-The-Bucket, who did not appear to have fared as well as her jockey.

"That stupid nag only had another 150 yards to go," unfeeling Gus moaned.

"We were that close to $2,000 a piece," Bob lamented.

They all began to stare at me with menacing glares. A moment later a large diesel bulldozer with a cavernous front-end scoop bounced down the dirt track. It swept up poor departed Drop-In-The-Bucket without so much as a goodbye prayer and disappeared into a nondescript barn, the words *Acme Dog Food* printed above the doorway.

There was a long, silent ride home. I was the only one who hadn't lost any money. That's because I had beginner's luck and knew when not to bet.

- - -

Stanley tapped me on the shoulder. "I lost again. Look, why don't-cha place a bet? Maybe ya'll have beginner's luck. Believe it or not, dat happens a lot in horse racing."

I wanted to explain why the odds of that occurring weren't quite as good as he thought, but as usual he wasn't listening.

"Der's nuttin to it. Just study dis next racing form, pick a nag, and give da guy at da window two bucks. A five-year-old can play."

He shoved the magical magazine into my hand, the periodical that guaranteed each winner of every race. What did I have to lose other than two dollars?

I located a solitary table, sat down amidst the mayhem of the surreal betting parlor, took out a pencil and studied the myriad, complex data. I had grey hair. I smelled of cigar smoke. I looked lost and clueless. I fit right in.

Now let's see ... It says here Broken Axel is going to win, Loose Change will place and Semi-Conductor will show. If I bet two dollars on Broken Axel, I'll make three dollars, or a return on my initial investment of 50 percent.

*"THREE MINUTES TO POST TIME,"* the ubiquitous, hidden Wizard of Oz announced from behind some curtain.

I proceeded with authority to one of the 20 clerks standing behind one of the 20 betting windows. I had my racing guide and two bucks. He probably thought I was a seasoned veteran of the wagering world. I put on my best James Cagney - Humphrey Bogart face and casually moseyed up to the window.

"Broken Axel ... two bucks." I handed him the cash like a pro.

"Say what?"

"Broken Axel ... two bucks." Was this guy new on the job?

"He scratched 15 minutes ago, Ace."

"What?"

"He ain't in the race, Einstein. Try another nag or step aside. There's other betters lining up behind you."

*"TWO MINUTES TO POST TIME,"* the wizard announced.

"But he has to be running. He's the winner!" I was beginning to feel like I was pleading for a way to return to Kansas.

"Call your congressman. Maybe there's something he can do. Now please step aside so these other ... "

"Okay. Here's what we're going to do," I stammered. "Two dollars on Loose Change."

The sarcastic little man standing in his protective cage looked me squarely in the eye. "Listen, pal, do you see the big sign hanging above this window, the sign with the instructions on how to bet?"

I looked up. It was printed in English and Spanish.

*Please place bets in the following order: the racetrack, the horse, the amount of your wager, the number of the race, and the type of wager.*

Where was Stanley when I needed him?
*"ONE MINUTE TO POST TIME,"* the wizard announced.
"Is it possible you know the racetrack in which Loose Change is making an appearance?" I inquired.
"Aquaduct."
"What is the number of the race?"
"174."
"Okay. Two dollars he'll win."
The little man typed the information into his state-of-the-art computer as he repeated my bet aloud. "Aquaduct, Loose Change, a *whopping* two-dollar bet, race 174, to win. Correct?"
"*Correct*," Bogart, Cagney and I confirmed.
The machine made a whirring noise and out popped a receipt.
*"NO MORE BETS ... NO MORE BETS,"* the wizard proclaimed.
I turned to walk back to my table. There were seven men standing in line behind me. I wondered if they were planning to bet on this *same* race.
"A two-dollar wager? Is that what you just bet, stud?" the menacing guy behind me inquired. "I was ready to plunk down $500 on Semi-Conductor to place. If that nag comes in, you and me is gonna have a little talk outside."
I felt as if I were back at Monmouth Raceway with the public defenders' staff. I had disappointed another gambler.
I located Stanley near the TV screen that was announcing the results of a race somewhere in New Mexico. The dejected people around us were throwing their receipts on the littered floor, despite the abundance of trash cans.
"Didja place your bet?" he asked.
"I'll tell you about it later. I'm ready to leave," I replied as I nervously looked over my shoulder.

"Me, too. But first I got a little business to attend to. You can help."

"Doing what?"

"Pickin' up some of deese here discarded receipts on da floor. Make sure dey ain't walked on or ripped."

"Why do you want useless pieces of paper?"

"Cause dey ain't useless. I send dem into da IRS with my taxes to prove I had losses to offset my winnings."

"Wait a minute," I stammered. "You want me to engage in a conspiracy to defraud the federal government by helping you submit receipts that have nothing to do with you?"

"Who's gonna know?" Stanley asked as he knelt down and began to harvest the precious paper scraps.

"Stan, there're more video cameras in here than in all of Atlantic City!"

"Conspiracy ta defraud," Stanley laughed. "You lawyers always come up wid da weirdest technicalities."

I didn't stay long enough to learn if Loose Change won the race. I don't know if Semi-Conductor placed. Maybe I made three dollars, or maybe I saved the guy in line behind me 500 bucks. It was a gamble I preferred not to take.

## Chapter Fourteen

### Sic Transit Gloria

If you were important during some point in your life, it is possible that something might be dedicated to your memory *post mortem*. If the "something" is in short supply, that's an indication that you were probably very important. There aren't that many counters around, so Geiger probably was very important. The same might be said about scales. Not many people have one named after them: perhaps the best known is Richter. Vaccines: Salk. Vacuum cleaners and dams: Hoover.

- - -

"They're selling the last original farm left in Bethlehem," my aged mother noted as she scanned the morning newspaper, magnifying glass in hand.

"There's a farm somewhere in Bethlehem?" I innocently inquired.

Mom was genuinely affronted by my stupidity. "People like you are the reason there are no more dodo birds or carrier pigeons."

"I caused their extinction?"

"This is the last colonial-era farm left for miles around. Some *developer* wants to level the place and put condos and a mini-mart there."

Never had I heard Mom pronounce one specific word with such anger and disgust.

*Developer!*

"How are kids supposed to learn about the history of this region if the historic structures are bulldozed? Whatever happened to common sense?"

My mother's next crusade had just been hatched before my unsuspecting eyes. She didn't have the five million dollars needed to purchase and preserve the farm, so she did what everyone running for judge or mayor does. She became annoying. First, she hit up our local congressman. His office was located downtown, about four miles from the farm.

"Do you have an appointment to see the congressman?" the pretty receptionist asked.

"I'll wait," Mom assured her. She took out her magnifying glass and started to read the newspaper.

When Mom ordered lunch on her cell phone, the office staff decided it might be wise to have the congressman meet this rather persistent constituent. He finally made an appearance as Mom was finishing her tuna hoagie.

"How nice to see you again, Mrs. Fox," he assured her.

She searched in vain for a napkin, licked her fingers and shook his hand. "Look, Congressman, it's like this. They're going to bulldoze the Burnside Farm, so we'll need five million dollars quick if kids are going to see history firsthand. Can I count on you?"

The next day Mom made a similar unannounced journey to the county administration building. One tuna hoagie later, she gave the chief executive her pitch to save the farm and our local history. The day after that, she visited the mayor and our state representative. Then it was time to call the newspaper and tell the editor the local politicians were balking at a mere five mil even though kids' educational needs hung in the balance. The local TV station agreed to an interview. Mom advised her audience that it was time for our nearsighted officials to save history from another unnecessary convenience store. The letters, lots of them, started pouring in and so the politicians began to reassess the situation. Maybe five million wasn't that much after all.

And so the county, with the help of the federal, state and city governments, bought the farm before it was leveled and turned it into an historical site.

Similar to Moses, Mom had led the people to the Promised Land, but she was not to enjoy the fruits of her labors. She died before the preservation work began in earnest. She would have been proud.

A board of directors composed of members of the community returned the derelict farm to its simple colonial serenity. The dilapidated barn became the object of a thousand dedicated, loving hands. The farmhouse underwent a similar transformation. The outbuildings were refurbished to reflect their original purposes - corn crib, smokehouse, chicken coop and all. An operational colonial farm with authentic herb garden, walk-in fireplace, slate roof and horse stalls rose up among the handsome split-rail fences. And once rebuilt, they came: the teachers with their students, the Boy Scouts, the history buffs, the tourists, the Blueberry Festival people, the beekeepers, the colonial cooking instructors and the busloads of crafters. Every weekend seemed to welcome yet another influx of celebrants.

When my older brother, Richard, visited from Florida, naturally his first request was to see the place Mom had helped to save. I drove him to the pasture named after its first owner and now known to all as the Burnside Farm. We walked together in silence, soaking in the magnitude of what the community had unselfishly accomplished. Some school children were studying the unusual botanical names printed on identification tags lining the herb garden. A gaggle of geese waddled near the meandering Monocacy Creek. I could hear one horse nicker to another in the barn.

And then came an unexpected surprise. Attached to the base of a black cherry sapling was a small brass plaque. It read *Dedicated To The Memory Of Gertrude Fox*. It became harder to read the inscription as my eyes began to tear. Same with my brother. We just stood there, staring. Mom's name was affiliated with a sapling. Granted, it wasn't a dam or a two-lane bridge, but the thought was just the same, and Richard and I were deeply touched.

- - -

Somebody named Taylor Hathaway was on the phone.

"Your mother, Gertrude, God rest her soul, was the 'sparkplug' that resurrected Burnside. Without her foresight and common sense, that historical site wouldn't exist today. I am honored to serve on the board of directors. We believe that a member of the Fox family should serve on the board as well. I'm calling to ask you to join us and your late mother's worthy cause."

Some entreaties should be answered only in the positive. Just last week, a junior Brownie sporting a pair of merit badges appeared unannounced upon my doorstep.

"Hey Mister, you wanna buy a box of Girl Scout cookies?" the 9-year-old voice implored.

I would have given her the initial down payment on the Brooklyn Bridge.

Taylor Hathaway was awaiting my response. "Mr. Hathaway, I am deeply honored by this unexpected invitation, but I already serve on six ... "

"We only meet once every three months, the first Monday of the third month ... "

"Mr. Hathaway, I hesitate to take on a commitment I may not be able to ... "

"The members of the board unanimously chose your name over 15 other candidates."

My goose was cooked. I had been outmaneuvered by a pro. "I'd be honored to join the board," I gushed.

- - -

It was time to attend my first board meeting, time to sit as a pretender to the throne among truly important people who legitimately deserved to have important things named in their memory. I sat silent and humbled as this group of community leaders assembled in the hand-cut, wooden-beamed meeting room located in the barn one floor above the horse stalls. I was about to become privy to the inner workings of this august body of dedicated citizens.

Hathaway gaveled the meeting to order. "Do I hear a motion to accept the previous minutes?"

"So moved," Colin Fletcher responded.

Wasn't he the mayor's personal assistant?

"Is there a second?"

"Second," Bloomhilda Snarlssted volunteered.

Wasn't she recently pictured on the society page, resplendent in her flowing holiday gown at the hospital's black-tie gala?

"All in favor of the motion?"

The show of hands suggested that the motion would be unanimous, if I also stuck my little paw skyward.

"The next order of business is the maintenance and grounds committee report," Hathaway announced.

Anclova DeLorenta stood up - THE Anclova DeLorenta. Some of her Rubens and Picassos were on loan to the Tri-State Museum of Art. She cleared her delicate throat.

"It is with great sadness that I report the demise of yet another sapling. This time the beavers took the Gertrude Fox black cherry."

Anclova stood stoically silent as the collective gasp of 15 community leaders filled the room. Downstairs, I thought I heard a horse sigh as well.

Anclova - THE Anclova - turned and looked me right in the eye. "I am sure I speak for the entire board, Mr. Fox, when I express my heartfelt sympathy for your family's loss. I believe the finance committee will be placing on their next agenda the purchase of a beaver-proof replacement sapling."

There are times in life when one should not burst out laughing. Standing in the viewing line at a funeral comes to mind. As Anclova described the demise of my mother's sapling, I secretly hugged my sides with my elbows as I bit my lower lip, trying desperately not to insult all these caring souls, the assembled Who's Who of Bethlehem. I must have done a passable job. One of the board members, upon seeing my tortured face and a tear falling from my cheek, rushed to my side and gently patted me on the shoulder. Another flashed a tissue before me.

"There, there, Mr. Fox, we'll find a beaver-proof sapling, don't you worry."

I bit my lip harder as my body again began to shake.

"Thank you all," I whimpered.

- - -

Were there actual beavers in Pennsylvania? After recovering from the meeting, I decided to conduct a brief investigation of my own. As the Cadillacs and Mercedes left the parking lot, leaving my dented Dodge to fend for itself, I walked over to where my mother's memorial sapling had been growing. It wasn't there. What remained was a stump surrounded by some stray wood chips. I followed sapling drag-marks through the tall grass leading to the Monocacy Creek. I felt like Davy Crockett tracking a bear.

Down by the creek, some geese noted my approach and waddled out of harm's way. I walked along the bed of the tributary, not exactly sure what it was I was looking for. And then, another 40 feet downstream, I noted an unusually large collection of sticks, logs, branches and, yes, recently cut saplings, all packed together in the middle of the creek. I could have sworn a beaver was paddling nearby.

My mother loved this creek. In one of her other crusades, she had fought successfully to minimize the sources of pollution entering the tiny waterway. Now fish and geese abounded, and apparently a beaver or two.

I had never actually seen a beaver dam before. What I saw was an engineering marvel. These little mammalian developers had bulldozed part of the Burnside Farm and had created their own aquatic condominium.

I was about to leave this idyllic setting when something affixed to the top of the mound caught the reflection of the evening's setting sun. For a moment, a beam of light shot across my face. I inched slightly closer as I tried to find stepping stones protruding from the muddy creek bank.

There, partially obscured by a recently chewed branch, sat a brass plate still clinging to part of a sapling, like a diamond tiara adorning the head of a princess. The words were barely visible: *Dedicated To The Memory Of Gertrude Fox.*

That pile of sticks might not have been as grandiose as Hoover Dam, but there was nothing else that could compare to it in all of the Monocacy Creek. Mom would have been proud of her beaver dam.

# CHAPTER FIFTEEN

## The Heat's On

How could he have been so treacherous? How could she have been so naïve?

Aged widow Sophie Walkernagel rented a second-floor walkup from Denny Davis, her fast-talking, unscrupulous landlord. Rumor had it that Denny was well-off, and that his wealth had been amassed in part by cutting corners.

Sophie paid top dollar for a modest four-room apartment, and yet Denny was always slow to respond to her legitimate requests. The water failed to drain out of the sink. He didn't seem to care. Several electrical outlets were useless. He never had the time to hire an electrician. But the big problem was the heat, or more specifically, the lack thereof. It was winter, and Denny kept the downstairs thermostatic control under lock and key. It took two days of telephone calls before Sophie received a response.

"It's very cold in here," she pleaded. "Could you turn up the heat a little?"

"Cold? You must be mistaken. I've got the control set at a balmy 72 degrees," the con-artist responded. "Are you wearing a wool sweater?"

After Sophie contracted double pneumonia, Denny reluctantly appeared at her door. She was enveloped in two sweaters.

"Now here's what I'm gonna do," the snake in landlord's clothing offered. "As you can see, I brought my toolbox. I'm gonna install a thermostat right here in your apartment. Nobody else in the building has one. When you feel cold, you can turn up the heat."

"Splendid," Sophie coughed as she repositioned her hot-water bottle.

"Now you go in the kitchen and make us some nice tea. When you come out, the thermostat will be installed. But you've got to promise me one thing in return."

"Anything, whatever you say," the shivering elderly woman agreed.

"Don't turn the dial above 72 degrees. I can't afford to operate a sauna."

"I promise," Sophie confirmed as she headed toward the kitchen.

When she emerged ten minutes later, the installation was complete. A new thermostatic control graced her living room wall. Denny drank his tea and departed.

A few days later, Sophie called Denny.

"It's still cold in here," she protested.

"What do you mean? I gave you your own thermostat. Isn't it working?"

"Well, I guess it got a little warmer, but ... "

"You didn't turn it past 72 did you?"

"Oh no. I promised I wouldn't."

"Then what's the problem? It's got to be much warmer than it was."

Two days later, Sophie's neighbors called the hospital. Her pneumonia had become life-threatening. As the ambulance attendants wheeled her out of the apartment, the thermostat Denny had installed fell off the wall, since it wasn't connected to anything. The suction cup Denny had used to attach the fake device was defective as well.

- - -

I graduated from law school in 1973. I was penniless. I had no job, no prospect of a job, no place to live, no money and no car. I also had no debt, so I could buy anything, even a new vehicle. I took out a loan of $1,900 and bought a straight-from-the-assembly-line, robin's-egg blue Volkswagen "Beetle" right off the showroom floor.

"Are you sure you wouldn't prefer to purchase a Mercedes or Cadillac?" the bank loan officer had inquired.

"After all, you can afford it. You don't owe anyone a dime, and you'll be raking in the dough in no time."

"I'm destitute," I confessed. "I don't have a nickel to my name."

The wise loan officer smiled. "Take advantage of the situation, son. You may never be this well-off again."

He was, of course, correct. Soon I would also shoulder the responsibility of a law office, a monthly mortgage payment and the obligation to pay a secretary each Friday for the rest of my working life.

- - -

I drove my new car around town for a week as I looked for a suitable place to set up an office. Then I pulled into a gas station to get some fuel. The tank had a capacity of 10 and half gallons. I squeezed in 10 gallons, paid the attendant $2.85 and received a free coffee mug after he finished cleaning my windshield.

My new car had everything: a driver's seat that reclined in two different positions with just the crank of a handle, a steering wheel with a real simulated leather cover, a gas gauge, AM radio, ashtray with cigarette lighter (in case I ever took up smoking), a glove compartment (in case I ever bought a pair of gloves), turn signals, a low-oil-pressure light, and an engine in the rear. It even had a heater that could be operated on either a "low" or "high" setting. Cadillac - Schmadillac. My 64-horsepower, four-cylinder machine and I were now kings of the road.

Then came the winter and office overhead. I figured I'd probably be able to keep above the water line if I didn't buy anything else for the next 30 years.

I loved my VW Bug. It might not have had a radiator, but so what. Lots of people keep moving for years without a gall bladder. Maybe it didn't have air-conditioning, but there were those handy little wing-windows. And best of all, it would be paid off in just four short years despite the cost of gas having recently risen to almost 29 cents a gallon.

December turned into January. It was getting quite cold. There was no longer a need to roll down the windows. It was time to try out my new VW heater. The Beetle's designers had thought of everything. A small vent in the dashboard was designed to blow warm or hot air in the direction of the driver, and a similar vent projected warm or hot air upon the front passenger. With time, this heat would make its way back to the rear passengers, similar to the good old days when smoke infiltrated the non-smoking area of a restaurant.

I activated the heater button by turning the little white arrow to the "low" setting. I saw no reason to overtax the system during its maiden operation. The response was immediate and assuring. From somewhere deep within the confines of the dashboard I heard the unmistakable whirring of a fan, perhaps two of them. Instantaneously, forced air began to shoot from the dashboard vents. A strong current not unlike the Gulf Stream filled my little robin's-egg-blue encapsulated world. Curiosity got the better of me. I turned the indicator arrow to the "high" position. The interior fans responded without hesitation. A torrent of air poured forth as unseen spinning blades rose to a high pitch, proclaiming that winter drives in my new car would be toasty-warm.

- - -

Jake Brackenbill had once again been charged with passing worthless checks. He was one of those guys who had an answer for everything except how to take responsibility for his actions. I had represented him before on a similar charge, which became even more complex when he gave his probation officer a restitution check that proved to have been drawn on a closed account. His preliminary hearing was scheduled to take place before Magistrate Dooley in 45 minutes. He unexpectedly showed up at my office.

"Can I get a ride with you?" he asked me. "I don't think my car is inspected, and the place will be crawling with cops."

I grabbed his file, and we jumped into my VW. It was freezing outside.

"Shouldn't a lawyer be driving a Mercedes or a Cadillac?" he asked as he surveyed my Bug.

I turned on the heater. The interior fans came to life as they began their familiar whirring duet.

"It should be warm in a minute or two," I assured my client as I adjusted my scarf and earmuffs.

"Who are you kidding?" Jake responded. "This is a VW Beetle. There's no radiator and no hot-water circulation, ergo, no heat. Are you telling me you've actually felt something warm emerge from those microscopic vents?"

Come to think of it, I couldn't truthfully answer that question in the affirmative. I always had on my heavy jacket so I simply assumed the car's interior atmosphere was getting warmer. As we drove on, our visibly frosty breath continued to condense in ever thickening layers on the inside of the windshield. I removed one of my mittens and groped with a frozen hand toward the vent cover. There wasn't a trace of heat, just a torrent of cold, blowing air. Jake noted my surprise and concern.

"What you got here, counselor, is a psychological heater," he explained. "Perhaps we should roll down the windows to let in some heat."

"What type of heater?" I yelled over the drone of the spinning fans.

"A psychological heater. It makes a lot of noise, so psychologically you figure it must be producing some heat. As a result you feel warmer, even if you aren't."

I stared in shock through the only portion of the front windshield that wasn't obstructed by the interior build-up of ice, hoping the defroster would kick in soon.

"Look," he explained, "I know what I'm talking about. I give people psychological checks. The paper is worthless, but at least the recipient gets a warm and fuzzy feeling - temporarily."

# Chapter Sixteen

## Congratulations

Joe McCarty was my friend and one of the most knowledgeable CPAs in town. I could always count on him to lend a hand, even on weekends. A mutual client was the object of a complex IRS audit, so Joe and I met early Sunday morning to review a multitude of exhibits. We started at seven a.m. sharp, because Joe made it clear he had to wrap things up to attend 10 o'clock Mass.

We catalogued and indexed documents for more than two hours. Then Joe instinctively checked his watch.

"That's all for today," he announced, as he began to shove papers back into his briefcase. "It's time for church."

I thanked him for his time. As usual, his insights were invaluable.

"What are you doing with the rest of your morning?" he asked.

"No plans," I admitted. "I'll probably stay at the office and catch up on my dictation."

Joe closed his laptop computer as he turned toward me. "You know, Larry, you're always welcome to come to church. You might find the hour uplifting. No strings attached."

This was not the first invitation to Catholic Mass I had received this year. As a graduate of Villanova University School of Law, my presence was requested at the annual Red Mass, a celebration invoking the blessing of the Holy Spirit upon those serving the legal community. It was an elaborate affair, over which the Archbishop of Philadelphia presided. I rarely turned down sincere offers to gather with others where God was sure to be present.

"I think I'll go with you," I replied.

"Good," Joe responded. "It's just three blocks to St. Mary's."

We walked over to the towering, century-old church, each stone and beam of which had been transported by horse power and laid in place without the benefit of power equipment, computer drawings or college-trained architects.

We made our way to a pew where Joe knelt in prayer as I studied the ornate stained glass windows fashioned by the hands of an artist who had probably lived during the Civil War. The service was well attended, the music lovely and the sermon thought-provoking. I was glad I had accepted the invitation. It was time for the collection. Four men appeared on cue at the front of the church, each carrying a 14-foot pole to which was attached a one-foot-square wicker basket. Each of the four rows of pews was 15 feet long. As a result, one of the four baskets could be passed under the chin of each congregant, an act requiring some talent since retrieval of the basket could result in poking a hole through a stained glass window.

The four men, laden with ever-increasing wealth, systematically made their silent journeys to the back of the cathedral, where the contents of the baskets, now bending their poles as if they had hooked marlins on a fishing line, were unceremoniously dumped into yet a larger wicker basket held by a priest. This servant of God then walked the entire length of the church, ascended the altar, momentarily lifted the basket heavenward and then disappeared through a hidden backdoor, carrying the spoils of the morning with him. No one seemed to care, with the possible exception of me. My experience at Protestant services cried out for a more hands-on approach. Protestants pass one basket from congregant to congregant. Then the church treasurer and his assistant count the money and render an accounting.

I left Mass with more questions than when I had entered. Such is the mystery of great religions. I decided to inquire of my host as we made our way through the congregants now gathered on the sidewalk.

"Joe ... "

"Yes?"

"The money that was collected today ... "

"Yes?"

"I put some in." I wanted Joe to know that I felt I had standing, a vested interest, to ask the next question.

"It will be used for good causes," Joe assured me.

"Joe, who counts the money collected today?"

"A priest."

"Not the one on the pulpit? Not the one whose sermon inspired me to make a donation?"

"No, another priest."

"Where does he count the money?"

Joe, the certified public accountant, seemed confused by my question. "In the back office, I suppose."

"Is there someone with him, helping with the count?"

"I don't know. I never gave it much thought."

"When do you get an accounting?"

"An accounting?"

"Of the money?"

"If you put your money in your envelope with your name on it, you get an accounting of what you paid at the end of the year," Joe explained matter-of-factly.

"But you already know what *you* paid," I exclaimed. "When do you find out the total of what was collected?"

"You mean annually?" Joe looked at me as if I had just flown in from another planet. "Parishioners don't receive a statement of all the money collected."

"Why not?"

"Too much information."

"Protestants and Jews get an accounting."

"That's different. See, it's like this. Catholic churches are part of a parish. You must attend Mass each week in the parish where you find yourself. So, as an example, if you're on vacation at the Jersey Shore, you go to Mass there. Then your money that week goes to the New Jersey parish. You don't get an accounting of their money. They keep it in New Jersey.

"Now Jews, they're different. If they want to join a synagogue, they give 10 percent of their earnings up front each year to the rabbi. Then they can vacation free in New Jersey without going to another temple, and those who believe in heaven may still get in.

"Protestants are a collection of several sub-groups. Presbyterians know what they're doing. They build only one church in each community, so when the roof leaks, they've got a captive audience and money to fix it. Lutherans, Baptists and UCCers aren't business savvy. They build churches all over the place at the drop of a hat and then sell shoefly pies in competition with each other as they try to stay in the black. No wonder they need an accounting. Episcopalians don't care, what with all their endowment funds."

I was glad Joe had clarified things for me. This information would come in handy just one week later. Morley Stipple, who had recently been relocated to the Lehigh Valley, stopped by my office with an ecumenical accounting question of his own.

"It's nice to make your acquaintance," I assured my newest client as we shook hands in my law library. "Please sit down."

"I just arrived in the area," Morley explained. "I've been given the manager's job at a warehouse out in the industrial park, so last month I moved the wife and kids here from Ohio."

"I think you'll like the Valley," I confirmed. "I've lived here my entire life."

"Well, here's the situation," Morley continued. "We began to attend services at the Lutheran Church out near Seipstown. Been Lutherans all our lives. The church is only around the bend from our house. The minister and congregation seemed nice. After two Sundays, we felt right at home."

"So what's the problem?" I asked.

"Last week we joined the church. After services, everyone went to the social hall for cake and coffee. That's when the minister made an announcement. The place has termites and the roof leaks, so each family is going to be assessed $500 to help pay for the repairs. Is that enforceable, or can I quit and join the Lutheran Church three miles down the road?"

I wanted to tell Morley, who had probably failed to inquire as to whether his new church had a building fund escrow, about shoefly pies and why Lutheran churches compete with each other, but before I could, the hand of God took hold of me, as I heard these words being whispered in my ear:

*October 1, 1973 ...*

Arguably, it was one of the most magical days of my life. It was the day I learned I had passed the Pennsylvania Bar Exam. After 19 years of private education, 12 in a private Protestant school, four in a Lutheran college and three in a Catholic law school, I could now practice my chosen profession.

Things began to happen at a fast pace. I received notice that in just 48 hours I would be standing before the Northampton County Court of Common Pleas. My mentor and preceptor, Harlan Zipp, would petition for my admission as an attorney. Eight other lucky law school graduates would take the same oath, as proud parents, spouses, siblings and friends watched in Courtroom Number One of the Easton Courthouse.

The president judge, flanked by his black-robed brethren, uttered the joyful pronouncement.

"The Court, having reviewed the applications before it, finds all to be in order and is prepared to administer the oath of attorney. Gentlemen, raise your right hands and repeat after me."

At the conclusion of the oath, His Honor proclaimed that we were now attorneys, certified to practice within these hallowed halls. Spontaneous applause broke out among the audience. It was time for a speech or two. The president of the Northampton County Bar Association was introduced and stepped to the podium.

"Congratulations," he began. "The Northampton County Bar Association welcomes our newest attorneys and extends an invitation to attend the quarterly meeting scheduled tomorrow night at Hotel Bethlehem. There you may seek permission to join our local bar association as its newest members."

In the space of 48 hours, I had received word I had passed the bar exam. I had taken the oath of attorney, and now I was about to join the county bar association. Life was good.

The next evening, I donned my only suit and drove to the Hotel Bethlehem. Seventy lawyers were milling about in the grand ballroom, sipping drinks and boasting of courtroom exploits.

Then waitresses in crisp white uniforms brought out the entrees and everyone sat down to a sumptuous candlelit dinner. I was impressed.

There followed a business meeting. The nine new attorneys were introduced to the elder members of the bar. Each of us was asked if we wished to join their bar association. Without hesitation we all answered in the affirmative. A vote was then taken to determine if anyone wished to preclude our admission. We were given unanimous approval. I beamed with pride, the newest inductee of a select fraternity

"Congratulations," the bar association president proclaimed.

The business meeting continued.

"Gentlemen," (there were no women attorneys at this time) the association president announced, "there is another matter to discuss."

Those in attendance grew still as dessert was served.

"You will recall that last year Amos Grabonosky, one of our former members, was disbarred after he pled guilty to stealing $50,000 from his 90-year-old, blind, wheelchair-bound client. He is now in the county prison serving time for his crime."

Grabonosky ... disbarment! I thought to myself.

"We have a responsibility, as members of the bar, to show our community that we will not permit those practicing law to commit such wrongs. Therefore, the executive committee has passed a resolution whereby each member of the bar association will be surcharged $1,000 in order that the victim of this crime may be made whole again."

I began to squirm in my one and only suit. I had no job and had just taken out a loan of $1,900 so I could finally own a car. Shouldn't somebody have brought up the issue regarding the surcharge *before* they voted us in as members? What den of thieves had I joined? Was anyone else planning in the near future to rip off little old ladies? Was I as naïve as a Lutheran joining a church full of termites?

Three months later, I was assigned by the court before which I had sworn my allegiance to represent some indigent felon for free. I went over to the Northampton County Prison, interviewed the bum, then made my way down the secured corridor to the big iron gate that stood at the exit to the lockup. I waited to be released by the guard holding a huge brass key. So did another man, who was wearing a derby and dapper checkered red vest. He carried an umbrella and a suitcase. It hadn't rained in five days. The guard opened the last obstacle to freedom, and we both emerged into the sunlight. He looked about as if he were lost.

"You by any chance going toward Bethlehem?" the strange man, perhaps 60 years of age, inquired.

"Yes, as a matter of fact I am," I admitted, a little startled.

"Got room for another passenger?"

He had all his teeth and spoke coherently. For some reason I, who never picked up hitchhikers, did not fear him.

"All I've got is a VW Beetle."

"Beats walkin'," he responded.

We made our way to the prison parking lot.

"Amos is the name." He put his umbrella under his arm and stuck out his hand. I shook it.

"Larry ... Larry Fox."

We squeezed into the VW.

"You an attorney?"

"Yes," I confirmed.

"I'll give you some advise, counselor," Amos offered. "Don't drink, don't gamble and keep your trustee account balanced."

Amos Grabonosky was going home for the first time in a year. It wasn't like the movies. No one was there to greet him. We drove for a few blocks in silence, squeezed shoulder to shoulder in my VW Bug.

"Mr. Grabonosky ... "

"Call me Amos. My friends just call me ... come to think of it, I may not have friends anymore. Nobody came to visit me."

"Amos ... "

"Yes, son?"

"I was surcharged because of your crime."

"You were?"

"Everyone in the bar association has to pay $1,000. Since I make about $100 net a week, I may be paying in installments for the next five years."

"That's not fair," Amos mused. "And here you are helping me with a ride home. Maybe my only friend. Tell you what ... "

"What?"

"I'll send you a check for $1,000. I don't want you to be adversely impacted by my unfortunate indiscretion."

I dropped Amos off in front of his house. There was a foreclosure notice posted on his front door.

That was 30 years ago. I'm still waiting for his check.

## Chapter Seventeen

### Big

I paid a considerable amount of money during my pursuit of an education to attend countless lectures. I recall a small portion of what was discussed.

It's funny how often a chance fleeting conversation impacts you forever, even though you paid nothing to acquire the valuable insight imparted.

I finished my oral argument before the Justices of the Commonwealth Court in Harrisburg. Had they heard a word I said? Did they care? I had awoken at four a.m. to be on the road by five, then drove three hours to the capital of Pennsylvania, only to learn some city planner had obviously failed to make provision for me to park my car. Then I waited three hours until my case was called, whereupon I was given 10 minutes, and not a second more, to explain to this appellate panel why the junkyard existing next to my client's house constituted a non-conforming use for which no permit had been obtained.

It was almost noon, and I faced the long journey home, assuming my car was still there. Surely the one-hour time limit on the meter had expired, transforming my vehicle into a non-conforming object existing on a public thoroughfare without the requisite permit.

I ran down the fancy courthouse's marble steps constructed at taxpayer expense, jumped into my parked car and with little fanfare, no lunch and a three-hour drive looming ahead of me, headed back to Bethlehem. Hunger overtook me at Exit 27, so I turned into the Seipstown Diner. My life would never again be the same.

I had entered Pennsylvania Dutch country. This restaurant was not McDonalds and it wasn't Burger King. The animated staff served breakfast 24 hours a day. They had scrapple with eggs, scrapple with waffles, scrapple with pancakes, scrapple on toast with creamed chipped beef, and for the not-so-daring there was plain scrapple. I perused the six-page menu and then ordered the chef's salad.

"Would you like a side order of scrapple, then?" the enthusiastic waitress inquired.

Every waitress in Pennsylvania Dutch country ends most sentences with the word "then."

When in Rome ... I thought to myself. "Yes," I confirmed. "Scrapple and a chef's salad."

"Would you like that well done, medium, or mushy, then?"

"The salad?"

"No. The scrapple."

"I'll leave that decision up to you."

"Excellent," she affirmed as her face took on the glow of someone raised on scrapple.

There I sat in Seipstown, exhausted and alone. Or was I? The back of the high bench in my booth bounced back and forth as new occupants plopped themselves into the cubicle next to mine. My spine and head now rested inches away from the spine and head of someone facing the opposite direction, someone I could not see. It soon became apparent that two interlopers had invaded the solitude of my space, and that I had unintentionally become privy to their rather intimate discussion.

From the spontaneity of the giggles, the non-stop chatter and the sing-song octave changes in voice, I surmised that two lasses of college age, obviously close friends, had temporarily entered my life, yet were oblivious to my existence. One supplied most of the giggles, while the other provided a significant portion of the astonishment and heavy breathing.

"So, like, guess what?" (Giggle.)

"What?"

(Dead silence.)

"WHAT?"

I stopped munching on my last saltine. I could tell something important was coming, so I ceased breathing momentarily, lest I cause a vibration to ripple through the back of our shared seat, thereby revealing my presence.

"Ronny and I finally did IT last night!"

"NO!" (Astonished heavy breathing.)

"Yup." (Giggle.) "On, like, our three-month anniversary."

"NO!" (More heavy breathing.)

I was jealous, not of Ronny, but of the fact I couldn't share in the heavy breathing.

"Well, give me, like, all the details! I can't wait to hear!"

I was glad she said that. I wanted to, like, say the same thing.

"Wellll, it was, like, right after the basketball game let out, but we were still, like, sitting on the bleachers. He was wearing those blue jeans I gave him, and then ... "

"Excuse me, ladies. You'se ready to order, then?"

Damn! The waitress must have appeared at their table. This interruption might change the entire course of the discussion. The two scatterbrains might not pick up where they left off.

"I'll take a grilled cheese sandwich on white, a cup of pea soup and a diet coke."

"You want a side order of scrapple with?"

Waitresses in Pennsylvania Dutch country also sometimes end a sentence with a hanging preposition.

"Sounds good."

"What about you, honey?"

"The chicken stir-fry and a chocolate milkshake. Heavy on the syrup."

"Scrapple with?"

"Okay. A side order of scrapple."

The waitress had failed to ask if the lasses wanted the scrapple mushy. They probably were regulars who didn't need to say a word. I heard the server's footsteps trail off toward the kitchen. Would the interrupted conversation continue?

"So, like, guess what?"
"What!"
"It's true what they say."
"About what?"
"Big hands means he's got a big ... you know what."
(Astonished heavy breathing, or was that me?)
"You mean ... "
"Yup. Ronny's not that tall, and he only weighs, like, 130, but he has those really big hands. Well, that ain't the only thing that's really big."
"Little Ronny?"
"Hung like a door." (Giggle, giggle.)

My waitress was back. "Now let's see, honey ... a chef's salad, and a scrapple, medium. What do you want to drink, then?"

Nuts. The efficient waitress had given away my position. The conversation over in the other booth had suddenly become subdued as animated whispers became the primary means of communication.

The impact of this unique moment cannot be overstated. I tentatively looked down at my rather small or delicate - no, let's be honest about this - my little hands. The ones that had trouble striking an octave on the piano keys. Had thousands of women over the years, unbeknown to me, looked at these diminutive appendages and concluded, without offering me a chance to present rebuttal evidence, that part of me was less than ...

"Here's some water, honey," the waitress announced as I struggled to hide my telltale hands. Had she seen them? Had she and every other woman in this diner heard and accepted the theory that big hands meant a big ... you know? Did she believe in the opposite premise, small hands served as proof positive of a small ... you know?

- - -

I represented Amber. Maybe that was her first name, maybe it was her last. At the strip club where she danced, each girl was known by but one name. I became privy to her real name, the first, middle and last, because it was written on the criminal complaint charging her with prostitution.

I liked Amber, because unlike so many other clients coming in and out of my law office, she had nothing to hide, said what was on her mind, and paid my monthly legal fee without hesitation, usually by handing me a stack of crumpled one dollar bills. She was a breath of fresh air.

Amber made a living at the strip club, one dollar at a time, but she never seemed to retain much money. She didn't even own a car. As usual, she needed a ride to the courthouse, so I picked her up as requested at the corner of Fourth and Broadway. She was always on time for her arraignments. She crushed her cigarette with her stiletto shoe, took off her gold and silver sequin jacket and nestled into the front passenger seat of my VW Beetle. She looked about my compact economy car as if she had just entered an alien spacecraft. The car needed a new paint job, having endured eight hot summers and eight cold winters. There wasn't enough room for both her feet and her handbag, so she put her carry-on luggage in the abbreviated back seat, next to my briefcase. Her face was unable to hide her disbelief.

"Honey," she began, "I've paid you a king's ransom to represent me, and this piece of crap is all you can afford to drive? What'll it do - zero to 40 in five minutes?"

I was about to respond, but her attention had already begun to focus upon something else.

"Of course, the good news is you gotta have the biggest pecker in the Lehigh Valley."

She had caught me off guard.

"I beg your pardon?" I wasn't thinking fast enough. I should have said, "How ever did you know?"

"Honey, you're talking to a pro. Every gal in the business will tell you that guys who drive flashy, expensive muscle cars invariably are overcompensating for their microscopic you-know-whats."

I stared at my small hands grasping the steering wheel. Amber hadn't taken notice of them. She knew the true measure of a man, the size of his car.

The following week I traded in the VW and bought something a little smaller.

## Chapter Eighteen

The Midnight Star

Once upon a time a couple of centuries ago, doctors in this country were doctors. If the patient suffered from gout, shingles, diarrhea, headaches, heart palpitations, tuberculosis, broken bones, hernia, kidney stones, deformed toes, brain tumor - it didn't much matter since most of the remedies were the same - he visited his doctor for a cure. Then came specialization in medicine and everything changed. The ailing party needed a referral to get an appointment to consult with the foreign physician on the wrong insurance plan who "English I not speak so good."

There once was a time when a lawyer was a lawyer. If the client needed a last will and testament, slipped on a banana peel, thought he was slandered, intended to purchase a farm, was charged with a crime, finally found his true love and needed a simple divorce from the wife and six kids - it didn't much matter since most of the paperwork looked the same - he visited his neighborhood lawyer for a remedy. Then came personal rights and the IRS tax code, and everything changed. The troubled party needed a specialist for just about everything - securities fraud, capital gains avoidance, elder law and Medicaid disputes, municipal law, land use planning, copyrights and trademarks, matrimonial law, landlord-tenant arbitration, construction financing, bankruptcy protection, criminal law, contract drafting, personal injury and environmental law, just to mention a few topics. Some lawyers even specialize in suing doctors who "English I not speak so good."

- - -

Specializing in one area of the law or another grants unto the practitioner certain perks, some readily apparent, others perhaps more subtle in nature. As an example, the attorney defending drug dealers gets to visit exotic and interesting prisons and prisoners. The personal injury counsel gets to play with life-size anatomical manikins, the type where the muscles come off exposing the nervous system and then the skeleton. The sports and entertainment attorney enjoys collecting autographed pictures from famous football players and pro-bowlers.

I'm involved to a large degree in estate work, taking care of the numerous needs of dead people, who often have more legal problems than those of us who are still alive. Some dead people don't plan their funerals, or write last wills, or clarify exactly how many children they actually produced. Some dead people prefer to create riddles and let others search for the answers. Was the decedent married or just living with a roommate for the last 20 years? Where did he do his banking and maintain his clandestine investments, and why was that information such a guarded secret?

I am called upon to render an accounting of the decedent's money and worldly goods, and to distribute the bounty to designated surviving loved ones without the undesignated surviving loved ones killing the designated surviving loved ones.

There are perks to this job. Dead people don't telephone, complain much about legal fees, or demand that I pursue meritless appeals. Also, their mail is rerouted to my office so I can review incoming bills, dividend checks, and other important correspondence. At first I didn't realize what a personal benefit this might be, especially with regard to what some fools might consider to be useless "junk mail."

Erma LaBrook died last year. The quiet, unassuming 70-year-old widow lived alone in one of the row homes on $10^{th}$ Avenue. She bowled every Tuesday in the afternoon ladies league, volunteered at the local hospital, attended church regularly, and left a last will and testament giving everything to her two nearest living relatives, a pair of nieces who resided across the country in California. She had some modest savings at Keystone Federal and a small pension from the telephone company. She also had a three-year prepaid subscription to *The Midnight Star*, the tell-all weekly gossip newspaper that employs predatory paparazzi to take embarrassing impromptu photographs of the rich and famous. Why any normal-thinking human being would waste time perusing the nonsense lurking between the covers of this rag sheet was an incomprehensible mystery to me. Yet sweet, law-abiding Erma LaBrook not only immersed herself in this printed garbage, she sought out a long-term subscription at the preferred customer rate.

After Erma passed away, I was retained to assist with the administration of her estate. Her mail was forwarded to my office so my staff could timely pay her bills and account for any income derived from her modest investments. A week after her funeral, the first packet from the post office, all addressed to the decedent, showed up at my door. I unwrapped the bundle. There was a TV cable bill, so I dictated a memo to cancel that service. There was a water and sewer statement, a reminder that her car needed an oil change, a church picnic announcement and, finally, a copy of *The Midnight Star*. This last periodical caught my eye. Even if I had been scheduled for cataract surgery, it still would have captured my attention. The expansive cover, emblazoned in sweeping colors of fire engine red, pastel sky blue and sunset yellow, boasted no less than three separate front-page pictorials about important people and their interesting lives. Over on the right was a "before" and "after" snapshot of a famous soap opera star who had lost her pregnancy "baby bulge" in just six short weeks. The enclosed secret diet and exercise schedule were mine for the reading. At the bottom right was an exclusive photo of an unhappy movie star throwing her purse at some insolent bellhop who hadn't hopped quite fast enough. Over on the left was a half-page spread exposing the love triangle of a confused congressman and an unsuspecting cab driver who both dated a lesbian lover.

For years I have paid good money to have *The Wall Street Journal* and *The New York Times* delivered to my office. I have attempted at some cost to remain informed. How had these so-called sophisticated daily journals failed to report the important events captured by the *Star*? Didn't they realize that inquiring minds want to know stuff?

I had only two hours left to prepare for a complex afternoon hearing before Judge Hambrook regarding my motion for injunctive relief to preclude an abutting landowner from obstructing ingress and egress to an easement by necessity. I was pretty sure most of my exhibits were in order and properly labeled. But I wasn't quite done reading the *Star*. How had I become addicted so quickly? I turned one fascinating page after another. I don't drink coffee, yet my anxious fingers were now trembling with excitement. I had no idea rap stars made so much money. Maybe I could come up with a syncopated rhyme or two and leave the rat race behind. And this article on Liberace's piano collection - who would have thought the diamonds encrusted in the pink Steinway were real?

Life has meaning when something exciting lends anticipation to an otherwise humdrum existence. I could hardly wait for Monday. That's when the postman delivered all the wrapped packets of estate mail gathered during the week. Where was he? Didn't he realize I had an inquiring mind that had fallen behind on current events?

The receptionist was at my door. "Here's your - "

I jumped across the table that separated me from the indispensable news. The receptionist threw the bundles in the air and fled in panic. I scurried about on hand and knee desperately seeking the package that lay somewhere on the floor, strewn among useless dividend checks. My eye searched for intermixed hues of fire engine red, pastel sky blue and sunset yellow. I found them reposing together under a padded chair.

My trembling fingers ripped off the rubber band separating me from the news. A gas bill, a receipt from an undertaker, and a coupon for two bottles of mouthwash floated back to the ground. It didn't matter. The addict had found his fix. I sat down and soaked in the cover. There were three separate photo spreads, each focusing upon important events missed by lesser journals, whose subscriptions I was thinking of canceling.

*Psychic Sees End To Petroleum Supply By Next Century.* There was an accompanying picture of horse-drawn carriages.

*Murderer Confesses To Parrot Who Tells All.* There was a picture of a bird who obviously couldn't keep his beak shut.

*Self-taught Brain Surgeon Perfects New Procedure.* There was a picture of a maniac in surgical scrubs posing with a bloody scalpel.

My secretary stuck her head though the door. She had stumbled across *The Midnight Star* last week after I carefully secured it in the LaBrook estate file.

"Is that the new *Star*? Can I read it during - "

"Get away!" I screamed, as I clutched my prize. She retired in a hurried fashion similar to the receptionist.

I carefully turned scintillating photo-bestrewn page after page. *Fascinating ... Of all the nerve ... Who would have believed it ...?* I could hear myself say out loud.

And then it happened. Having digested the first 16 pages in less than half an hour, I turned to the next exciting exposé. There in the printed black-and-white word, accompanied by three exclusive action color photos, stood a headline like nothing I had ever read before.

*I Flew Half A Mile In A Tornado ... Clinging Onto My Toilet.* The byline helped to clarify things a bit. *Diana Jones tells how she was ripped from her home by a twister - and survived.*

She had flown farther on her first solo flight than the Wright Brothers, even though she was weighted down by a porcelain bowl. How far she might have traveled unaccompanied by the plumbing fixture was left unanswered.

*I don't know how long I was up there, but it must have been a few minutes,* Diana was quoted in the copyrighted feature. *Then I was struck by debris and lost my grip on the toilet.* That was understandable.

There was a full-color photograph illustrating Diana's involuntarily ascension into the funnel cloud accompanied by her life-saving ceramic anchor, and another picture showing the heroine re-enacting *how she clung to a toilet in a bid to withstand the force of the tornado. Her old toilet shattered and was never found.*

*I feel lucky I'm still here,* Diana confirmed.

I wonder if she reached that conclusion before she clicked her heels together and scooped up Toto. After all, there's no place like home. There's no place like home.

# Chapter Nineteen

## The Lost Thought

I'm the only one I know around here who is perfectly normal. That's because everything I do makes sense. Why other people don't think and act like me is difficult to understand. Yesterday was just one more example of what I have silently learned to endure.

It was a typical Tuesday at the law office. The phones were phoning, the fax machine was faxing and the e-mail was e-ing. I was standing in the secretarial area trying to coax a few more pages out of the hesitant copy machine. Laura sprinted down the stairs with that rare enthusiasm that is only possessed by recent law school graduates. Obviously there was something of great importance on her mind, and she needed to share it with us all. She would require our undivided attention, but both Tammy and Katie were tied up on the phones taking morning messages.

Laura was not one to waste precious time. She realized it would take a moment or two before she could address her audience, so she disappeared around the corner and headed toward the ladies' room while the opportunity presented itself. She emerged a minute later, just as the two secretaries ended their conversations, and I completed my paper shuffling.

"Listen, everyone, I've got to tell you something," she began as she motioned with her hands. I had never witnessed Laura speak unless she simultaneously moved her hands in a sign language known only to her. I had a theory I kept to myself that the only sure way to silence her was to tie her arms behind her back.

Tammy, Katie and I froze in our tracks. We had all previously experienced the consequences of ignoring impatient Laura, the poster child for instant gratification.

We didn't move a muscle, as we gave Laura the floor and our undivided attention.

"Listen, everyone, I've got to tell you something," she repeated with a hint of hesitation.

We were waiting. Then a look of profound loss began to spread across her face.

"I can't believe I forgot what I was going to say!" my young associate cried out in exasperation and embarrassment.

"That's okay," understanding Tammy said in her soothing, soft-spoken voice. "It happens to me all the time."

"But I had something important on my mind," Laura stammered.

"No problem. Where did you last have that thought?" helpful Tammy inquired.

Laura blinked her big eyes for a second or two as she pondered. "In the ladies' room."

"Good," helpful Tammy noted. "Just go back in the bathroom where you lost it, and you'll find it again."

Was I working with aliens from another world? Was that not the most ridiculous suggestion to have ever issued forth from a confused mind? Who, pray tell, loses a thought at a certain location and then returns to the scene looking for it?

"That's a good idea," Laura agreed as she headed toward the ladies' room. She returned 30 seconds later, the hesitation gone from her face.

"Okay. I remember now," she proudly announced.

I don't recall what she told us. Rather, I focused on the unsettling realization that I worked in a small office with strange women who apparently considered themselves to be quite normal.

## CHAPTER TWENTY

But They're Already Dead

The City of Bethlehem Public Works Department finally agreed to extend the municipal water line an additional two miles north along Appleblossom Road. By doing so, Woodland Acres, the new, exclusive, 500-unit gated private residential development would be able to construct three and one-half baths per residence, create a five-hole championship putting green and be assured of adequate fire protection.

I represented the *Rest in Peace Cemetery Association*, the northern boundary line of which was located just 200 yards from this new development. During the last 125 years, my client had overseen the burial of about 4,000 souls within its peaceful 90-acre tract, and there was room for yet another 4,000 dearly departed. The association kept a detailed map reflecting the location and identification number of each grave, the name of the deceased and the dimensions of each site. When a last resting plot was purchased, the owner received a deed describing all of this information. By law, the deed was not recorded at the courthouse nor was municipal subdivision approval required. Rather, the association was tasked with keeping such land records current and available for inspection.

The association maintained a small combination office-maintenance building in the middle of the cemetery. Mildred, the secretary, answered the phone there and met with customers shopping for a burial location. She used the same hunt-and-peck manual typewriter she first relied upon when she started 40 years ago. No glowing computer screen adorned her desk, since such gadgets were alien to her. The maintenance man kept his machinery in the back garage. There also was a small bathroom with one toilet and one sink. An on-site well and septic system dug a century ago supplied the water.

Mildred was confused by a letter the association just received, so she faxed it over to me for a response. The letter was from the City of Bethlehem Public Works Department, and it was bursting with news.

*Dear Landowner:*
*The City of Bethlehem has recently completed extension of municipal water lines along the boundary of your real estate abutting Appleblossom Road. Arrangements may be made with the City Plumbing Department to establish the location and cost of hookup. Pursuant to municipal ordinance 4-23-A, you are responsible for a one-time $5.00 per linear foot improvements assessment. This billing will arrive under separate cover.*
*Very truly yours,*

*Water Department*

Similar to a threat from the IRS, the letter was unsigned and referred to a department that had no telephone number or address.

"What exactly does all this mean?" Mildred asked through her black rotary telephone.

I decided I better call the city solicitor's office. They knew about such things. C. Corwin Newsam, Esquire, took my inquiry and explained the state of affairs so that even I might understand.

"See, it's like this. The statute provides that when new municipal water lines are installed, the property owner who benefits from the improvement is surcharged, based upon the lineal footage of real estate abutting the water line."

"What does that mean, exactly?"

"Well, according to our records, your client's real estate maintains a front footage along Appleblossom of 2,834 feet, and so you will be billed $14,170 for the improvements to your parcel."

"Wait a minute," I interjected. "The cemetery association doesn't own that front footage. It's filled up with hundreds of graves, owned by hundreds of dead people."

"Not according to the county assessment records. The only name recorded is that of your association."

"Of course. By law, individual cemetery deeds aren't recorded, but the people who bought the plots own them nonetheless."

"Then perhaps, when you get the bill, you may want to pass it along and charge each of the real owners for their fair share."

"But they're dead."

"And your point? Do you think that nullifies a valid assessment?"

"But none of these people will ever need any water!"

"That's of no significance. The value of their land has been enhanced."

"But they'll never sell it to anyone else! They don't plan to move."

"That's *their* decision."

- - -

Wendell Felspar, the self-proclaimed financial guru and author of three books on *The New York Times* bestseller list, was back in town. He was giving one of his popular financial planning seminars at the Holiday Inn. Last year he had instructed his loyal followers in the art of buying real estate at foreclosure sales while using other people's money. The year before he had enlightened his audience in the art of circumventing valid nursing home bills. Now he was about to discuss avoiding death taxes. That seemed like something good to know, so I decided to attend.

It was an over-75 crowd shuffling into the Holiday Inn, a crowd of people who looked like they might die someday. I fit right in.

Felspar proved to be an engaging and animated speaker, capable of captivating his audience. He pranced swiftly from one side of the room to the other, as he imparted his pearls of wisdom.

"Ladies and gentlemen, believe it or not, when someone dies as a widow, widower or single person in the Commonwealth of Pennsylvania, a minimum of four and a half percent of what he or she owns goes to the state before the remaining assets are to be transferred to direct lineal descendants. The tax rate is even higher if those who inherit are not directly related to the deceased. Furthermore, if at your death, you possess an estate of significant value, the federal government takes an even greater share.

"But there is a way to avoid these cruel, unjust and burdensome taxes. It's foolproof and yet so simple. Just place your assets in a trust. That way, when you die, they will not be part of your estate and thus not subject to tax. You can name yourself as trustee to administer the trust assets and that way you will know they are protected. As an example, you can transfer title of your house into the trust, with your stocks and bonds and anything else you wish. And it's so easy to do. For just $350, you may purchase my famous *Felspar Trust Book* and its accompanying audio tape, just as thousands of other tax-free trustees have done. Everything you need to know is in the packet, from amending you insurance policies to writing a meaningful obituary. Now are there any questions?" our instructor announced triumphantly.

Some little old man stood up and walked to where a portable microphone awaited inquiries. He appeared to have worked hard all his life. He looked as if no one had ever given him a dime. He cleared his throat.

"Let me see if I've got this right. I should pay you $350 so I can take everything I've worked a lifetime to earn and transfer it into a trust, so that I won't own anything anymore. Then because I don't own nothing, Pennsylvania gets no tax?"

"I wouldn't phrase it exactly that way," the surprised Felspar stammered.

"Well, how would you phrase it? You claim that I'll save big bucks in taxes. The way I see it, I won't save a nickel 'cause I'll be dead. And whoever inherits my estate won't save any taxes 'cause they'll get 94.5 percent of my estate as a gift without lifting a finger. So they spend nothing, they just receive slightly less."

"Well, I suppose you could look at it ... "

"Pardon me, Felspar. Is the house in which you reside titled in the name of a trust?" the old man inquired.

Felspar didn't answer that question. It wouldn't have mattered. There was too much noise created by the abrupt departure of most of the audience.

- - -

Humphrey Distlefink sat in my office, a confused look clouding his face.

"Last week I got notice from my insurance company that it won't insure my house until the deed is recorded in my name. Until then, they said they might provide 'renter's insurance' at a higher premium. But I own the house. I've been paying on that insurance without a problem for more than 30 years."

"The deed is in your name?" I asked.

"Sure is. I have it right here." Distlefink reached into an ancient envelope and produced a faded legal document. He handed it to me.

It was a deed from Distlefink's father to Distlefink. There was a problem, however.

"Mr. Distlefink," I began, "this deed is 40 years old. Unfortunately, it does not appear to have ever been recorded. There are no transfer stamps or imprinted county seals."

"So what?"

"A deed in your name must be recorded in order for title to be transferred to you."

"Why? In all them cowboy movies I've ever seen, they play high-stakes poker by wagering their deeds. Whoever wins gets the deed and owns the ranch. It was the same with my grandmother, dad and me."

"What do you mean?"

"My grandmother got the house from my great-grandmother. Then my grandmother gave the house to my dad."

He reached into the envelope and produced two more ancient unrecorded deeds. None of the handwritten deeds had been notarized, nor did they contain other minimal yet necessary recordation criteria. They were impressive historical documents, but not legally binding without the requisite recordation data.

I tried to explain that estates would need to be opened for both his grandmother and his father. Death taxes spanning the better part of a century were probably owed to the state. Distlefink found my remarks unsettling. He grabbed the deeds and returned them to the safety of their envelope.

"I'm not paying death taxes for a house I already own," he assured me.

I'm certain those souls reposing in the *Rest in Peace Cemetery* would have agreed with him.

# Chapter Twenty-One

## The Proposition

It was the fourth Thursday evening of the month, time once again for the Goshenhoppen Township Zoning Hearing Board to convene. I drove over to the municipal office, as I had on the previous fourth Thursday of each month during each of the last 10 years. I was the solicitor to the Board and, in that capacity, was called upon during hearings to field questions pertaining to zoning, evidence and procedure.

Most of the rural townships in the Lehigh Valley received only one or two requests for zoning hearings in any given month. Goshenhoppen averaged about five, and with good reason. Unlike other municipalities, it still possessed significant areas suitable for development, as well as adequate water and sewage facilities. Unending construction continued at a rapid pace.

The hearing room was packed. I took my place at the raised front stage with the five zoning board members and a stenographer, and faced the animated audience. The written zoning hearing agenda was positioned at each of our microphones. As I studied this document, it became clear we were in for a long evening.

Ferdie and Gretchen Pomperdink were petitioning to convert their old barn into a child day care center. Several objectors were present to voice their concerns regarding increased vehicular traffic in the neighborhood.

Ace Cement Company was seeking permission to construct a temporary batch plant in a proposed industrial campus so that the number of construction site deliveries might be minimized.

Sadie Bumberg wanted to add a sun porch to the back of her house, despite rear yard setback restrictions. The First Baptist Church needed a temporary permit to hold a bazaar in a mammoth portable tent. Dr. Gamo Blamha had returned with yet another inadequate site plan to explain why his new medical office could function with only eight parking spaces.

The final hearing dealt with the application of Igor Teprokasovich. He hoped to operate a butcher shop from the basement of his private residence. All of the surrounding neighbors were present to voice their concerns about the proposed sale of liverwurst and kidney pie in what was a quiet, residential setting.

I decided I better duck into the bathroom, since it would be a long night. Igor followed me into the cramped quarters to introduce himself.

"I Teprokasovich," he announced in a thick Russian accent.

"Nice to make your acquaintance."

"Are you big boss?"

"I beg your pardon?"

"You person in charge for getting permit?"

"Mr. Teprokasovich, this is not the place to discuss ... "

"I understand system. Just like in old country. I give you big juicy steak each week for next year if you ... "

Clearly, it was time to exit the bathroom. I was upset that this idiot thought he could purchase my soul for a couple of lamb chops. I was angry that he had attempted to compromise the hearing process with a bribe. Apparently, this was how he did business in a far-off land.

The hearings dragged on through the evening. The democratic process is never quick. All parties were heard. Those who could demonstrate the valid need for a remedy were granted relief. Those without a legitimate cause of action were rebuffed.

It was just past midnight. I was starving and exhausted after another 18-hour day. Thankfully, there was *Sunderman's*, the yes "we're open 24-hours, 365-days-a-year, gourmet, big-as-a-city-block $8^{th}$ wonder-of-the-world, any-gastronomic-dream-will-be-fulfilled" emporium. When I was growing up, "ma and pa" corner grocery stores predominated. They closed evenings and Sundays in observance of the blue laws. The selection of consumables was sufficient to meet the basic needs of the average white, middle-class, non-immigrant family. There were Frosted Flakes, Jello, Tastykakes and other necessities. Everything was located in one small room from which a husband and wife could eke out a living.

Things have changed. *Sunderman's* employs several hundred people laboring in three different shifts. There are eight full-time Japanese chefs cutting and packaging raw fish. Ten food handlers maintain the kosher deli. All of the food is blessed once a week by a rabbi. The Chinese buffet displays dozens of Asian delicacies, all cooked on premises in a kitchen the size of a basketball court. Down another aisle, four chefs stand next to a grill, ready to serve any steak or fish delicacy to order. Several dozen chickens and turkeys turn on barbeque spits on a neighboring wall. The cheese department boasts over 1,000 selections from around the world. For the well heeled, truffles sell for $199 a pound. Black sea caviar is slightly more per ounce. There is nothing that can't be ordered, prepared and eaten.

The do-it-yourselfer is not forgotten. The brass-inlaid elevator transports the famished consumer to the second-floor lounge area where each of five designer dining rooms boasts microwaves, sinks and kitchen utensils for those who wish to reheat their own food.

I decided to patronize *Sunderman's*. It might have been past midnight. Perhaps most of the world was sound asleep. But at *Sunderman's*, a lobster tail, a goat cheese Cobb salad, smoked eel with black olives - anything I could name and some things I couldn't - awaited me, just two miles away.

I drove into the 700-vehicle parking area with the additional 30 designated handicap spaces. Obviously, Mr. Sunderman had purchased a parcel of real estate big enough to accommodate the minimum parking requirements mandated by the zoning code. Everything about this place complied with the code, including half a million dollars in sculptured buffer plantings composed of deciduous vegetation, and an underground drainage system leading to a retention pond with a 30-foot sparkling fountain.

I entered the expansive Italian-tile lobby area and was immediately faced with a decision which would impact me for the next 15 minutes. Left, and I would enter the world of vegetables, fruits, cans and cartons. Straight, and row after row of breads, frozen foods and dietary supplements would confront me. Right, and I'd begin the journey into the world of cooked and prepared delicacies.

A barbequed chicken with bread stuffing, corn on the cob and spinach salad would sure be nice. I turned right and walked about 400 feet past 20 rows of well-stocked shelves. I spotted the rotisserie area and began to evaluate all the golden, turning chickens. Pavlovian slobber would soon drool out of my mouth if I didn't grab one of these birds and set up camp in the dining area.

It was the hour after midnight. With the exception of one cashier and a floor polisher person back at the entrance, I hadn't seen a soul. I was alone, dressed in my three-piece zoning hearing board suit, clutching my pad of paper containing scribbled notes. I intended to review my work product as I ate the chicken. But my concentration was about to be broken.

"May I help you?"

The voice startled me. I turned around to face a chef adorned in full white cooking uniform, including a foot-tall, pure white, stovepipe hat. Where had he come from?

"May I help you?" he repeated in earnest. "If there's anything at all I can do, I'd be pleased to honor your request."

It was clear to me why *Sunderman's* was a successful enterprise. I may have been the only customer for half a city block, and yet, here was a chef standing at the ready to assist me at one o'clock in the morning.

"That's very kind of you," I assured my new friend. Then I turned and pointed. "I just came by for a chicken and some stuffing."

No sooner had I announced my intentions than a second chef dressed in similar style emerged from behind the rotisserie machine and approached.

"How can we make your stay here a pleasant one?" number two asked as number one stared at the note tablet in my hand. "I'm just finishing some veal medallions in wine sauce. Care to sample some?"

How very accommodating. Did they treat every customer this way?

"Look," number one explained, "we know who you are."

"You do?"

"The three-piece suit, the note pad, the subtle powder-blue tie, the visit here after midnight," number two interjected with a wink of his eye.

I was beginning to wonder exactly who I really was.

"You're the secret inspector from *Sunderman's* corporate headquarters. There's no reason to try to hide the fact," number two explained.

I looked at the note pad in my hand, as I adjusted my powder-blue tie. "Forgive me gentlemen," I corrected. "I'm not an inspector. I'm just here to eat a chicken."

"Tell you what," number one offered, "we'd like to buy you dinner. You name it. Anything in the store. In return, if you enjoy what you eat, just send a complimentary evaluation back to headquarters. Fair enough?"

"I'm not an inspector."

"We know. We know," number two confirmed as he focused upon the pencil in my other hand. "We got a deal?"

Earlier this evening I had been offered some steaks by Igor the Russian to swing a zoning decision in his favor. It was a bribe that if accepted would have landed both of us in jail.

This *Sunderman's* situation was slightly different. I had tried to clarify a misconception. If these two guys still insisted on serving me dinner, I saw nothing criminal in that act, if, as requested, I completed the bargain by drafting a complimentary letter.

"You have any fresh lobster tails?" I asked.
"Just flown in from Maine," number one assured me.
"Any drawn butter?"
"Sir ... "
"Yes?"
"Why don't you go upstairs to the dining area. We'll bring up a feast you won't soon forget."

I entered the inlaid brass elevator and ascended to the second floor, where I studied my zoning notes while number one and number two withdrew to the kitchen to prepare my dinner. They didn't exaggerate. The lobster lay in a bed of crabmeat stuffing, along with corn on the cob, clam chowder and chocolate mousse. It was one of the most memorable meals of my life.

The next morning I kept my promise. I located the *Sunderman's* headquarters on the Internet and sent a letter advising that the two chefs at the local store were the finest cooks in the northern hemisphere.

A month later, I attended zoning hearings at the township municipal office. They ran late. I was hungry, so I drove over to *Sunderman's*. I was staring at a chicken on the rotisserie when the two chefs appeared out of nowhere.

"May we buy you dinner?" number one offered.

"Your favorable evaluation landed us both a raise," number two explained.

"You got any pheasant under glass?" I inquired.

# CHAPTER TWENTY-TWO

## The Valley Of The Weedwackers

There are five residences in the cul-de-sac where I live. Four of the households are occupied by retirees. The guy living to my left put in 30 years with the power company. He started at age 25 and quit when he turned 55. The fellow living to my right did something for the federal government. He received a gold watch and an annually escalating pension from Uncle Sam when he reached 50. The former school teacher on the other side of the cul-de-sac ended his career at the ripe old age of 56. Now he takes off more than just summers. The airline pilot was put out to pasture when he became 60.

I bought my home some 20 years ago, just about the time these folks retired and began their second full-time careers in earnest: lawn maintenance.

This metamorphosis was subtle at first. The former electric company guy threw down the gauntlet by purchasing a simple riding mower to cut his quarter acre of grass. Prior to that, the unspoken law was that everyone walked, similar to professional golfers. This blatant violation prompted the federal employee to acquire an all-purpose all-terrain all-season four-speed combination riding mower-snowblower. Not to be outdone, the former school teacher proudly displayed something similar to a tractor that was able to cut his quarter acre, or with the flip of a switch could toss manure about in less than half an hour. That prompted the former pilot to add to his arsenal, including a gas-powered motorized weedwacker with self-sharpening hedge clippers, and a computer programmed fertilizer spreader with accompanying global navigation system that assured distribution of chemicals in unwavering geometric patterns. The lawns in our little cul-de-sac began to rival in appearance the manicured green carpet inside Yankee Stadium.

There was, of course, one exception: my lawn, the unkempt fast-growing lawn with more than a few sprouting weeds. I planned to crank up my pushmower as soon as possible, even though working six days a week sometimes delayed the process. Surely my neighbors understood, since I was the only one still funding their Social Security checks.

The former federal guy was waiting for me as I drove into my driveway after another 12-hour day. There was something on his mind. He pointed at a cluster of brilliant golden dandelions sculpted by the very hand of God.

"The prevailing winds are gonna throw all your seeds on my lawn," he announced with the desperate look of someone who had the time to study the Weather Channel. "Something has to be done."

I agreed with him and then crawled into bed so that I might awaken at six a.m. to start another 12-hour shift. No government-subsidized pension plan awaited my loyal service.

The next evening I returned home exhausted, only to become confused as I entered unfamiliar territory. There wasn't a dandelion to be found in my front yard, which had been mowed in perfectly straight lines as if with the assistance of a global satellite navigational system. The grass clippings that I usually scattered about had been meticulously collected and carted away. It appeared that the border of my driveway had been edged and trimmed as well.

I was very thankful. Apparently some unknown stranger had come to my rescue. What's more, when I had to work seven days in a row the following week, my mysterious benefactor again came to my assistance.

- - -

That August proved to be unfortunate for some inhabitants of the cul-de-sac. In the space of just two short days, both the power company guy and the federal government guy unexpectedly died. I took off from work to attend their respective weekend funeral services. They lowered the coffins into waiting holes in the ground and covered the caskets with dirt that formed large mounds. I wondered if the dandelions growing on the nearby grave sites might dare to send some of their progeny in the direction of these fresh piles of earth.

Upon my return from the cemeteries, there still was sufficient time to mow my lawn. I looked to my right and then to my left. Dandelions were beginning to sprout up in both of the decedents' neighboring unattended yards. The shifting winds would probably blow those inevitable flying seeds in my direction. The hand of God is everywhere.

# CHAPTER TWENTY-THREE

## The Helpful Grandnephew

I can still recall the legal conundrum offered by Professor Dobbs during my first week of criminal law class. Was it possible to charge a person with attempted murder if a sack of potatoes was mistaken for the "victim?" Dobbs outlined the facts as he stood next to his wooden podium at the front of the law school lecture hall.

"Suppose, class, that I wish to kill Mr. Victim. I know where he lives and I know that each night precisely at 10 p.m. he retires to his upstairs bedroom, the bedroom with an open window. So I buy a gun and, in the cover of darkness, I place a ladder against the side of Mr. Victim's house and climb up to the open window. With weapon in hand, I peer into the bedroom and view the sleeping Mr. Victim under his bedcovers. I take deadly aim and empty six rounds into the slumbering body of poor Mr. Victim. Unfortunately for me, Mr. Victim suspected that I might try to murder him and so he devised a clever plan. He placed a large bag of potatoes under the covers to give the appearance that he was sleeping. The only thing I shot was a bunch of spuds. Can I be charged with attempted murder?"

I stopped taking notes and looked up, hoping that unlike the last 17 questions Dobbs had tendered, this one might have an answer somewhere in its future. There were 248 other "I-wanna-be-a-lawyer" aspirants in this lecture hall. But I was the only one sporting a confused look. What was I doing here, a pretender hidden among all these barristers and judges of tomorrow?

"Now class, we will consider the case of *Commonwealth versus Gasaway*," Dobbs announced without skipping a beat.

Wait a minute, I wanted to scream. What happens if a client shows up at my office some day accused of shooting a bag of potatoes? Might I tell him there's a possible defense?

Dobbs didn't seem to be concerned about my future clientele. He was on a roll.

"In *Gasaway*," he continued, "the defendant steals five dollars from the victim's purse." Dobbs paused momentarily and began to study the class roster. "Is Mr. Hendricks here?" our learned mentor called out.

Some poor schnook three rows behind me tentatively acknowledged his presence.

"Mr. Hendricks, kindly relate to the class what happened in this case," Dobbs commanded.

Luckless Hendricks gave it his best shot. "Well, Professor, it was like this. Gasaway stole five dollars from old Mrs. Frankferter's purse when she wasn't looking. Then he took the gambler's express bus to Atlantic City and placed the stolen five-dollar bill on number 28 at the roulette wheel. It was the winning number. By the end of the day, the defendant had parlayed the pilfered five-dollar investment into $26,000 and change. But his luck ran out when Mrs. Frankferter realized she was missing her five dollars. She knew that only Gasaway had been in near proximity to her purse, so she had him arrested."

"Right you are," Dobbs confirmed. "Now why is this case important, Mr. Hendricks?"

"Well," Hendricks pondered aloud, "Gasaway was ultimately convicted of the theft. So the judge ordered that Gasaway return to the victim the money that he had stolen. But old Mrs. Frankferter's lawyer argued that Gasaway should not be permitted to benefit from his criminal act, and that since Gasaway only amassed the $26,000 by stealing Frankferter's five dollars, she should also receive the fruits of the crime, or an additional $25,995, plus interest."

"An intriguing issue, indeed," Dobbs remarked. "If I steal a dollar from you, buy a lottery ticket with the dollar and hit for a million bucks, is the million yours? What if I steal a dollar from you, put the dollar in my wallet with another dollar of my own, then buy the winning lottery ticket, but can't say for sure whether I used your stolen dollar or not?"

I was starting to get that queasy, confused feeling again. Did Dobbs actually know the answers, but simply wasn't inclined to share? Why didn't they just call this place "Riddle School" and place a big question mark over the front door?

- - -

My good friend Serena Gibbons was on the phone. We had attended high school together. She ultimately became the manager of one of the local nursing homes. I, on the other hand, had chosen the legal profession so that I might confront a lifetime of riddles.

"Hi, Serena," I began. It was good to hear her friendly voice. We exchanged the usual pleasantries. Then the conversation became serious.

"Larry, a resident here at Sunnydale may have a problem. I'm calling to see if you might help her. She's all alone in the world."

"What type of problem?"

"Some of her money is missing - we think."

"How much?"

"About half a million, maybe more. It's hard to tell, since the theft probably occurred over a long period of time."

"Who is the victim?" I asked.

"Betty, Betty Wienches. She'll be 97 this month," Serena explained.

"How long has she resided at your nursing home?"

"Two, maybe two-and-a-half years. When she first came here, she suffered only from partial blindness. Then she lost most of her hearing. Recently, she broke her hip, so now she's confined to a wheelchair."

"Who reported the theft?"

"Betty did. She may not be able to see or hear so good, but her mind is as sharp as a tack. She was an accountant or bookkeeper in her previous life. She determined unassisted that some of her money was missing."

I decided a visit with my newest client was in order, so the next morning I drove to the nursing home.

Serena met me in the spacious lobby and affixed a "visitor" tag to my suit coat lapel so that people would know it was my intention ultimately to escape. There were several wrinkled, wheelchair-bound bodies slumped at the front door. How had they found their way to the lobby? Some ancient faces had that look of unspoken anticipation, similar to an attentive tropical fish studying the passing world from the confines of its aquarium. Some were asleep, or dead perhaps.

"So nice to see you again," my guide sang out in a cheerful voice. How was she able to remain so cheerful?

The ubiquitous TVs were on in the lobby, down the hall and in the dining room. The same soap opera danced on each unwatched screen.

"I'll take you to Betty," Serena confirmed, as she led me to an elevator large enough to accommodate four bodies on stretchers. The automatic door closed, and we ascended inch by labored inch to the second floor. I could have commuted to downtown Philadelphia in the amount of time it took to reach the next floor.

"Our guests don't do well with sudden movement," Serena explained.

We exited the temporary prison and stepped into a hallway filled with more wheelchairs supporting more bodies. Some of the mobile seats sported clear plastic tubes leading to clear plastic bags. These transient people weren't going to waste what little time they might have left standing in line for a restroom.

"Betty's room is right around the corner," Serena assured me.

Some of the forgotten people tried to interact. "Do you know where my lunch is?" one frail angel inquired.

"Am I going home now?" another implored.

I empathized with this poor soul's plight. I, too, wanted to leave. I felt as if I were a participant in a scene from some forgotten horror movie, like *Night of the Wheelchairs*.

"This is Betty's room," Serena announced as she knocked on the half-open door. No one answered, although I thought I saw the outline of someone in a wheelchair sitting inside. The room's dim light gave few clues regarding its mysterious occupant.

"Betty, I brought a visitor."

There was no response. No movement. No indication of life.

Serena approached to within a few inches of Betty's fragile face, her eyes closed, her breathing short and labored.

"BETTY! I BROUGHT A VISITOR!"

The body jolted slightly.

"What? Who's there?"

"BETTY! YOUR LAWYER IS HERE TO TALK ABOUT THE THEFT."

"My lawyer? Is he in the room?"

Blind and deaf. How was I supposed to interview Wienches? How could she possibly know if anything had been stolen from her? I decided to give it my best shot as Serena nodded her encouragement.

"MS. WIENCHES ... " I began.

"Who said that?" my client demanded.

"I DID. MY NAME IS LARRY FOX."

"Hairy Locks?"

"FOX."

"You're a Fox?"

"YES, I AM."

"Come closer and stop mumbling," she instructed.

I sat down on the bed and faced her, no more than two feet from her nose. With effort she succeeded in opening one eye.

"I think I see part of you," she said.

And so our first of many conversations began. Betty had quite a bit on her mind, a mind that, I would soon discover, was sharp and focused.

"Ms. Wienches," I inquired, "did someone take money from you without your permission?"

"Of course, you fool. Why do you think I asked for a lawyer?"

Arguably, Betty's skills at diplomacy might have used some polishing.

"Listen, pal, I may be half-blind and half-deaf, but I'm not half-witted," she informed me.

"No, ma'am," I agreed.

"Now here's the story ... I SAID 'HERE'S THE STORY,' BUB! Are you going to take notes, or just sit there?"

I snapped to attention and reached for my tablet and pen.

"I'll be 97 next month ... " She paused to see if I was writing.

I scrawled "96 years old" on my pad. This flourish of activity had a temporary calming effect on the cantankerous narrator.

"Ninety-seven. Worked most of my life as a bookkeeper. Never married. Saved my money and invested it ... " She gazed at me with that one eye.

"Invested it," I scribbled furiously.

"Am I going too fast?" she asked sarcastically.

"No, not at all."

"Where was I?"

"Invested it."

"Oh, yes. Invested it. So when I retired at 85 ... "

"Excuse me. You retired in 1985?"

"No, you idiot. Stay focused. I retired when I *turned* 85 ... " She waited to see my writing hand move again.

"Retired at 85," I noted.

"By then, I had a nice nest egg, maybe two million."

I stopped writing and looked up.

"Now what's wrong? Just put down the 'two million.' I'll tell you when to stop."

I did as commanded, while formulating my next question. "Ms. Wienches, did someone steal your money?"

"Millhouse. He's the culprit. Find him and you'll find my money."

"Who is Millhouse?"

"Millhouse Grossbeak, my nephew and only living relative. And to think I actually trusted that worm!"

"Where is Millhouse now?"

"How should I know? After he cleaned me out, he split."

"How did he gain access to your accounts?"

"See, it was like this. A couple of years ago, I decided to view the autumn foliage here in Pennsylvania, so I drove from my apartment in New Jersey to the Poconos for the day. After that I don't remember much. The cops say I missed a curve and hit a pole or something. Anyway, I woke up here. Been at this stinkin' carcass camp ever since. I can't go home. There's nobody to care for me. Then about six months ago, Millhouse appears out of the blue. Says he's my long lost nephew and asks if I needed any help."

"Is he actually related to you?"

"In a distant way. My departed sister had a son who also died. That son had a child, this Millhouse, but I never met him until he showed up here. I can't image how he found me. Well, anyway, he pops up out of nowhere and says he wants to help his poor old great aunt. I fell for it."

"What happened?"

"He started coming around each Sunday, just as nice as you please with gifts like soap bars and hairbrushes. He began asking questions about my finances. One day he brings this document along with some guy he claimed was a bank representative from Union Fidelity where I keep a small checking account. Millhouse said if I signed this joint 'signature card' then he could use those limited funds to pay my bills in New Jersey. My landlord wanted his rent, my car registration was due, stuff like that. So like a fool, I agreed. Turns out the document was a general power of attorney, and the so-called friend was a notary. Millhouse helped me with my mail, so he knew every bank, credit union and stockbroker I dealt with."

"And you think Millhouse used the misrepresented power of attorney to access your money?"

"After I signed what he assured me was merely a signature card on a checking account holding only a few thousand dollars, my loving great nephew stopped coming around. He telephoned each Sunday to tell me that he was on yet another unexpected business trip. Some of his travels took him to the West Coast. Others were out of the country."

"What did he do for a living?"

"I don't quite know. Anyway, a month goes by, and I received my bank statements. That's when I began to suspect something was wrong. I don't see so good, so I had a nurse read me each account number and the balance. Guess what?"

"What?"

"That snake-in-the-grass removed half a million dollars from my Federated Transcontinental account! The next Sunday, he calls to say he's putting some deal together in Minnesota and can't stop by. I says 'Where's the $500,000 you pilfered?' He says the cell phone is breaking up and he'll have to call back. That was the last I ever heard from him."

"Do you have your current bank statements?" I inquired.

Wienches pointed to a small nightstand near the head of her bed. "All 12 should be there."

I began to sift through the small collection of computer printouts. They totaled about one and a half million. The Federated Transcontinental statement reflected a recent withdrawal of $500,000.

"So far, he hasn't taken anything else," she confirmed.

My blind and feeble hostess was about to surprise me.

"The bank acknowledged the withdrawal on the 8$^{th}$ of the month. At 6.75 percent straight line interest, that means I'm out $87.23 as of today."

I stopped taking notes. "I beg your pardon?" I stammered.

During the next five minutes, I learned that Betty was able to recite from memory each account number, the date and amount of deposit, and the interest accruing thereupon. Was I dealing with an idiot savant?

"I was a bookkeeper before the days of calculators and computers," she said almost as an afterthought.

- - -

The Federated Transcontinental's bank fraud representative was cooperative and made his files available for inspection. Millhouse had not engaged in some unfortunate innocent mistake. He was a thief. The financial data confirmed that great nephew Millhouse had, on the third of the prior month, entered the branch bank in Kresgeville, with power of attorney in hand. Twenty minutes later, he emerged with a cashier's check made payable to himself for $500,000.

The check was endorsed by Millhouse and then counter-endorsed by the Amalgamated Title Company Of The Poconos, into whose account the proceeds were deposited.

Amalgamated's secretary was also helpful. She recalled that about a month ago, Millhouse Grossbeak had purchased a vacation villa in the north end of the county. The price was $500,000, and Grossbeak had not required any mortgage financing.

My next call to the courthouse recorder of deeds office confirmed that one Millhouse Grossbeak had recently become the new owner of a vacation villa located on seven secluded acres. The tax and assessment records listed Grossbeak's mailing address as the vacation villa.

I contacted the police, who swore out an arrest warrant. The cops drove over to the villa in order to serve the warrant, but Grossbeak was nowhere to be found. He had fled the jurisdiction, leaving the villa strewn with a substantial amount of furniture, clothing and dishes.

The vacation villa soon began to show signs of abandonment. A broken front window was in need of repair. The heating oil tank was empty, and water from a frozen pipe had entered the basement. Some squirrels had taken up residence in the attic, and vandals had stolen some of the furniture. The homeowners insurance policy had not been paid in full, and that important coverage was about to be cancelled. I had to do something, or the real estate purchased with Betty's money would fall into significant disrepair.

I filed a petition with the court seeking a constructive trust so that I might sell the villa at auction to some legitimate buyer. This raised some complex issues. The deed was still recorded in Grossbeak's name. If a new purchaser bought the villa, would another state transfer tax have to be paid for a new deed to be recorded so that Wienches might finally recoup the money stolen from her? In Pennsylvania, a tax equal to two percent of the purchase price must be paid when a new deed is recorded. Usually the seller pays one percent and the buyer pays one percent. Grossbeak had purchased the seven-acre villa from a lady named Henrietta Ridge, a widow who had no idea Grossbeak had stolen the half a million dollars used to purchase her real estate. Innocent Mrs. Ridge paid a one percent transfer tax of $5,000, as did the criminal Grossbeak.

The deed placing title in Grossbeak's name had been obtained with Wienches' stolen funds. Would another transfer tax need to be paid to correct this criminal act? I knew this issue required resolution before I might petition the court to permit an auction, so I telephoned the Pennsylvania Department Of Revenue Real Estate Transfer Tax Office. Revenue Agent Clyde Porterfield graciously took my call.

"This is Larry Fox."

"Porterfield ... Clyde Porterfield ... Revenue Agent. What can I do for you?"

"Mr. Porterfield, I'm an attorney practicing in Bethlehem. I have a question regarding payment of the state real estate transfer tax."

"What's the question?"

"If title to real estate is obtained by a criminal act, must another two percent transfer tax be paid to the commonwealth if the real estate is ultimately re-sold to an innocent third party purchaser at an auction?"

"Depends on the facts. We've had many cases of criminal conduct where some crook forged a signature on a deed and recorded it. We don't charge another transfer tax to put the deed back in the rightful owner's name."

I was starting to feel optimistic. I began to tell him the story. "A few months ago, Henrietta Ridge innocently sold a seven-acre parcel of real estate to Millhouse Grossbeak for $500,000. The $500,000 was stolen by Grossbeak from my client, Betty Wienches, a 97-year-old nursing home resident."

"How very unfortunate."

"Now I want to obtain a court order creating a constructive trust that will permit me to re-sell the real estate at auction."

"That makes sense. What's the problem?"

"When the widow Ridge sold the land to Grossbeak, they paid a total of $10,000 in transfer tax. Now Grossbeak has disappeared, but title is still recorded in his name. To get title out of his name, and get my client's money back, must I pay another transfer tax if Grossbeak acquired the real estate by a criminal act?"

"Hold on just a minute, counselor. I understand that there was a criminal act. Grossbeak stole half a million dollars. But the purchase of the real estate was legitimate."

"I'm not sure I follow you."

"The widow Ridge wanted to sell her land at a fair price, and Grossbeak wanted to buy it at a fair price, so they paid the lawful two percent transfer tax. The fact that Grossbeak stole the money from Wienches, however unfortunate that is, is not the concern of the state revenue division. That's something for the district attorney to investigate. And so when you re-sell the property at auction to someone else, another transfer tax will be due."

"Wait a minute! That's the whole point. Grossbeak is a crook and has fled the jurisdiction. I want to sell the land at auction to get the stolen money back. Why must I pay another $10,000 in tax so that Mrs. Wienches can reclaim her stolen half a million?"

"I understand," bureaucrat Porterfied assured me, "but there was no fraud between Mrs. Ridge and Grossbeak. When the real estate is re-sold at auction, another transfer tax will be due. But for what it's worth, I've got a little advice, if you'll permit."

"Certainly."

"Set a minimum sale price of $510,000. That way Wienches gets back her $500,000, and Pennsylvania will receive the necessary $10,000 tax."

Maybe Porterfield wasn't such a bad guy after all. I thanked him for his counsel. Within a week I obtain a court order authorizing the auction. I sent a copy of the order to the seven-acre villa address, so that Grossbeak couldn't claim he had not received notice his real estate was being sold. A month later, I attended the auction.

- - -

"What am I bid for this beautiful, secluded dream home?" the Pennsylvania Dutch auctioneer shouted through his hand-held bullhorn. The animated crowd came to a hush as everyone strained to see who might bid. Was there actually someone in this group of nondescript onlookers capable of tendering a legitimate offer? I hadn't seen a single Rolex or diamond necklace anywhere in the audience. I looked at the broken front window. Perhaps if I had repaired it, someone would have offered ...

"$400,000," some guy in a torn overcoat called out.

The auctioneer took a deep breath. He had a fish on the line. "I've got four hundred towsund, four hundred towsund, four hundred towsund. Do I hear four-tventy? Four-tventy?"

"Four-tventy," the farmer dressed in bib overalls responded.

Two fish on the line.

"I've got four tventy, four tventy, four tventy. Do I hear ..."

"Four forty."

This newest offer had originated from a young couple holding a baby.

In less than three minutes, the biding had reached the sum of $520,000! There would be enough money to pay the Commonwealth of Pennsylvania, the auctioneer and Wienches. I was ecstatic as I fought to maintain a poker face.

"Ladies and gents," the auctioneer proclaimed, "we have reached the minimum sale price as established by the court-appointed trustee. I'm pleased to announce that this is an 'absolute auction' and someone out there is about to become the owner of this fine estate."

"Five forty," the farmer shouted.

"Five fifty," the owner of the torn coat announced.

"Five sixty," the father of the baby chimed in.

Apparently Millhouse had negotiated quite a bargain when he purchased the villa from the widow Ridge for a mere half a million. Two minutes later, the biding had reached $620,000.

"All in? All in? I've got six tventy, going once, going tvice, going thrice ... Sold to Mr. Naglebacher for $620,000." The auctioneer banged his gavel and, at that very instant, the young couple lost their dream home, while the bidder who couldn't afford proper outerwear became the owner of a country estate.

I introduced myself and asked if he would join me inside to sign the agreement of sale. Moments later I received a down payment check for 10 percent of the purchase price.

- - -

"Sebastian Prolkup is on the phone," my secretary informed me.

"Who?"

"Says he was at the auction last weekend."

I took the call. "This is Larry Fox."

"Sebby Prolkup. My law office is in Philly. I saw you at the Millhouse Grossbeak auction on Saturday."

"Did we talk?"

"Nope. I was just an interested bystander, you might say."

I didn't know this joker, but I was starting to get an uneasy feeling. "What can I do for you, counselor?" I inquired.

"Nice place, that seven-acre spread. I represent the owner, Mr. Grossbeak."

"Millhouse? Where is he?"

"Not so fast, counselor. I just represent him civilly. I'm not involved in his criminal case. I don't know where he's hiding, and I don't care. He calls me on a throwaway cell phone. Anyway, I received your notice of the auction and was glad I attended. Who would have thought that the place would have increased in value $120,000 above what my client recently paid?"

"Is there something on your mind?" I asked.

"Actually, there is. Assuming you've got to pay transfer tax, the auctioneer, your incidental expenses and the old lady is reimbursed her half million, there should still be 50 grand or so remaining. Uncle Sam may want some of that in capital gains. Now here's the point: my client wants the rest. He alone generated that net profit by buying the house at a good price."

Broken windows, frozen pipes, squirrels, intruding vandals, countless hours with Wienches, the insurance agent, the auctioneer, debates with Porterfield, petitions to the court, the drafting of auction documents - and now this Philadelphia bottom feeder wanted a net check representing the fruits of theft committed by his sociopathic client who preyed on a 97-year-old blind woman imprisoned in a nursing home.

"Mr. Prolkup ... "

"Call me Sebby ... "

"Your client's a crook. I won't give him a penny!"

"That's why he needs the money. So he can come out of hiding, hire a good criminal defense attorney and post bail. I guess I'll be seeing you in court for an accounting."

I hung up the phone and turned to my secretary. "If someone steals five dollars from you and wins the lottery with your money, how much does the thief get to keep?" She looked confused.

- - -

That night I had a dream that I purchased two 50-pound bags of potatoes and stood them up against the tree out back. I made believe one bag was Sebby and the other was Millhouse. Then I loaded my .45 caliber semi-automatic pistol and pumped several rounds into each unsuspecting bag. No one came to arrest me, so it probably wasn't attempted murder.

# CHAPTER TWENTY-FOUR

## The Security Clearance

I represented Smedley Gorski. When he wasn't in jail, he burglarized houses for a living. Apparently it had not yet occurred to this 23-year-old miscreant that perhaps it was time for him to get a legitimate job and become a productive member of society. His chosen lifestyle did not require that he ever plan more than three or four hours in advance. As long as he could smoke some pot and bum a meal, he seemed content. Jail was not seen as a deterrent, but rather as a type of restricted spa where he received three meals a day between exercise sessions in the prison gymnasium.

It was time for my client to be sentenced by crazy Judge Ishmael Blatt for Smedley's latest criminal venture. He had broken into a residence and was caught when he tripped the silent alarm. He couldn't make bail, so I drove to the Northampton County Courthouse to discuss his options.

At one time 30 or 40 years ago, Judge Blatt might have been a legitimate run-of-the-mill jurist. But over the years, the judge's demeanor had taken on a bizarre, unorthodox twist. His Honor was now certifiably crackers. Luckily for those of us forced to appear before him, crazy Blatt was fast approaching mandatory retirement. The county voters wouldn't be able to put this maniac back on the bench for yet another 10-year term.

I stopped into the prison for a little talk with Smedley before they escorted him to the adjoining courthouse. He looked quite at home in his county-issued orange jumpsuit and flip-flops.

"Smedley ... "

"Yo?"

"This is the third time I've represented you on a burglary charge."

"What's your point? Guys like me keep lawyers like you in business. I hope you're grateful."

"Listen, Smedley, it's time for you to turn your life around. You've got to find and keep legitimate employment. Otherwise you'll be looked upon as a career criminal, and the next time you're arrested, the judge may not be very lenient."

Did Smedley hear a word? An hour later, we stood side by side before Judge Blatt for the sentencing hearing. His Honor emerged from his chambers wearing a black robe accented by a pink bow tie decorated with a background of green amoebae. He took his seat upon the bench and stared at Smedley and me.

"This is the sentencing hearing for Smedley Gorski. Are you Smedley Gorski?" His Honor inquired.

"Yes," the defendant responded.

"You have previously pled guilty to the crime of burglary. We have now convened for the formal imposition of your sentence. But ... before we do, I'd first like to note one thing for the record. I ordered a ham and cheese sandwich on rye for lunch today from the cafeteria downstairs. They delivered it on white bread, and there was no tomato. Counselor, would you have found this type of service to be acceptable?"

"I beg your pardon, Judge?" I responded.

"Please be candid. Would you have sent the sandwich back?"

For the next 10 minutes, deranged Blatt bemoaned the sandwich's other deficiencies, including too much mayo and an unwanted thumb print. Then he grew silent for a lovely moment, after which he sentenced Smedley, for no reason in particular, to time served. My client left the courtroom a free man.

- - -

I have practiced law at the Northampton County Courthouse for 35 years. I've been witness to some significant changes. The original stately portion of the courthouse, constructed just after the Civil War ended, exists as a testament to classical architectural design. It is a masterpiece of Greek revival, with its massive columns and rectangular features. It is a privilege to walk in its hallways and practice in its courtrooms.

By 1975, the original courthouse was no longer able to serve the needs of a county population that was growing exponentially, and so an adjoining "annex" twice the size of the original edifice was constructed. The county commissioners voted against the idea of constructing a new governmental complex on an undeveloped 150-acre tract in the middle of the county, since the cost was prohibitive and the annex would adequately provide for all services for the foreseeable future.

In order to accommodate this project, the old gravel parking lot bordering the courthouse was converted into a construction site. As a result, convenient parking for 300 vehicles vanished. So they built an inconvenient claustrophobic three-tiered parking deck next to the prison so that limited parking would still be available. However, as the courthouse staff continued to increase in number, these coveted spaces began to be reserved primarily for the use of the irreplaceable county employees. A mere 50 spaces remained available to the lucky taxpayers who chanced upon them.

By 2005 the annex was jammed to capacity, so the county commissioners commissioned as commissioners so often do a "second annex" onto the first annex. The second annex was twice the size of the first annex. In order to create a construction site, they condemned the streets servicing the courthouse and the first annex. As a result, all the on-street meter parking vanished. This meant that when 300 jurors were called to the courthouse to serve on jury duty, they had no place to park. So the county commissioners condemned an old hotel six blocks away, had the jurors park wherever they might find an elusive space downtown, walk to the condemned hotel, and then ride a bus to and from the courthouse. Unfortunately, there was no space to park the bus, since the new entrance to the courthouse complex existed at an intersection where no bus or handicap parking had been provided.

One other minor detail had also been overlooked. There was now no place to park for more than 1,000 daily visitors, including defendants, witnesses, attorneys and citizens. And, so, the county commissioners condemned a city block a quarter-mile downhill from the courthouse and razed the homes on it to create a paved parking area. Now the relatively healthy patrons visiting the courthouse who did not suffer from heart conditions, asthma, arthritis, or poor sight had a place to park just a brisk 15-minute walk up a 600-foot hill, assuming it wasn't snowing or raining.

The original courthouse had five entrance and exit doors. They all worked. The main classical Greek revival doorway boasted 20-foot-tall side-by-side mahogany doors through which an elephant could have passed with room to spare. Upon entering, the guest of the county proceeded into the ceremonial entrance hallway for easy access to the courtrooms and row offices.

The first annex also possessed four public entrances. Then the 9-11 disaster turned the world upside down, and security concerns became paramount. The second annex was intentionally constructed with but one entranceway. The other nine means of ingress were, in the blink of an eye, forever sealed. To enter the courthouse complex required that an individual pass by a video camera to the security scanning booths and conveyor belts to undergo a search similar to that experienced at an airport. Often over 100 people seeking entry, many of whom had walked for 15 minutes, would stand outside in the elements for an additional 15 minutes as the time-consuming security clearance process dragged on. Similar to an airport, it became necessary to arrive an hour early to appear in court on time.

To alleviate this burdensome situation, the sheriff's office issued security passes to those county employees who entered the courthouse on a daily basis. For the rest of the "regulars," the lawyers, the title searchers, the service people making hourly deliveries, one could, for a mere $10, obtain a photo identification pass, complete with accompanying fingerprint verification. That seemed better than waiting in line, so I filled out the application, had my photo and fingerprints taken, and soon no longer suffered the indignities experienced by the hordes of the great unwashed masses milling about at the one and only entrance.

Things were now secure at the courthouse. With each passing day, the implementation of the newest surveillance technologies assured that no terrorist would gain a foothold in the hallowed halls of justice in Easton, Pennsylvania. A Girl Scout on a school tour tried to sneak a nail file past the scanner. She was caught and detained for questioning.

- - -

A month passed. I was scheduled to serve on an arbitration panel at the courthouse. Two other attorneys and I were appointed by the Court to act as a panel of three to hear a dispute involving less than $80,000. Elected judges consider such matters too insignificant to waste their time, so arbitration panels are assigned to conduct the hearings and render decisions. I rushed to the courthouse and arrived at 7:15 a.m. - an hour and 45 minutes early - hoping to secure one of the 50 elusive unrestricted parking spaces located in the parking deck. I slowly drove through the ground floor level, past the first 100 empty reserved spaces.

"Reserved for Judge" took up the first 30 spaces. True, there are only eight judges in the entire county, but perhaps more were about to be elected. "Reserved for County Council" claimed another six spaces. Then came those with individual recognition:

"Reserved for Court Administrator."
"Reserved for Computer Programmer."
"Reserved for County Forester."

"Reserved for Warden."
"Reserved for Probation Administrator."
"Reserved for Domestic Relations."
"Reserved for Prothonotary."
"Reserved for Sheriff."
"Reserved for Recorder of Deeds."
"Reserved for Clerk of Civil Courts."
"Reserved for Clerk of Criminal Courts."
"Reserved for County Executive."
"Reserved for County Solicitor."
"Reserved for Clerk of Orphans' Court."
"Reserved for Office of Weights and Measures."
"Reserved for County Coroner."
"Reserved for County Health Inspector."
"Reserved for County Controller."
"Reserved for District Attorney."
"Reserved for Public Defender."
"Reserved for Animal Control Officer."
"Reserved for Department of Roads and Bridges."

The second level was no different, concluding with reservations for the Department of Parks on the left and Insect Control on the right.

The third level promised the 50 discretionary spaces, right after the Department of Environmental Resources, the Pollution Monitoring Administrator and the stenographic pool.

This was the third straight year the county treasurer announced a sizable budgetary shortfall. Was I the only person in the entire county to perceive a simple solution without the need to increase taxes? Just auction off the damn parking spaces annually to the highest bidder. Come to think of it, what secret tribunal had determined who was so essential that he or she deserved a reserved space?

I advised the Court Administrator and the President Judge of my budgetary solution as they passed me in the hallway. They were not amused. I had not meant to be funny. Logically, the President Judge and his cronies should have constituted the one group with no reserved parking. After all, they can never be late for court, since it can't start without them. So let them walk a little.

- - -

Glory be, I found a space in the corner of the third tier. Life was good. I proceeded a mere 100 yards to the new exclusive courthouse entranceway. I whipped out my photo and fingerprint-bedecked $10 identification card and put it through the familiar slot in the computerized turnstile. Nothing happened. The octogenarian security guard with the cataract in his remaining good eye somehow began to sense my presence.

"Are you an attorney?" he asked as he tried to focus.

"Yes. Remember me? I've been coming here for 35 years."

"That card probably don't work no more. From now on, you'll have to be scanned and searched."

"Why? Who took my security clearance away?"

"Don't know. Ask the sheriff. He's in charge of stuff like that. Now bend over and open your briefcase."

- - -

After my arbitration concluded, I sought out the sheriff.

"I couldn't use my security clearance card this morning. Is there a problem?"

"It was decided attorneys shouldn't have clearance anymore. Too much of a threat, you know."

"Who decided that?"

"I'm not sure."

"Can I appeal the decision?"

"Doubt it. Terrorism. It's everywhere."

"But I haven't felt like blowing anything up until now. Has clearance been taken away from everyone? Are we all to be treated on an equal basis?"

"Not quite."

"What's that mean?"

"Courthouse employees - they can still get through."

"What makes them less of a security threat than attorneys?"

"I'm not sure, but I'm a courthouse employee, and I happen to think I'm pretty safe."

- - -

A week after my security pass was summarily revoked, I drove to the Northampton County Courthouse to again act as an arbitrator on behalf of the Court. I parked a quarter-mile away, trudged up the hill, and stood 40-people-deep in the security clearance line. It wasn't moving very quickly. Another damned metal hip replacement. As I languished, a familiar face walked by.

"Smedley," I yelled out almost as an involuntary reaction, "is that you?"

"Attorney Fox! It's good to see you again," the professional house burglar responded.

"Don't tell me you're in trouble again."

"Actually, Boss, I decided to take your sound advice."

"What was that?"

"Get a job. The burglary business had no future. Now, I got me full-time legitimate employment with benefits and a pension plan."

"That's wonderful news. What exactly are you doing?"

"I'm a dishwasher downstairs in the cafeteria. I get a paycheck every two weeks. I even got my own parking space and security clearance. They tell me I'm indispensable."

It took me 15 minutes to get through the security check. Had I been a reformed house burglar turned pot scrubber, I probably could have avoided the delay by using one of those elusive security clearance cards.

## CHAPTER TWENTY-FIVE

### The Guilty Party

After more than 30 years in the law business, I've developed a sixth sense regarding *el stinko* cases - litigation that no lawyer in his or her right mind would ever touch. If a client announces he's pursuing a case because "it's the principle of the thing," think twice. If a pretty young lady asks for a discount because her divorce is sure to be "real simple," tell her politely to take her six minor children and the family's delinquent mortgage to the new attorney down the street. If a potential litigant intends to sue her veterinarian for her free cat's botched appendectomy and wants you to take the case on a contingency basis, run.

Sunrise Housing, Inc. was a good client. The corporation operated 15 apartment complexes across the county. With more than 300 rental units, I was often called upon to resolve legal issues affecting tenants. I had found over the years that just about any matter could be settled amicably if the tenant did not willfully attempt to destroy my client's property.

Lulu Bunker was not such a reasonable person. After I was forced to evict her for non-payment of six months' rent, my client found, upon entering the vacated apartment, that the residence had been destroyed. There were gaping holes in the walls, windows were broken and cigarette burn marks could be found in every square yard of carpet. And she and/or some large animals appeared not to have been housebroken. Rumor had it she had been operating a daycare and spa for dogs and cats without any permits or litter boxes.

"Sue her," Bart Renaldo, vice-president of operations, shouted over the phone.

I understood his anger, but things weren't quite so simple. Lulu had left no forwarding address, so the task of serving her with legal documents would be daunting. Then there was the fact that she was judgment-proof. She owned nothing, so any attempt to collect an award most likely would prove futile. Perhaps of greater concern was the fact that the eviction had taken an additional six months because she was penniless and, therefore, qualified for free legal assistance at taxpayer expense. Some legal aid attorney who got paid every Friday had taken every form of meritless appeal imaginable. Lulu knew how to work the system. Her next luckless landlord was surely in for a similar surprise.

"Mr. Renaldo," I cautioned, "I doubt that it is cost-effective to - "

"Listen," he interrupted, "it's the principle of the thing. She can't get away with this. Now are you the lawyer for the job or aren't you?"

I sure was glad I had recently hired an associate. She was fresh out of law school and was as energized as a bunny full of batteries. Just perfect for this kind of -

"And don't hand this file to some green teen recruit in you office," Renaldo interjected. "I haven't been paying you the big bucks all these years so you can sit back and drink the cream. Got it?"

Drink the cream? Sit back? Big bucks? I hadn't felt so guilty since moving out of my parents' house to attend college. Different parents employ different motivational techniques to push their offspring toward a specific goal. Some bribe with candy. Other use a belt strap. My mother manipulated through guilt - an art form she developed with time into a fine science.

I remember at age 10 sitting on our one and only toilet. Back then, they built homes with just one john. I was minding my own business when I heard the unmistakable clomping footsteps of a woman in distress. My mother was heading up the stairs and in my direction.

"Are you in there?" she bellowed.

" ... yes ... "

"Well get out this very instant."

"I ... can't ... yet, Mom. I need another minute or two."

"There isn't any time left. You should have thought of that in the birth canal when you permanently wrecked my bladder."

- - -

And so I was stuck with the Lulu Bunker case. I tracked her down in an apartment outside of town and served her with a formal landlord-tenant complaint alleging $8,000 in damages. The magistrate scheduled a hearing and three weeks later I showed up with Renaldo and our six witnesses. Lulu made an appearance as well - this time without legal counsel. Apparently she had exhausted her source of free services. Nonetheless, she was prepared. She brought a shopping bag overflowing with official-looking documents. The carpenter, plumber, painter, rug installer, window repair guy and plasterer each testified that they completed repairs to the damaged apartment. The cost approximated $8,000. Lulu cross-examined each witness. Then I rested my case. The magistrate found in my favor. The hearing had spanned about three hours.

"I'm takin' an appeal," belligerent Lulu announced.

And appeal she did. I received notice of an arbitration to be heard at the courthouse by a board of three attorneys. On the designated hearing date I presented my six witnesses and finished with Renaldo, who testified that the landlord paid $8,000 to these craftsmen. Lulu cross-examined each witness, after which the arbitration panel ruled in my favor. The whole process had taken about three hours.

"I'm filing an appeal," pugnacious Lulu announced as she shoved the official-looking documents back into her shopping bag. And appeal she did. I received notice of a jury trial. Five months later I appeared at the courthouse as required, accompanied by my six witnesses and Renaldo. Judge Hainesworth was assigned to the litigation. He met the parties in open court.

"What's this case about?" His Honor asked from the bench.

"It's a landlord-tenant dispute over damages to an apartment," I explained to the court.

"How long will your testimony take?" the court inquired.

"About two and half hours," I estimated.

"You have any witnesses, Ms. Bunker?" Hainesworth asked.

"No, sir."

"Good. Then we'll pick a jury this morning and begin trial immediately," the judge announced.

Moments later, they brought in the jury panel - about 200 citizens. From this crowd Lulu and I would choose twelve members of the community to sit in judgment.

This was a simple trial. Judge Hainesworth knew that and so did I. Apparently Lulu felt otherwise. I stood up and asked the standard five minutes of jury selection questions: did anyone have strong feelings one way or the other regarding landlords; would they listen to the evidence fairly and impartially; did anyone know the parties or the witnesses? Then I sat down.

Lulu was more thorough in her approach. She directed over a hundred inquires to the panel to determine who among those she addressed had ever been tenants or been sued or been accused of damaging an apartment. She asked how they perceived the act of taking an appeal and whether there could ever be a reason not to pay rent. She waxed eloquent for over two hours and then it was time for lunch.

"Are we ready for trial?" Renaldo inquired over a delectable courthouse cafeteria grilled cheese sandwich. This would be the third time I would present the same evidence with the same witnesses.

"Yes," I confirmed.

We shuffled back into the courtroom at 1:30 p.m. I called my first witness to the stand, a plasterer named Herman Grindle. He testified regarding the damage he had observed in the apartment and the nature, extent and costs of the repairs he undertook.

I turned to Lulu. "Your witness," I said.

She stood up. "I don't got no questions, 'cause that testimony is irrelevant. The witness never testified that he saw me damage them walls. Anybody coulda wrecked the place."

She started to gather several papers strewn across her desk and shoved them into her grocery shopping bag. Then she turned to the judge. "I'm outta here, Your Judgeship."

"I beg your pardon?" startled Hainesworth responded.

"I said I'm outta here. I've got a hairdresser's appointment across town and I'm not gonna miss it. Despite what that landlord would have you believe, I'm a responsible person and always honor my obligations. If Lawyer Fox hadn't taken so long pickin' a jury, we woulda been done on time."

Lulu hoisted her shopping bag into her arms. "You can mail me the verdict, Judge."

"Where do you live?"

"Here and there. On second thought, I'll drop by fer it sometime."

With these words, she turned, saluted the jury and walked out of the courtroom. The large, ornate black walnut doors closed behind her.

His Honor motioned for me to approach the bench.

"That makes things a lot more simple, doesn't it, counselor."

"Judge, you mean to tell me a party can just up and leave in the middle of a trial?"

"Not in a criminal proceeding. We chain 'em to the seats if necessary. On the civil side, things are a little different. The plaintiff can proceed with the case, even if the defendant voluntarily chooses to absent herself. You still have to prove your case."

"How very unusual," I mused to myself as I looked at Lulu's abandoned seat.

"Which brings me to the next procedural point," the judge continued.

"Yes, Your Honor?"

"Tomorrow at the crack of dawn is the beginning of bear season. I haven't missed opening day in 20 years. I thought this little trial would be over before lunch. You've still got another five or six witnesses."

"That's correct, Your Honor. But I'll be done in less than two hours," I promised.

"I'm sure you will," the court agreed. "But I could use a small favor myself. I'd like to leave now to prepare for my early day tomorrow. I've got to get up at three a.m."

"I understand, Your Honor. I don't object to a continuance until you return."

"No, you don't quite understand. See, I'll be gone about a week. The jury might forget most everything by then, so I don't want to send them home. I took this trial because I thought it would wrap up in an hour."

"I apologize to the court."

"No need to. Now here's what I want you to do. Continue on with the trial without me."

"I beg your pardon?"

"So long as you agree on the record, I don't think that the rules require that a judge be present."

"But Your Honor ... "

"Look, it's simple. Suppose you ask one of your witnesses an irrelevant question. Just object, and then make a ruling on your objection. I've made rulings in my sleep for years. There's nothing to it, believe me. Now go back to your seat. I want to explain our little understanding to the jury."

And he did. He told the 12 citizens an emergency had come up requiring his immediate attention, but that he would consider it a personal favor if they would stay to hear the rest of my case. At the rate people were leaving the courtroom, I hoped the jury would show some mercy and stick around.

Then his honor reached under his bench, pulled out a large caliber rifle, a pair of boots, and a red cap with a hunting license attached. He motioned to the tipstaff and they both proceeded toward the rear exit door.

"Just leave the verdict slip on my desk," Hainesworth called out.

If I had objected to the judge's proposal, he would have missed the first day of bear season, and I would have felt more pressure than a 10-year-old sitting on a toilet seat in near proximity to a woman with a defective bladder. I didn't want to be the guilty party at this trial.

# Chapter Twenty-Six

## The Outsourcing

Why is it that most of the lawyers in Philadelphia act like Philadelphia lawyers? It's annoying. Somebody should tell them it's annoying.

I had been dreading this encounter for weeks. Today Bernard Setzer, Esquire, was scheduled to appear at my office. He was a low-echelon worker bee buzzing about in the 400-lawyer hive known as Seligman McClintock. Although we had spoken by telephone, this would be our first face-to-face meeting.

I tried to count my blessings. At least I didn't have to fight my way into Philadelphia, and thank God our discussion wouldn't be adversarial. We were on the same side of a complex construction case in which he represented the architect and I represented the contractor. The owner of the building claimed our clients designed and installed an inadequate HVAC system. Setzer wanted to view firsthand the disputed system and to discuss our mutual trial strategy.

I looked out the back window as a Boston Green BMW automobile raced into our parking lot. The driver was gesticulating wildly as he conducted a discussion on his earpiece cell phone. Bernie had arrived, and only 15 minutes late. I waited to see if he had brought the obligatory Philadelphia-lawyer-extendable-shiny-black-fold-up-airport-travel-file-box-carrying-device with the 360-degree ball-bearing wheels. He did not disappoint as he closed his cell phone, touched a button on his key ring and headed toward the yawning trunk lid. He looked to be about 36 years old, but a receding hairline and two protruding veins pulsating in his forehead spoke volumes about his blood pressure.

As I walked into the conference room to prepare for introductions, I wondered whether he would violate the sacred Philadelphia code by failing to discuss vehicular congestion.

He stuck out a free hand as he dragged two boxes of files into the room.

"Hi," he began. "I'm Bernie. Sorry I'm late. You would not believe the traffic on the Schuylkill out of Philly."

This observation, offered by most Philadelphia lawyers who found their way to Bethlehem, always intrigued me. It was similar to being advised, "It's not the heat ... it's the humidity."

- - -

I must admit that to his credit, Bernie was a worker who wasted no time. From the moment that he and his files commandeered my conference room table, he was all business. We reviewed witness lists, architectural renderings, construction diagrams and countless potential trial exhibits. Then we journeyed to the job site to personally view the disputed installation. We returned to schedule depositions and prepare interrogatories. Whatever the Philadelphia queen bee was paying her little worker bee Bernie, it probably wasn't enough.

Ten grueling hours and two pots of coffee later, Bernie still didn't show any signs of slowing his pace.

"Listen," he suggested, "why don't we draft a short memorandum outlining what we've done today and what we need to do by next month."

"I think my secretary left two hours ago," I apologized.

"No problem," Bernie assured me. He flipped open his cell phone, hit speed dial and began to dictate. He didn't come up for air for about half an hour. He nailed everything we had discussed in the correct chronological order, including accurate observations as to the specific pre-trial responsibilities I had agreed to shoulder.

Bernie snapped shut his cell phone and rooted about in one of his files. I figured we were done for the day.

"Now if you'll check your e-mail, that memo should be done," he instructed.

I stared at Bernie in shocked silence. I walked over to my computer and instantly retrieved a 15-page memo from the law firm of Seligman McClintock. The document appeared to be flawless.

"That's some secretary you have," I observed.

"Wouldn't know," Bernie replied, distracted, as he began to pack his files into his carrying case. "Never met him or her."

"You've never met your secretary?"

"Nope. She might be in India some place. Bombay. Calcutta. Don't know for sure."

"Seriously?" I protested as Bernie looked up and stopped shuffling papers. "The person who just drafted this memo is halfway around the world?"

Bernie appeared genuinely puzzled by my obvious naïveté. "Outsourcing, counselor. Ever hear of it?"

"Of course, but ... "

Bernie continued. "Philadelphia salaried secretaries? You gotta be kidding me. Nope. Our support staff is, for the moment, in India until we find a cheaper option. This memo cost just a penny and a half per word. In Philadelphia, assuming you can find a high school grad who can actually read, write and type that same document, adding in 12 paid holidays, plus sick and personal days, pregnancy leave, workers' comp and medical insurance, would equate to the down payment on an oceanfront condo."

"You don't have any secretaries at your office?" I repeated in disbelief.

"Look, pal, there's 400 lawyers. To house 400 additional secretaries would approach the national debt. In Calcutta, the rent is manageable, since they don't have indoor plumbing and most people bicycle to work. Anyway, who needs a secretary in the next room? I take all my calls by voice-mail and generally get back to clients within three days."

Of course, deep down, I knew he was right. I had over the years unwittingly created at my office a clientele of whining, overindulged, me-first brats who expected to talk to *the lawyer* at a moment's notice. Simultaneously, I had unwittingly become an enabler for badly behaved clients. We all know there's no actual need for such instant contact with any attorney, as most questions can always be answered with the same simple phrase.

"*Lawyer Fox! Thank God you're there. Listen, the IRS just showed up and they're inspecting my second set of books. Can they do that?*"

"*Most likely.*"

"*Is it possible I could go to jail?*"

"*Most likely.*"

"*Will they put a lien on my vacation condo?*"

"*Most likely.*"

The more I though about it, the more I realized the wisdom of Bernie's simple, yet logical, office procedure. The reason I wasn't remotely as efficient as worker bee Bernie centered around the fact that I was tending to the needs of my clients, rather than to my needs. If clients stopped interrupting me with damn fool telephone calls, I might actually get some billable work done. Obviously I needed to turn over a new leaf. No secretary, just voice-mail. It was a foolproof formula that might apply to just about any personal service profession.

"*Hello. You have reached Munkfeller's Funeral Home ...*"

"*(Sniff ... sniff) This is Ethel Bumgarden. Grandpa passed on this afternoon.*"

"*Your call is important to us and has been transferred to our instant voice-mail. We'll be calling you back before you know it. Until then, follow these simple directions: If the loved one has died at home, pack the body in ice. If you're not in possession of a thermal bag, any large garden or lawn bag will do. To leave a message with our crematorium, press 1 ...*"

It had been a rough day. Bernie had sucked every ounce of energy from my body, like some vampire dining on the life juices of his prey. I stumbled through the door, four hours late for dinner. My wife didn't seem to mind. She was used to such delays, given the fact that I was in a service industry requiring that I unselfishly tend to the needs of my flock. She began to reheat the abandoned pot roast. An overnight courier package designed for those in need of instant gratification lay on the table.

"The new pants you ordered arrived this afternoon," she explained.

L.L. Lentle. What an amazing company. Yesterday I went on-line, and with a click of my mouse and the submission of a credit card number, my wardrobe had become enhanced, as the website catalog assured me, by attractive, yet practical, navy blue casual trousers. Such convenience. No mall. No traffic. No pushy crowds. Just pants.

Having finished my delayed dinner, there were but a few precious minutes left before bedtime and the press of new stresses awaiting me tomorrow at the office. I reached for the professionally wrapped L.L. Lentle overnight courier box that had winged its way from the rocky shores of Maine to the Commonwealth of Pennsylvania. It was time to see if my new pants fit as well as those worn by the handsome guy in the catalog.

I opened the package and withdrew a pair of navy blue casual trousers. But in an instant my short-lived enthusiasm turned to concern as I realized three or four of me could easily fit inside. The interior waistband boasted a length of 94 inches, while the legs measured a mere 12 inches. Pants intended for a circus sideshow freak. Or perhaps I could use them as a protective outdoor cover for the second car that didn't fit in the garage.

As usual, my wife displayed her flair for understatement. "It's possible you may have moved the mouse the wrong way," she theorized. "Why don't you tell L.L. Lentle there's a problem. They advertise total customer satisfaction," she explained. "You can call them right now."

"Now? It's eleven in the evening. I'll get a recording."

"Lentle boasts that it's open 24 hours a day, 365 days a year," my wife assured me.

*Calcutta*, I thought to myself. Some guy in charge of taking messages about returned pants was probably sitting one console away from the guy typing memos for Seligman McClintock.

I dialed the 1-800 number printed on the red and blue L.L. Lentle box. The phone only rang once.

"L.L. Lentle," the pleasant voice with a rocky Maine accent announced.

I waited for the recording to kick in telling me to wrap my pants in ice until someone got back to me.

"L.L. Lentle," the perky female said again.

Who could be so happy sitting in Calcutta, without the benefit of indoor plumbing?

"Hi," I tentatively offered. "This is Larry Fox."

"Hi. This is Priscilla. How may I help you, Mr. Fox?"

"I received some pants today, but the waist is too big and the legs are too short."

"How unfortunate, Mr. Fox. Here at L.L. Lentle, customer satisfaction is our primary goal. We will gladly correct the problem at no cost to you."

"You will?"

"You have three options. You can return the pants and we will return your money. If you wish, we will send you pants that fit properly. Thirdly, you can take the pants to your favorite tailor, have them altered, and we will pay the bill."

That last option sounded enticing. There was enough material to make three or four pairs of pants, and a matching vest, perhaps.

I chose the second option, and 24 hours later I was the proud owner of pants that fit perfectly. I looked every bit as handsome, from the waist down, as the guy strutting about in the website catalog.

Priscilla had taken care of everything without fanfare, and without hesitation, even though she didn't reside in Calcutta. Because of her personal, caring service, I planned to buy more L.L. Lentle pants. In contrast, if ever I needed a lawyer, I had no intention of calling Seligman McClintock or their outsourced wait-three-days secretarial staff.

About a month later, I stumbled home late. My wife reheated some chicken. There on the dining room table lay a discreetly wrapped package similar to the clandestine missives sent by the better lingerie companies. Inside reposed a special L.L. Lentle catalog entitled *The Stylistically Challenged Man*. The cover picture displayed some handsome guy with a 94-inch girth and 12-inch legs. Apparently L.L. Lentle had kept my special measurements on file.

# Chapter Twenty-Seven

## The Copper Caper

It would be the perfect crime. Egbert had the brains. Morton had the blowtorch. The caper was simple, yet foolproof. The two drinking buddies planned to enter the mammoth abandoned blouse mill below the old trestle bridge and remove hundreds of yards of copper piping, some of which ran the entire length of the quarter-mile-long derelict building.

"We'll make a fortune," Egbert said as he scribbled on a napkin in the dim light of Hogan's Bar and Grill.

Morton took another gulp of beer. "How much?" he asked.

"Ten, maybe 20 cents a linear foot," Egbert estimated. "If'n we loads the rear bed of your three-quarter-ton truck to the brim, it'll be like hitting the lottery!"

*What's a "linear"?* Morton silently pondered to himself.

"Now listen up," Egbert instructed. "I know that mill like the back of my hand. Twelve good years of my life ... Anyway, there's just one chain and an old lock securing the back fence. We can break through both with bolt cutters. And here's the beauty part: no night watchman. Some electric power is still hooked up so we won't need a generator for the welding equipment. We can start cutting and dismantling after midnight, and no one will be the wiser."

The high-level planning session was interrupted by a musical interlude as Morton's cell phone came to life. A depression-era theme song began to fill the air, announcing an incoming call. *We're In The Money - We're In The Money* could be heard across the entire barroom. Morton reached for the phone tucked away in his shirt pocket and placed the singing device next to his good ear.

"Yeah ... What? ... I'm with my friend, Egbert ... You want a quart or a half gallon? ... Skim or 2% low fat? ... Okay, as soon as I'm done here, Sweetie ... Yeah, I love you too."

Egbert tried to hide his displeasure with the telephonic interruption. He had important things to discuss and preferred that his train of thought not be derailed.

'Now here's the plan," he lectured. "We'll hide your truck behind the trees at the end of the old mill's loading ramp. That way no one will ever know we're inside. As you cut the copper pipe with the welder, I'll carry pieces out to the truck. We'll have a full load in less than three hours. We'll be rich!"

"Rich!" Morton echoed as he stood up to leave the bar. Then he drove over to the all-night grocery store, picked up a half gallon of milk as requested, and went home. He would need his beauty sleep, since the big copper escapade was planned for just after midnight in less than twenty-two hours.

At the appointed time, Morton loaded his arc welder onto the bed of his patched pickup truck. Then he drove over to Egbert's trailer and beeped the truck's horn once and then twice - their special secret signal.

Egbert emerged from his mobile residence carrying a leather electrician's pouch bursting with burglary tools. He had wire cutters, a flashlight, duct tape, pliers, a police radio scanner and other essential equipment. Nothing would be left to chance. He opened the passenger door and positioned himself in the truck's passenger seat, the seat with the coiled interior spring that had been attempting during the last decade to protrude through the ripped padding.

"Haven't you fixed this seat yet?" Egbert lamented. "It feels like I'm at the proctologist!"

*What's a proc-tonist*? Morton thought to himself.

They drove under the star-studded April night to the unsuspecting blouse mill where copper tubing awaited extraction. The perfect plan unfolded without impediment.

They hid the truck among the trees next to the parking lot, now overgrown with protruding weeds. They cut the lock and chain with bolt cutters. No watchman, no security cameras, no problem.

The burglars crept into the gaping basement of the blouse mill, the dancing beams of their flashlights leading the way. Morton dragged the arc welder behind him. Above them stretched hundreds of yards of shiny copper tubing - there just for the taking. Soon the two thieves began their labors in earnest. Morton cut the precious metal conduit into 15-foot sections, as Egbert lugged the booty to the hidden truck. Similar to lobster and crab fishermen, they worked diligently through the night, knowing that each additional pound of line they netted would bring them further riches.

It was indeed the perfect crime. By four a.m. the truck was crammed with cut tubing, and the felons were exhausted. It was time to go home. Morton dragged the arc welder back to the truck and dumped it on top of the glistening load of stolen goods. Their clandestine mission had been a rousing success.

That same morning, about 10 a.m., I received a telephone call from the county prison. The corrections officer advised me that a Mr. Smithers and a Mr. Wirtman wanted to retain me as their legal counsel with regard to their pre-dawn arrest.

"Who are they?" I asked.

"I doubt you know them," the prison officer conceded. "They said they found your name and number scratched in the wall over the toilet in their cell. The etched hieroglyphics proclaimed 'for a really cheap lawyer, call'... "

"I get the picture, officer," I interjected.

The proper location of a discreet advertisement makes all the difference in securing new clients. Had I paid for a similar phrase in the local newspaper, I probably wouldn't have received a single call.

I drove over to the jail. The guard escorted the tired-looking conspirators into the visitors' room. After the usual introductions, we got down to business.

Egbert explained how they had been involved in the perfect crime, stealing copper pipe, and how they had planned for every possible eventuality. From where I sat, their planning seemed to be somewhat flawed.

"So what happened after you left the blouse mill?" I inquired.

"We was standing in the woods loading the arc welder back onto the truck," Egbert explained. "It was as dark as the inside of a cow. You couldn't see nothin.' All of a sudden, this cop pulls into the parking lot. I can't imagine what caused him to show up unannounced. It didn't matter, though. We was hidden from view. So we stood there real still, hardly breathing. We didn't move a muscle for over 15 minutes. The cop snooped around a bit, but I knew he'd never find us. We was flossed like a camel."

Egbert probably meant "camouflaged," but I decided not to dwell on this minor point.

"Then how did you get caught?" I persisted.

Morton momentarily adjusted his hangdog body language and looked up. "My girlfriend called for some milk."

"I don't quite understand," I interrupted.

"On my cell phone. It plays this song until I answer the call. The cop heard the music."

"You committed a burglary and didn't put your phone on silent mode?"

"I guess I forgot. Anyway, she gets mad if I don't take her calls."

- - -

I find it curious that they call them "cell phones." Egbert and Morton will be in a cell for a long time, but their new home won't come equipped with a phone. And the girlfriend is sure to be inconvenienced, too. Who's going to buy the milk for the next one and a half to three years?

## CHAPTER TWENTY-EIGHT

Please Take A Number

Certain rules are universally recognized and need never be written. I hesitate to give examples, because they have never been written down before. There's an unwritten rule against doing so. But here goes:
Never leave the toilet seat up.
Turn around after entering an elevator.
Toilet paper hangs over, not under.
Don't step on a judge's robe that's dragging on the floor.
Always check the coin return slot.

- - -

Sometimes unwritten rules may be subject to interpretation and possible dispute.
Sunderman's deli department was having a sale on liverwurst. I missed the last sale. I ran right over.
I still get a rush each time Sunderman's exterior automatic doors magically open on cue and invite me in. Entry into the massive shopping-cart storage area is a moment to be savored and experienced by all five senses. There's the piped in music - not exactly classical, nor is it rock - just Sundermanesque, the type of relaxing background melody that makes one want to buy yet another cantaloupe. The sense of sight is impacted next. Just inside the gaping store archway reposes the daily unadvertised special. Today it's row after row of apple pies with perfect little red bows on top. The olfactory receptors take over, as shopper after shopper breathes in the aroma of cinnamon and other delicate spices. I can almost taste the apples as I tenderly examine one of the pies, entombed within its very own see-

through-plastic pie-carrying case. For a moment, it feels like Christmas Day back at Grandma's house.

I decided to take a shopping cart, just in case I needed something else besides liverwurst. There were several makes and models from which to choose. Let's see, I didn't need one with the infant seat where a mommy could stick her little darling's squirming legs through the two holes. I didn't need one shaped like a car so a five-year-old could sit inside and play with the useless steering wheel. I didn't need the motorized combination shopping cart-wheelchair. I didn't need the two-foot-high miniature cart with a pole and attached flag that read: *For our junior customers in training*.

The sights and smells welcomed me once again as an octogenarian motored on by in her shopping cart-wheelchair. I grabbed a regular cart of my own and headed toward the deli department. Similar to golf, you're not actually in the game unless you're walking.

The deli counter was busy. Two overworked clerks wearing baseball caps emblazoned with the red "S" logo sliced meat and scooped out macaroni salad. Five patient customers stood facing the clerks waiting for their number to be called.

I squeezed by a young boy making race car noises in a sporty race car shopping cart. I secured a number and took my place in the back of the line. I was number 89.

"Number 84?" a clerk shouted as he restocked a tray of deviled eggs.

"That's me," some lady snapped from the front. She inched forward in her motorized wheelchair-shopping cart, no simple task, since she was morbidly obese. "I'll take two pounds of sliced salami, cut an eighth of an inch thick, three pounds of hot dogs, and the rest of that creamed cucumber salad."

The clerk reached for a large cylinder of meat and made his way to the slicer. Simultaneously, the second clerk handed off his order and stood poised for the next customer.

"Number 85?" the second clerk announced.

"That's me," the same obese lady confirmed. "Get me three pounds of domestic Swiss, two pounds of potato salad, and a pound of pickled eggs."

This beleaguered clerk was unaware that an unwritten rule had just been broken.

This, however, was not lost upon a tall gentleman at the front of the congregation who possessed number 86.

"Wait just a minute, lady," he stammered. "The first clerk is processing your order. You can't take two numbers in a row. I've been waiting here for ten minutes."

Fanny couldn't, and wouldn't, be pushed around by some lightweight.

"Hey, Twig, where's it say you can take only one number?"

"I beg your pardon?"

"You heard me, Stick. Who made up the rule that says I can't take two numbers?"

By now, both clerks realized what curious manipulation had overtaken their efficient operation.

"Ma'am," the first clerk observed, "I'm taking care of you."

"I know that," Fanny agreed. "And now so is your dumb friend."

"I can't do that," clerk Number Two interjected. "There are other people waiting."

"Exactly," Stick exclaimed. "I'll take a pound of low-fat, low-salt turkey breast."

"You will over my dead body," the offensive woman announced in a menacing tone. "Hey, Doofus, stop staring and start slicing," she hollered over the counter.

This heated verbal exchange had caught my eye, and judging by the astonished looks on the faces of numbers 87, 88, and now newcomers 90 and 91, the collective eye of everyone else who had gathered to secure the liverwurst special.

What *was* the rule regarding the taking of a number? Was it written anywhere?

- - -

For a moment, I thought back to an article I had read in the *Wall Street Journal* about another nut who snagged two reservations and made a good living doing so. Apparently, the airplane built by Lear Jet was at one time so popular that a two-year customer waiting list existed. Moreover, to lock in the purchase price, an order had to be accompanied by a $100,000 good faith down payment. One enterprising young man had $200,000 saved up, so he ordered two jets at a specific locked-in price. Two years later they were ready for delivery. By that time, the price of a Lear Jet had risen another million dollars. So he sold his place in line to two new customers who didn't want to wait and who were willing to pay him an additional $500,000 to save themselves $500,000. He got back his $200,000, netted $800,000, and never bought a plane.

I had one client, Elmo Schwartz, who made money by not waiting to be served. He would go to real estate auctions and determine who was there as a bona fide bidder.

"Give me $100," he'd tell each potential buyer, "and I won't bid up the price." Once he collected his fees, he left.

- - -

Stick had no intention of relinquishing his perceived vested right to turkey breast. "Lady," he yelled, "maybe if you used just one clerk and bought half as much, you'd be half as wide."

This comment was not seen by Fanny as an olive branch. She reached into her shopping bag, produced a chocolate croissant, crumpled it in her pudgy hand, and pitched it between Stick's eyes.

Stick thought for a moment, then methodically rooted around in his shopping cart and produced a jar of sweet brown molasses. He slowly unscrewed the cap as someone in the crowd gasped.

I like liverwurst, especially when it's on sale. But I also know that being a witness to a criminal assault may require that the onlooker testify under subpoena at some jury trial that might be rescheduled four times. I gave my precious number 89 to a college student who had joined the crowd, similar to a moth drawn to a flickering candle. I hadn't been paid $800,000, or even $100. I walked toward the grand entranceway where the apple pies were stacked. In the background I could hear the cheer of the mob as food began to fly.

## CHAPTER TWENTY-NINE

What's Your Sign?

It was a better than average day until the mail arrived. Another wedding invitation. If I decline, one of my most important clients may never talk to me again. What now looms is a 300-mile trip to sit in some over-priced reception hall, making small talk with people I don't know and will never see again. And there's assigned seating, so I can't even sneak away for at least an hour.

They sat me between fellow rejects Aunt Tabatha and family friend Eloise. I tried to look occupied as I examined my paper place setting, but there was no hiding from the inevitable. Tabatha peered at my name on the fancy printed card.

"An attorney!" The cross-examination was about to begin.

"I'm Larry Fox."

"You with the bride or groom?"

"I know the bride's parents."

"Nice people, I guess. Listen, what's your date of birth?"

"I beg your pardon?"

"When were you born?" Eloise chimed in, as her earlobes and oversized pearl earrings swayed back and forth. "It's all in the stars, you know."

"You're a Sagittarius, aren't you?" Tabatha postulated. "The silent, strong type with a nomadic tendency to see the world. And you prefer to avoid confrontation."

"He's an Aries, silly. Look at the way he carries his shoulders, and he's here alone. Definitely an Aries, or possibly a Cancer," insightful Eloise corrected.

Trapped. This was not the first time I had endured the misfortune of astrological inquiry. Of course, if one of these true believers were able to look me up and down and correctly announce the actual month in which I was born, I'd become a convert in a heartbeat. But that has never happened. Rather, invariably the astrologer first demands to know the date of birth, and only then begins to describe demeanor and characteristics attributable to the subject of the study.

Astrology is a science the object of which is to expend no energy or effort in determining the true nature, talents or capabilities of the individual. By pre-judging and categorizing someone based solely upon a birth date, meaningful interaction with a fellow human being can be avoided, since every trait becomes an instantaneous, foregone conclusion.

There was only one other critical piece of information required of me, and then there would be no need for further inquiry. I knew what was coming.

"What's your background?" Eloise insisted.

I played dumb. "I work in an office."

"No. No. I mean where did your grandparents come from?"

"Bethlehem."

"No. I mean in what country did your ancestors reside?" Eloise insisted as she studied my blond moustache and hazel eyes. Armed with this information, the pre-judging would be complete. Italian, Nordic, East European, each had its individual immutable character flaws. Or was I a mutt, the product of unbridled cross-breeding, a chance muddying of the ethnic waters?

"Please pardon me for a moment, ladies," I announced, as I stood up to leave. "I must give my respects to the bride and groom."

"Definitely a Sagittarius," Tabatha whispered to her friend. "Secretive and humorless."

- - -

Godfried Pendergast had been a good client for years. I had assisted him and his wife with the acquisition of their new house, an estate plan, and a zoning issue. As usual, he showed up at my office on time. He was carrying a packet of documents that measured about one and a quarter inches in thickness. Given the fact that a quarter-inch of paper usually generated about one hour of legal services, it appeared that he was involved with a problem that would take about five hours to resolve. The look on his face suggested that he suspected as much. He dumped the pile of papers on my desk.

"Well, here's the story," he began. "My two young daughters wanted a dog. I couldn't talk them out of it. I figured the smaller the dog, the smaller the pile of poop. So I did a little Internet research and found this Chihuahua breeder near Philadelphia. You can hold these puppies in one hand. So three months ago we all drove down to Philly. It was love at first sight between the dog and the kids, and so I bought the little runt for $875."

"$875!" I blurted out. "They've got dogs at the city pound for next to nothing."

"Don't I know it. But it's sorta like buying a watch. The smaller they are, the more they cost. Anyway, the breeder gives me papers that this dog is a purebred registered Chihuahua. The kids named her 'Trixie,' and she became part of the family."

"What's the problem?" I inquired.

"Well, about a month ago, I received a certified letter from the American Kennel Club." Godfried pushed an official-looking document across the table in my direction.

*Dear Mr. Pendergast:*

*This letter is written regarding your recent purchase from registered litter R47B38-200742. Inquiry by other purchasers has brought into question the purebred status of the puppy acquired by you. Kindly submit a dorsal and lateral full-length color photograph of your puppy and return the photographs to the undersigned in the enclosed postage-paid envelope.*

*Very truly yours,*
*R. Thurston Terwilicer III*
*Bloodline Registration Specialist*

I read the letter twice. Then I looked up at Godfried, who had something to say.

"This guy Terwilicer, he's questioning the authenticity of my dog. Who the hell gave him this authority? We were actually thinking of breeding her ... "

An hour ago, I had met with a client who wished to establish a million dollar trust for a university lecture series. Now I was discussing alleged defective genes in an eight-ounce mongrel. It's a living, I suppose.

"Did you send in the requested photos?"

"Of course not. First of all, the dog's too small to have both a dorsal and a lateral anything. Furthermore, if there was a problem, it's between me and the breeder, not some nervy Terwilicer guy I never met, who writes unsolicited letters from midtown Manhattan."

"Do you have a picture of the dog?"

Godfried rummaged through his pile of papers and produced a photograph.

I studied the image. Any similarity between the small mutt smiling back at me and a Chihuahua was purely coincidental. But what did I know?

Prendergast wasn't done relating his story. "Then a couple of weeks ago I get another certified mailing from this persistent Terwilicer guy." Prendergast handed me a second document.

*Dear Mr. Prendergast:*

*Please consider this letter as formal notification that your bitch # L2214K37-BQR, sired in litter R47B38-200742, has been decertified as a purebred Chihuahua.*
*Her registration has been nullified.*

*Very truly yours,*
*R. Thurston Terwilicer III*
*Bloodline Registration Specialist*

"Can he do that?" Prendergast demanded. "One minute I own a purebred Chihuahua. The next minute, without a trial, judge or jury, Trixie is blacklisted? I want to sue!"

"Sue who? For what damages?" I asked.

"Well, for starters, that idiot Terwilicer and his whole snotty organization."

"But Godfried, you just said Terwilicer has nothing to do with your dog. Are you going to hire a lawyer in New York to force Terwilicer to put Trixie back on the AKC Chihuahua registry?"

Prendergast started blinking his eyelids at me in rapid succession as he began to review his limited options. "Well, then, we'll sue the breeder. I paid him big bucks for a purebred dog. Now I've got a five-dollar mutt."

"Have you told the breeder about this problem?"

"Sure. I called him after the second letter arrived. He said to ship back Trixie, and he'd return my money."

"So ... what's the problem?"

"I can't do that! The kids love the dog."

"Look," I stammered, "I'm not sure you have any damages. The breeder says he'll take back the dog and reimburse you the money."

"But I got ripped off. It's not a purebred, just some mongrel!"

"Not as far as your kids are concerned," I corrected.

- - -

An official-looking document just arrived at my office. It's from the United States Census Bureau. Another decade has faded into history. The government wants to know all about me. There are several rather personal questions about my bloodline.

Am I:

- ☐ White
- ☐ Black or Negro
- ☐ Indian (Amer.) (Print the name of the enrolled or principal tribe.) _____
- ☐ Eskimo
- ☐ Aleut
- ☐ Asian or Pacific Islander (API)
- ☐ Chinese
- ☐ Filipino
- ☐ Hawaiian
- ☐ Korean
- ☐ Vietnamese
- ☐ Japanese
- ☐ Asian Indian
- ☐ Samoan
- ☐ Guamanian
- ☐ Other API _____
- ☐ Other Race (Print Race) _____

Decisions ... decisions. Perhaps I should have my dorsal and lateral views taken, send the photos to the Census Bureau and let them figure it out.

Last night I watched Notre Dame football on T.V. A limber O'Malley completed a pass to O'Brien for a seven-yard gain. Both participants were black. Thankfully, they both had their names printed on the back of their jerseys. That sure makes it easier to pick out a true Irishman in the crowd.

## CHAPTER THIRTY

### The Trail Of Evidence

Cappy Drinker wanted to see me about filing an appeal. He had just been sentenced to 23 months in the county prison for retail theft. Since his freedom of movement was now rather limited, I agreed to visit him, despite the incessant heavy rain.

I scampered with umbrella in hand to my car and began the familiar journey to the Lehigh County Jail - Broad Street to Union, then up Linden. It was near the intersection of Airport Road that I noticed a most curious thing. To the right of the parallel double yellow "no passing" lines positioned in the middle of the road lay yet another line. It was white and wove at times from one side of my lane to the other, while maintaining a width of about two inches. It appeared as if someone had splattered paint in a haphazard manner as the unknown dribbler drove down the highway. The substance seemed unaffected by the elements, for neither the rain nor the thousands of tires proceeding in heavy traffic had loosened its grip on the highway.

A week later, I again noticed the same irregular white line, glistening in the sun, as it proceeded for more than three miles.

- - -

"Ziggy Reinsmith referred us here. Says you've been representing his trucking company for years," the older fellow sitting in my conference room explained.

I extended my hand and introduced myself. He did the same.

"I'm Amos Winkle, and this here is my son, Devon. We operate *Winkle Transport*."

"You folks drive trucks for a living?"

"Been teamsters all our lives," Amos proudly confirmed. "And my father before me."

I studied my newest clients. Amos may have tipped the scales at just 175 pounds, yet his hands were large, like leathery baseball gloves, and they were caked with oil. This man had dismantled and reassembled every internal combustion engine ever designed.

Devon's clean and petite hands were probably inherited from his mother. He might have driven trucks for a living, but he didn't fix them.

"How might I help you gentlemen?" I inquired.

"Yup. Been truckin' all our lives. It ain't getting any easier. What with the cost of diesel going up each week, it's been harder and harder to make a living," Amos explained.

"Why do you need a lawyer?"

"Well, see, it's like this. They done an audit. Never been through one before."

"Who did an audit?" I asked.

"A guy from the IRS. He took a look at our books."

"And?"

"I deducted the cost of diesel fuel as a business expense."

"Sounds legitimate to me, since you use the fuel to run your trucks."

"We do."

"Then what's the problem?"

"See, here's the thing. Our records show we operate three tank trucks."

"You don't hitch your rigs to trailers?"

"Nope. We run single unit tank trucks carrying liquids. Mostly we transport milk to the big dairies. Recently, we've also been using one of the tankers to deliver aviation fuel to the smaller airports. We've got all the interstate permits."

"So you use two trucks for milk and one for fuel. Do you ever use the milk tankers to transport fuel?" I asked.

"Nope, 'cause the fuel tanker ain't refrigerated," Amos explained.

"So did the IRS say there's a problem?"

"Well, you see, I reported that we put 450,000 miles on our tankers last year, and I submitted legitimate fuel bills to back that up. But then this hyperactive IRS guy checks the odometer reading on the three tankers. He comes up with only 380,000 miles. 70,000 miles were missing."

"I thought you said you had legitimate fuel bills reflecting 450,000 miles?"

"I do. See, the other 70,000 were put on another tanker that isn't registered."

"You operated a fourth tanker without the permits?"

Devon looked up for the first time. "We use it for special trips nobody knows about. We put 70,000 miles on it last year."

"Wait a minute," I blurted out. "Now I'm confused. It's not possible to operate a tank truck without the local, state and federal permits and licenses. There are inspections, sales taxes, highway use taxes, weigh stations and safety checkpoints."

"That's why we're here. We might have a problem," Amos confirmed.

Amos looked at Devon. Devon returned the stare. Then Amos lowered his voice.

"If we tell you something, it stays in this room?"

"Yes, of course. The attorney-client privilege precludes me from divulging what a client discloses."

Amos thought for a moment. "Here's the story. We got this fourth tanker hidden in the warehouse. That's because it has the same vehicle identification numbers as the aviation fuel tanker."

"How did *that* happen?"

"Do you really want to know?"

"You're right. I don't."

"When we operate the fourth rig, we take all the license plates, registration, and interstate log books from the licensed tanker and stick them on the unregistered rig."

"But why are you operating an unregistered fourth tanker? What are you transporting?"

Amos lowered his voice again and looked me in the eye. "With the increase in fuel prices, we were running at a loss. Nobody pays you what you're worth. Just look at the transportation industry. The cost of crude went up a dollar a barrel, and half the airlines filed for bankruptcy."

I knew how he felt. Rarely had I ever been adequately compensated by anyone.

Devon decided to join in the explanation. "Then one day this guy drops by our office and tells me he pays top dollar to certain tanker drivers. I didn't know what he meant. But then he showed me.

"Showed you what?"

"He takes me to this abandoned quarry up in Krucksville. Every once in a while, somebody shows up in a pickup truck and dumps a couple barrels of toxic waste into a sub-surface storage tank. The guy says he wants me to come by at night and fill up my tanker with that goo. He'll pay me $5,000 a load. *Cash.* I can't make that type of money in a month hauling milk.

"Where am I supposed to take the goo? He says that's the beauty part. The next day he shows up at my office and drills a one-quarter-inch hole in the bottom of my tanker. Then he installs a release valve I can operate up front in the cabin. All I got to do, he says, is drive from here to California and back, a one-week trip. Whenever I hit 20 miles per hour or better, just open the valve and let the waste drain out. When I come back empty, he'll have another load waiting."

I sat in silence.

"This guy thought of everything." Devon said. "Even cops. He installed a five-gallon drum inside the tanker. It holds aviation fuel. If someone wants to check my cargo, I pull another lever and petroleum is released."

"How long have you been dribbling waste between here and the West Coast?"

"70,000 miles worth."

"Did you report the income you earned?"

"It was cash," Devon smirked. "What do you think?"

The scenario to which I had just become privy was more complex than an all-day bar exam question. What laws hadn't these two co-conspirators broken? Environmental statutes? IRS regulations? Department of Transportation licensing requirements, or criminal conspiracy? Of greater concern to me were the ethical conflicts they had, without warning, dropped on my desk. Just who did I represent? The father, the son or the trucking company? Two out of the three would probably end up in jail.

They were waiting for a response.

"What should we do now?" Amos repeated after his son.

I thought back to the first time that question had been asked of me. Curley Johnson had just shot his wife through the head and was calling me with a question or two.

I decided to answer in the negative. "For starters, don't transport any more waste," I blurted out, "and for God's sake, stay the hell away from the guy at the quarry."

Devon's face took on an uneasy grimace. "That's a problem," he confided.

"Why?"

"I had no idea who I was dealing with." He glanced at his father and looked back in my direction. "It's the Mob. They told me if I talk to the IRS, or tell anyone about the quarry dump site, I won't see the sun come up."

I told the duo to go home and decide who, if anyone, I was to represent. I would await their call. A week later, Amos telephoned.

"I don't think we'll need your services," he advised.

"Really?"

"The guy at the quarry sent us to his special CPA over in Jersey. The CPA amended my IRS filing for last year by withdrawing our claim for the additional 70,000 miles. There is no deduction, and no fourth tanker."

"No tanker?"

"It's gone."

I decided not to ask. I went a different direction. "What if the IRS subpoenas your son to review his financial records?"

"He's gone, too."

## Chapter Thirty-One

Two Races Well Run

Desperate calls. Happy calls. Angry calls. Psychotic calls. At some point they all find their way into my office. Last week it was a sad call, prompted by the relentless angel of death. The receptionist was out to lunch. I picked up the phone on the third ring.

"Law offices. May I help you?"

"Lawyer Fox, is that you?" the familiar voice of an exhausted woman inquired.

"Frieda?"

It was my office cleaning lady, gentle, unassuming Frieda Bunkiss. She had been my loyal custodian for more than 30 years. She was one of only a handful of people walking the earth whom I could trust with a key to my office. She was industrious, punctual, efficient and never complained. Two mornings a week following her visits, the place sparkled and somehow it made the whole office staff a little happier.

"Frieda ... is something wrong?"

Her voice was subdued. "They took my Harvey to Cedardale. I think he may need a will and them legal papers that say he wants to die without being kept alive. Will you help me?"

Sad call. There was nothing good about the word "Cedardale." County run Cedardale marked the last stop for the impoverished and infirm. The last stop before the undertaker.

"Harvey had a stroke last night, so the ambulance came and took him," Frieda explained. "Now the social worker says we need papers wrote up."

"A medical directive?"

"That's the words. Yup, a medical direction."

It was all becoming painfully clear. I had little doubt of the answer to my next question.

"Frieda, does your husband have any medical insurance?"

"Who can afford that? We used to until his union pension contract turned to dust after the mill went bust."

It's funny how one's mind works. I've never had a problem visiting clients in prison. For the most part, they deserve to be there. They get three squares a day and play basketball and cards. Club Med with bars on the windows. I've never had a problem being called to the hospital. Usually the emergency is correctable, and often the sick recuperate.

But ... Cedardale. It's where they take you when there is no place to take you. It's the poorhouse.

When I'm at Cedardale, a temporary but deep sense of depression envelopes me. Not because of the unrelenting urine smell that slaps my face even at the front door. I've smelled urine before. It's not the disturbing sight of forgotten, aged and discarded human beings slumped over or strapped into county-owned wheelchairs. I've seen old people before. No, if truth be told, I am saddened because I know that with each beat of my heart, I am one second closer to falling into the abyss with each of these once alive, now withered souls. Miserable wretch that I am, I don't feel sorry for them. The bell tolls for me! Who dies at home any more? The chances are very good there's a seat being saved for me right here.

"Lawyer Fox ... are you still there?"

It was Frieda. "Will you go see Harvey at Cedardale and take them legal papers? He'll draw an X if you hold his hand."

Time was critical. If Harvey suffered another stroke, his ability to communicate might be further compromised. I dictated a medical directive with accompanying power of attorney. My secretary, Cindy, typed it up after lunch.

A few years ago, some over-zealous county solicitor ruled that employees of Cedardale may no longer act as witnesses to documents signed by residents of the home. Apparently, some defenseless resident lost her meager savings when a rogue last will and testament popped up in court, a document allegedly witnessed by a bedside nurse's assistant. My secretary Cindy would have to tag along.

As we drove into the Cedardale parking lot, the melancholy took hold of me. Insightful Cindy noted my change in mood. She knew of my ridiculous phobia regarding diapers and drool buckets.

"Every time we come here, you get sullen and morose," she observed. "Listen, Larry, if you ever end up here, I'll come and visit you if you give me a little extra time off during lunch."

I felt better, but did I really want her to see me dressed in one of those little blue hospital nighties that comes undone in the back at the most inopportune times?

We asked the lobby receptionist for Harvey's room. She pointed to an elevator.

"Third floor. Turn right. Number 34."

As we entered the elevator, the smell of death was already upon us. Urine. Feces. Decay. Filth. I wanted to leave.

We walked down a wide corridor where residents sat slumped in wheelchairs, their gazes fixed. Their faces showed no life, no reason to live. What had these people done before they were condemned to this place? Had any been lawyers who during brighter days had drafted medical directives?

Cindy and I entered number 34, a rather large room, painted in shiny white institutional gloss for ease during annual wall scrubbing. There was a hospital bed with raised siding in each corner. The only frosted window, boasting a safety bar for those planning to escape, added to the illumination cast from a single naked overhead lightbulb. There was no bathroom. The communal showers and toilets were centrally located somewhere down the hall.

Only two of the four beds were occupied. I looked at the body on my right.

"Mr. Bunkiss ... Harvey Bunkiss?" I called out. A moan issued forth from under the covers.

"Mr. Bunkiss," I began, "I'm Larry Fox, an attorney. Your wife asked me to come. I have a medical directive for you to consider. Mr. Bunkiss ... can you hear me?"

It would be a long afternoon before an "X" might make its way from Harvey's hand onto the legal documents I carried. And patient, good-hearted Cindy knew it. As I continued to explain the reason for my unannounced appearance to Mr. Bunkiss, Cindy turned to the man in the next bed who was staring at the ceiling.

"Hello," she began.

His eyes moved to meet her.

"Hello," he managed.

"I'm Cindy."

"Nice ta meet ya. I'm Gerald. Gerald Wilson."

There was a long pause.

"What day is it?"

"Thursday," Cindy confirmed.

"Thursday," Gerald repeated. "It's hard to tell the days apart. I wish I was home."

"Where's home?"

"Seventh Street Bridge. I had a box all to myself, out of the rain."

"Who brought you here, Mr. Wilson?"

"Cops ... said my feet was frozen. I lost two toes. Never had a problem with the cold before, but then some kids took my sneakers. Then they trashed all my clothes at the E.R. If I had sneakers, I'd walk out of here right now before someone gets my spot."

"We'll have to come back tomorrow," I interjected. "I think Harvey here just fell asleep."

"That's understandable," Cindy said knowingly. "Your dictation has the same effect on me."

- - -

Friday was little different from Thursday. The elevator smelled like urine, and Harvey and Gerald were still the only residents in unit number 34.

"Mr. Bunkiss," I inquired, "can you print an X on this line?"

Cindy walked over to Gerald's bed and withdrew a plastic bag from under her winter jacket. Gerald's eyes followed her every move.

"Hello, again," he offered. "What day is it?"

"Friday."

"What's in the bag? Did you bring something for us to eat? The food here ain't so good. They got me on a diabetes diet."

Cindy handed Gerald a shoebox wrapped in a ribbon. He reached out with shaking hands - hands that had not received very many gifts. He fumbled with the bow and opened the lid. New sneakers. He took an astonished breath.

He gently lifted the unexpected gift to his face. "Sneakers," he whispered. "New ones."

He smelled each one several times, as if he were breathing in the aroma from a bouquet of roses. He looked up at Cindy with his watery, old eyes.

"For me?" he asked.

"Yours forever."

It took an hour, but Harvey finally executed the medical directive. Cindy witnessed the event, and so we were free to leave. Gerald had since fallen asleep, one sneaker now lying on the left side of his pillow, the other to the right. It had been an exhausting afternoon for everyone.

Three days later, Cindy had to deliver the completed paperwork back to the client. Things had changed. Harvey now resided alone in unit 34. A Coast Guard petty officer could have bounced a quarter off Gerald's empty bed. Cindy ran to the nurse's station.

"I'm so sorry for your loss," Nurse Flannagan commiserated as she produced a small envelope. "He left you a note."

*Make sure you give the sneakers to someone who can use them. They shouldn't go to waste.*

- - -

It was poor old widow Beanstoffer calling from the Cedardale community payphone. I had known her for 40 years. Once upon a time she had worked in our local blouse mill, before the jobs went to China or somewhere. Now she existed on a $45 per month pension from the International Ladies Garment Workers Union, and Social Security.

"Larry," the feeble voice began as if its owner were a million miles away, "can you stop by? I need a living will, in case I linger."

The word *linger* reminded me of the story about the carrot and the cucumber walking down the street. The cucumber gets hit by a car and is taken to the hospital. The carrot is his best friend and visits the cucumber every day at the intensive care unit. Thirty days go by but the cucumber isn't getting any better - he's still in a coma. So the carrot summons up his courage and approaches the attending physician. "Give it to me straight, Doc. Is my friend the cucumber going to pull through?" The doctor looks the carrot in the eye. "He could improve," the physician surmises, "but he'll probably be a vegetable the rest of his life."

The widow Beanstoffer didn't want to share the cucumber's fate, so I drafted a medical directive and took it to her for signature.

How could some architect have possessed the nerve to charge a fee to design this place, a sterile, square, five-story fireproof cinder block building? I've visited prisons that generate more warmth. Cedardale was more depressing than ever. The angels of mercy who worked there so diligently would all someday surely pass effortlessly through the gates of heaven. One of the attendants showed me to Beanstoffer's room, shared with eight other ladies.

Beanstoffer struggled to remain independent her entire life. Now she needed assistance putting on her nightie and bunny slippers, her usual daytime wardrobe.

"You know what bothers me the most?" she explained.

"No. What?" I responded as I placed her executed documents in my briefcase.

"Being useless ... doing nothing of any importance. My life may have been insignificant, but it's only since they dumped me here that I've taken up space for no reason."

I wanted desperately to give her a litany of insightful reasons why her existence had meaning. None came to mind.

"You know what it comes down to?" she continued. "Nobody stuck in here has anything anybody on the outside wants. We've got no money for the kids to fight over, no magical wisdom to impart, and no funny jokes to tell - just adult diapers that need changing. Did God give us longevity for this?"

- - -

Billy Wanamaker and I grew up together. He went off to the police academy and 30 years later left on full pension as a local chief of police. He invited me to his retirement party at the downtown Hilton. Everybody was there, holding champagne glasses and trying to be heard above the commotion.

"I've been thinkin'," he confided to me.

I looked at the best man at my wedding, the guy who chose me as godfather of his son. "About what?"

"What am I going to do now?"

Here was someone who could lie on the beach for the rest of his life and have his pension checks deposited via electronic fund transfer. He had an opportunity to step off the treadmill, something few people can ever hope to achieve.

"I've got an idea, but I'll need your help. Can I count on you?" he asked.

Godfather ... best man ... Without question.

And, so, in one irreversible instant, I got sucked into the unthinkable. I became the chairperson of the *Billy Wanamaker for Magistrate* election committee. Me. The guy who had, without exception, actively avoided every political conflagration on all levels, local, state, and national.

Billy had decided to run for the open magistrate position vacated by the old district justice who was ill. The elective office of magistrate in Pennsylvania is, in a sense, rather unusual. The successful candidate need not be a high school graduate - just someone imbued with common sense. This public servant presides over the lowest level of judicial proceedings: recipients of speeding tickets, dogs pooping on lawns and people cited for tall weeds.

Billy figured he could render an appropriate amount of justice, so he threw his hat in the ring. So did Manny Grumbowski, a retired mobile home salesman. It would be a contested campaign.

I quickly realized why I had never maintained the slightest interest in politics. I was now organizing coffee klatsches, attending "meet the candidate" nights and mailing brochures. The weekly strategy sessions stretched into the night.

"Now let's see," Billy enthusiastically calculated from across my kitchen table, "during the last magisterial race, the winner received 847 votes and the loser amassed 540. We have just about the same number of registered voters. If I get 650 votes, I'll probably win. Of course, Grumbowski's already got most of the religious vote wrapped up. His church has sent mailers to every parishioner. That means we'll have to go door to door."

Door to door! I was starting to have unhappy thoughts about the political process, when an unexpected miracle occurred, one of those moments that renew one's faith in democracy.

"There's a Danny Bookmaker to see you," my secretary announced.

"Who? I don't have any appointments until three p.m.," I advised her.

"He says he's a political science major at the community college, and he'd like to get involved in the magisterial race so he can write a paper about his experiences."

Angels began to sing in the background.

"Show the gentleman in," I beamed.

There before me stood an 18-year-old energetic, smiling, well-groomed student, perfect for ascending porch steps and putting political flyers under doormats.

"It's so nice of you to drop by," I assured the sophomore as I shook his hand and patted him on the back.

We became instant friends and confidants. Danny soon joined us at each important strategy session and ultimately took over the responsibility to schedule political rallies. Sometimes as many as six potential voters remained afterward for the complimentary egg salad and petits fours.

It was anybody's guess who would win what looked like a tight race. On election day, Billy, Danny and I each stood like cigar-store Indians at different polling places handing out those stupid flyers with our candidate pictured among official-looking law books. I don't think Billy had ever read a statute or case in his life. When the polls closed at eight p.m., we journeyed over to Finnegan's Pub to watch the election returns on local TV.

"And with 60 percent of the districts reporting, Grumbowski would appear to have a comfortable lead over Wanamaker," the local news anchorman observed.

"Yes," his blonde co-anchor sidekick with the really red lip gloss confirmed. "Three hundred twenty votes to 240. It's too early to call, but Grumbowski has a commanding lead."

I put my elbows on the bar and buried my head in my hands. We had worked hard, and yet defeat appeared imminent. Our despondent candidate began to drink another beer.

"And with 80 percent of the precincts reporting, it's Grumbowski 544 and Wanamaker 403. Looks like a victory for Grumbowski, Kate."

Ms. Lip-gloss agreed. "I don't think Wanamaker can overcome that deficit. We project Grumbowski the winner."

With those words, Billy on my left began yelling at the TV screen as if the newscasters could hear him. Danny, the college political science major, however, began to laugh.

"What's so funny?" I moaned.

"We've won, probably by a landslide!" he remarked.

I looked at the boy political strategist and then studied the TV screen. "What the hell do you mean? With 90 percent of the vote counted, it's 670 to 490. It's hopeless."

"Not so fast, counselor," bright-eyed Danny said wryly. "They haven't added in the *absentee* ballots yet."

"What are we talking? Maybe 10 votes one way or the other," Wanamaker lamented.

"So you'd think," he said. I visited Cedardale two weeks ago. It's located in our voting district, you know," Danny noted.

I looked at Wanamaker, who put down his half-empty beer glass.

"What about Cedardale?" I asked.

"All those senior citizens, they're permanent residents in our district. Everyone is under doctors' orders and immobile. They all qualify as absentee voters. I went over there to canvass the place."

"You did what?" Wanamaker stammered.

"The assistant administrator told me to leave. I told her she was violating the Federal Age Discrimination Voters Registration Act if she tried to stop me from going room to room."

"I've never heard of such a statute," I noted.

"Actually, neither have I," the boy genius replied. "Anyway, the third lady I met, Mrs. Beanstoffer, she said she was thrilled she had something I wanted - her vote. She said it gave her life renewed meaning. She introduced me to about 600 other voters. They were thrilled, too. We held a rally between bingo sessions."

The next morning Grumbowski issued his concession speech.

## Chapter Thirty-Two

Fish

I take one day off a week - Sunday. No one ever said running a law office would be easy.

Personally, New Hope, Pennsylvania, is not where I would choose to spend my few precious hours of freedom. Funny how that small borough hidden along the Delaware River seems to constantly beckon all the women in my life. My wife, my paralegals and my partner's wife had once again conspired to drag all the husbands downstream for an unforgettable afternoon of shopping, to conclude with the obligatory late lunch at a charming turn-of-the-century tearoom. If I didn't join them, I'd never hear the end of it.

I don't understand the allure. What is it about this place that makes a woman's heart pump faster? We entered some quaint spice-scented kitchen shop filled to the brim with overpriced bread mixes, oven mitts and cookie cutters. Potential gifts abounded, all proclaiming that the lucky recipient was about to be blessed with another useless dust collector. But what cook wouldn't want an egg whisk with a pig-in-a-chef's-hat handle? Another shop (they all had the word "shoppe" stenciled somewhere on their reproduced colonial signboards) limited its inventory to cute, cuddly cat-things. Cat pillows with protruding whiskers, cat earrings, cat lampshades, cat postcards and stationery, cat welcome mats, cat wall hangings, cat sweatshirts bearing clever cat sayings like "Mouses beware," cat beach balls, cat storybooks, and a multitude of other cat-related inventory. The men shanghaied to this place all share the same look of quiet desperation. The women don't notice.

"Pardon me," the elderly lady pushing me to the side hissed as she and her partner in arms scrambled to reach the display of grinning calico cat beanbags. "This pillow will go perfectly with the wallpaper in my granddaughter's nursery!" Other interior decorators agreed, despite the lack of a formal introduction.

At any rate, I was in the way. I would again prove to be in the way at the natural honey and beehive byproduct shoppe, the nut and fudge shoppe, and the organic pottery and canning utensil shoppe.

Soon, we found ourselves at the antique shoppe. I thought about waiting out on the sidewalk, but that suggestion was summarily vetoed. I joined my fellow fun-seekers inside the cramped store, an emporium in which no usable space was left vacant. Copper pots hung from the ceiling rafters, century-old handsaws were nailed to the wallboards. Cuckoo clocks sat on window ledges. Display cases were jammed with arrowheads and trinkets, hex signs, glass bottles, pocket watches and butter churns. I felt strangely jealous of the spirits of those who had originally owned these simple relics. The torn Raggedy Ann doll had probably belonged to a little girl who had never been induced by Madison Avenue to believe that Disney World was the center of the universe.

And then I saw it, leaning in the back corner, a forgotten cloth mat or picture rolled into a tight cylinder. This artifact was tall, perhaps six feet in length. Its edges were frayed and time-worn where threads composing the ancient fabric had begun to unravel. Still, for the most part, the matting appeared to be intact. What image was hidden within?

I gently lifted the wound scroll from its hiding place and gingerly uncovered the first foot of material. To my surprise there appeared a title in bold black lettering: *Map of Northampton County, Pennsylvania.* I could feel my heart beating rapidly, an understandable reaction for any lawyer who has both resided in and completed hundreds of title searches within that very same county. How old was this aged document? How had it found its way here? Would I become its next owner?

After 15 minutes of negotiation and several surprised looks from my entourage, I tenderly carried the new-found treasure to my partner's van. That night I carefully unrolled the old chart on my living room floor. It measured six feet by four feet and was made of a heavy canvas with a cloth backing. Dated 1850, it depicted every county road, farm, residence and structure then in existence. Although hard to imagine, the last name of the family residing in each location was also clearly indicated. The cartographer's detailed labors included the identification of all public buildings, and the tracing of all rivers, creeks and tributaries, railroad lines, canals, bridges and local governmental boundaries.

Ultimately, after I'd preserved, cleaned and framed this historically significant find, the colorful rendering became a permanent display on the wall of my office.

Without the benefit of satellites or aerial photographs, the map accurately indicated the location and size of quarry operations within Northampton County. Several centuries-old slate quarries and limestone excavations were identified by name. The extraction of limestone near the Borough of Kreidersville has continued to the present day. Product from that quarry has been used for almost two centuries to manufacture cement. But recently, skyrocketing labor costs and the imposition of more stringent federal safety regulations have called into question the future economic viability of this mining operation. The quarry owner initiated a meeting with the cement workers' local labor union officials to determine if the work force might consider concessions in its hourly wage and medical insurance coverage.

"Without some reduction in overall operating expenses, we may be forced to close the quarry," Duane Kirkpatrick, vice president of operations, announced to deaf ears.

- - -

The widow Martha Freudenberger lived alone on her farm near the Borough of Nazareth. She had been born there

101 years earlier. She still collected and ate eggs produced by a few confused but loyal chickens, while lunch and dinner were delivered to her on a daily basis by Meals-on-Wheels volunteers. When her sight and hearing began to fail, the Area Agency on Aging became concerned for her well-being and petitioned the court to appoint a guardian so that she might be relocated to a nursing home. The judge assigned me as Freudenberger's guardian and ordered that I marshall her assets, sell the farm and place her in a safe environment. I drove out to her residence to meet my newest ward and to advise her that her care required that she leave her old stone farmhouse, each stone of which her great-grandfather had fashioned into place.

"I got to go?" she inquired, her blind eyes looking beyond me. "Why?"

"It's not safe for you to remain here. You need daily food and medical attention, ma'am."

"But I've been doin' okay so far."

I looked around at what once passed for a kitchen. Three feral cats sat in the cracked porcelain sink. There was no refrigerator, only an abandoned icebox. Thousands of discarded newspapers lay in crooked stacks, some reaching five feet high. Similar to trenches in a grainy World War I picture, one could only walk from room to room by passing between the mounds of newspaper filling the interior of each area of the unpainted farmhouse. Rain and snow entered freely through the broken slate roof and missing windows. I could not locate a heating system, source of electricity or running water. I found footsteps leading to a forlorn outhouse. Martha appeared to be wearing her one and only dress and winter coat. Neither appeared to have recently been cleaned. Her gray unkempt hair fell past her hips. She had no teeth.

"Mrs. Freudenberger ... "

She turned toward the direction of my voice.

"What?"

"It's not feasible for you to live here alone. This house doesn't comply with local health and safety codes, and you need immediate medical assistance."

"That's your opinion. Who will take care of my cats? I can't just leave them. Maybe I'll take them with me. Where am I going?"

"Presbyterian Hall, a pleasant community that provides elder care, including independent, assisted and skilled nursing living arrangements."

She scratched at her face with two-inch-long fingernails. "Been here a hundred years," she said wistfully.

"I know. You have a right to be proud."

"Great-grandpa, he built the place. Staked out 30 acres. Never had a mortgage. Never sold off any of the land. City people building up around here have tried to buy it. We never sold. Great-grandpa, he could have taught Frank Lloyd Wright a thing or two."

"The architect?"

"Great-grandpa built this house right smack over the creek so he could fish anytime from the kitchen. We used to catch native-born trout."

"There's no creek or pond, Mrs. Freudenberger. This farm is dry as a bone."

"Shows what you know. Anyways, Great-grandpa is gone, the fish is gone and now I'll be gone."

The next day a nurse and ambulance driver transported Martha to her new home. She received a bath, a hot meal, a manicure and clean clothes. She decided to stay.

I was tasked with the responsibility of selling the farm so the proceeds might be set aside to care for Martha. I obtained a court order to conduct a public auction. Then I began to prepare for the sale. Very little in the house could be salvaged. It took three refuse haulers the better part of a day just to rid the place of all the mildewed newspapers and magazines. The SPCA representatives came and gathered up about 20 roaming cats. The chickens found new quarters at another farm. I boarded up the windows and doors, and advertised the sale with the assistance of an auctioneer.

Freudenberger's strange words continued to ring in my ears. How could her family catch fish on a farm with no creek or pond? I decided to conduct a flood zone search at the courthouse, and I wrote to the state and federal authorities. All sources confirmed the absence of a waterway, flood zone or flood plain. If Martha's creative imagination led her to believe she caught fish in a stream, they must have been flying fish.

I drafted the mandatory Seller's Disclosure Statement to advise potential purchasers of those known adverse conditions impacting the farm. I attached a copy of the present deed, a survey and a disclaimer reflecting that the residence was not serviced by running water or public sewer, and did not meet minimum housing code standards. Buyers were cautioned to complete a full title search and to determine if flood insurance was required. No warranty regarding underground tanks or other environmental issues was given.

As might have been expected, interest in the auction was substantial. I received dozens of inquiries weeks before the sale date. After all, the 30-acre tract of land, improved by a picturesque stone farmhouse, represented the last working farm within city limits. Urban sprawl now surrounded the pristine pastures on all four sides. It was possible that this auction would transport penniless Martha into the ranks of the well-to-do.

- - -

The rank and file members of the cement and quarry laborers union did not consider themselves to be overpaid. A proposed reduction of $1.50 per hour was met with anger and an unwillingness to compromise. However, the cement company could not continue to operate in the red. Limestone could be quarried and transported from Mexico for a third of the cost. Sadly, the ancient quarry near Kreidersville would be shut down in 120 days. Seventy workers would lose their jobs.

- - -

"What do I hear for this magnificent farm?" the auctioneer called out over the animated faces of about 200 people. Both legitimate buyers and the merely curious sought to peek into the old house. Local governmental officials waited anxiously to learn if a developer would gobble up the valuable land on speculation. Couples hoped to purchase their dream farm, and the environmentalists prayed the place might become a park.

"Do I hear one million?"

"One million," somebody called out without hesitation.

"One and half," another bidder yelled.

"Two million," a third voice confirmed.

Three minutes later Martha was five million dollars wealthier. She could now purchase the entire west wing of her nursing home. Some guy from East Orange, New Jersey, bought her farm so his kids could raise their horses. I shook his hand, had him sign the agreement of sale, and took his certified bank check representing the 10 percent down payment. Half a million bucks, and he didn't even blink an eye.

A month later the same successful bidder showed up at settlement and paid the remaining balance due. I handed him and his beaming wife the deed to the premises and a key to what was left of the boarded-up door. He confided that they would gut the structure while retaining the exterior stone walls, and turn the place into their dream home - a gentleman farmer's showplace.

And that's just what they did. They hired a staff of architects and a construction site team, and got down to work. They installed new floors, roof, windows, kitchen, dining room, three full baths, six bedrooms, maid's quarters, guest rooms and a recreational family room in the basement. Money was no object. After all, the buyer, Timothy Witherspoon, owned a dozen car washes near East Orange, and most of the cars there got dirty.

---

I remember the phone call as if it were yesterday. It came just three days after the cement company shut down the quarry. It was Witherspoon, the gentleman farmer. He sounded upset.

"My basement rec-room - there's native trout swimming in it. Maybe a whole school. The water floated our bed into the kitchen. The wife and I woke up next to the dishwasher."

"What water?"

"The water that has filled the basement and two feet of the first floor. I was told the farm wasn't near a flood plain. I have the documents from the state and federal agencies. That is, I had them until my home waterproof safe floated out the front door."

For an instant my memory harkened back to that rambling conversation with delusional multimillionaire Freudenberger. Hadn't she said something about building a house over a stream and fishing from the living room?

---

"It's really quite simple," the hydrogeologist tried to explain to Witherspoon and me as we gazed from the top of Witherspoon's fancy new stairs into the farmhouse's flooded basement. Some native trout near the surface swam by in the crystal-clear water. I could peer down to where a TV and a family recreational center lay at the bottom of the newly formed pond.

"See, they ceased cement plant operations last week about three miles north of here. They stopped pumping out the water collecting in the quarry as well. The water has to go somewhere, so it followed the ancient underground aquifer back here. Them fish is native trout. Most sportsmen would consider you a lucky guy, Witherspoon."

I went back to my office and studied the old tattered map hanging on the wall. The farm was clearly outlined. The name "Freudenberger" was imprinted within its 30-acre boundary. And if one took magnifying glass in hand, it was possible to make out a small creek originating just to the side of the farmhouse, a creek that disappeared underground a few feet from the stone foundation.

Sometimes the older maps are more helpful than their new, sophisticated satellite-enhanced counterparts. It depends upon one's cartographic perception. I recall a recent interview on TV. The president of the *International Earth Is Flat Society* was fielding questions. They showed him a picture of our planet taken from 300,000 miles in space.

"Looks flat to me," he replied.

# Chapter Thirty-Three

## Bullshit Bullshit

I have inherited many traits from my parents: my surprising good looks, my Fred Astaire-like grace and high blood pressure. I don't mind high blood pressure. It doesn't hurt, and if truth be told, I'm actually quite grateful for it. After all, it's significantly better than no blood pressure. I take medication and then the numbers go down for a while. This daily ritual, in turn, keeps the blood pressure of pharmaceutical executives in check.

I don't think my high blood pressure has occurred solely as a result of transferred parental genes. My chosen profession is partly to blame. Sometimes I have to deal with idiots - people who stumble through life by being irrational or irascible. These are the ones who, as an example, decide without warning retrospectively to renegotiate issues previously resolved. It happened again last week during a real estate settlement.

My client, Morton McKnight, had signed an agreement of sale to purchase a rather fancy home in the prestigious Sherwood Oaks development. He was paying big bucks for a spacious house and expected everything to be in working order. So I drafted the standard due diligence provisions in the agreement empowering McKnight's professional structural inspector to test and evaluate each system servicing the residence, including the on-lot septic system. We agreed to pay for all of the testing costs, including the termite, radon and septic dye test examinations. But the septic tank was hidden somewhere underground, so the seller, Myrtle Wittaker, agreed that if the cost was no more than $250, she would pay to dig up and later replace the top soil in order to locate the holding tank.

On the day of the septic system evaluation, our inspector met the septic man who brought along a laborer who dug up the top soil. They ultimately found the tank, which we paid to clean so that our inspector could confirm that it functioned properly. I also received a separate bill for the laborer's services in the amount of $220, a $30 savings from what we expected.

The residence, with an interior living area of 4,800 square feet, a three-car garage and an in-ground pool, cost $1,200,000. Myrtle had decided to take her money, get away from the cold and move to Florida. On the day of settlement, everyone arrived at my office for the formal transfer of the deed, keys and money. Myrtle came with her realtor and some other guy. Morton was accompanied by the title insurance agent, his realtor and the mortgage lender's representative. As was always my custom, I had, well prior to settlement, faxed to each participant in the transaction a copy of the formal arithmetic computations so that each person could review and confirm in advance that the figures were correct. Because there was no present mortgage encumbering the real estate, Myrtle would, after payment of her realtor's commission and taxes, receive a net check in the amount of $1,105,834.

We all gathered at my conference room table and started to shuffle stacks of papers as introductions were made. The realtors, the lender, the title agent, the buyer, the seller and my overworked secretary all smiled and nodded at the appropriate moment of introduction. But there was an extra person seated at the table.

"This is my husband," Myrtle explained. "Howard Longenacre."

That remark stopped me in my tracks. The lender and title insurance clerk suddenly sat upright as well.

"Ms. Wittaker," I blurted out, "the title search certified you as a widow."

"I was for about 20 years, until last week. Howard and I just got married."

I looked at what passed for Howard. What could I say?

"Congratulations?"

Howard, to be kind, wasn't exactly a handsome groom. He had protruding reptilian eyes that moved independently of each other, a bulbous nose and thick sagging lips. His skin was a mine field of age spots, and during most of the first moments of this settlement, he appeared to be dozing off.

"Nice to make your acquaintance," I ad-libbed.

"Umph," he said as he stared while blinking one eye at the wall across the room.

"That's why I sold the house," Myrtle beamed. "We're starting a new life together in Florida."

New life? With him? Then again, they say that love can find itself in even the most unsuspecting of unions. Who was I to judge? I began to regain my composure.

"Ms. Wittaker," I explained, "all of the settlement documents have been prepared with the assumption that you are a single individual. The deed is drafted in your singular name with the understanding that no one else is the owner of the real estate."

"That's correct," Myrtle affirmed. "Howard has no legal title or interest in the real estate. Isn't that right, dear?"

"Umph," her spouse confirmed.

"Very well," I announced. "Let's proceed with settlement."

I asked my secretary for a copy of the formal accounting statement reflecting the proposed distribution of the settlement funds.

"Ms. Wittaker," I began, "my client and the other parties to the settlement have approved these figures. I sent you a copy as well. Would you like me to review the computations with you?"

"Yes, if you don't mind," the polite seller replied.

"Very well. You will note that there is deducted from the purchase price of $1,200,000 certain costs and fees incurred by you resulting in your net check of $1,105,834. These include realtor fees of $72,000, a transfer tax of $12,000, the apportionment of township, county, and school taxes in the amount of $9,941, a notary fee of $5, and finally a $220 reimbursement for the laborer who removed top soil and located the septic tank. Do you have any questions?"

"I don't think so," Myrtle confirmed.

"Good. Would you please sign here indicating your acceptance of the - "

"Bullshit ... bullshit ... "

I spun around to locate the source of this unexpected proclamation. It had come from Howard. He was still staring at the opposite wall.

"I beg your pardon?"

He slowly turned one of his eyes toward me. "You heard me, Bub. The bill from the laborer for $220 - it's bullshit ... bullshit ... "

"Now Howard, dear, we've already discussed this," Myrtle mediated.

"Bullshit ... bullshit ... Don't sign until they remove that charge."

"Howard, dear, it's not that much money. The lawyer's ready to cut a check for over a million dollars."

I thought Myrtle had made a valid point. She certainly convinced me. Apparently Howard wasn't quite as gullible.

"Bullshit ... bullshit ... The septic system works. They didn't have to dig it up."

"But dear, we agreed to pay for that excavation."

"Bullshit ... bullshit ... Don't sign."

This little tiff was beginning to take its toll on the two realtors, who stood to split a $72,000 commission. The last thing either of them needed was to have a million-dollar deal placed in jeopardy by some $220 septic bill. It was Myrtle's broker who first made the magnanimous suggestion that each realtor deduct $110 from their modest fees.

- - -

That night I had an unusual dream. I was shopping in a grocery store and had gathered together in my cart a rather substantial assortment of food and other necessities. I proceeded to the checkout area and began to place my purchases on the cashier's conveyor belt. That's when I spotted the can of baked beans near the bottom of the pile.

"BULLSHIT ... BULLSHIT!" I announced to anyone within earshot.

The cashier was caught off guard. "I beg your pardon?"

"BULLSHIT ... BULLSHIT!" I repeated slightly louder so that my ranting might be heard in the store manager's office. I obviously startled the people waiting in line behind me in the crowded market.

"Is there something wrong, sir?" the innocent, hard-working, full-time high school student and part-time cashier inquired as she stopped the conveyor belt.

"These beans!" I yelled louder. "Eighty-nine cents! Who the hell would pay eighty-nine cents?" I turned to both the astonished lady with the two small kids and the FedEx guy shifting from foot to foot behind her, the new involuntary prisoners of my raving.

The store manager appeared out of nowhere. "Can I be of assistance?" he asked.

"BULLSHIT ... BULLSHIT!" I bellowed as the veins in my neck started to bulge. "This can of beans! Eighty-nine cents! My bill is already $147. I'll take what I purchased, but the beans - they're free."

"Sir, if we did that for you, we'd have to let everyone ... "

"I'll buy the beans for him if we can get the hell outta here," the FedEx guy interjected. A happy solution for everyone.

In retrospect, Howard was no fool, and he taught me a valuable lesson. If you're slightly belligerent or just crazy, somebody will pay to shut you up. It ultimately lowers everyone's blood pressure.

# Chapter Thirty-Four

## She Might Squawk

Representing newlyweds buying a first home is exciting. Their whole lives, filled with hopes and dreams, stretch before them. Assisting the young lovers with the acquisition of a house they will transform into a home, perhaps with a nursery and a little basket-bed for a puppy permits me vicariously to feel that I'm part of something important, and that my chosen vocation serves a legitimate purpose.

Estate administration generates a similar sense of fulfillment. Working with bereaved families who have suffered the loss of a loved one gives the lawyer a unique opportunity to lend a helping hand at a time of need. Few other professions permit the practitioner to experience a similar sense of satisfaction.

Giving advice to the aged with regard to geriatric legal issues, counseling the needy of the community, sharing in the drama of an adoption - these and other scenarios grant the small town lawyer the rare privilege to do something useful. In many instances, those whose lives I've touched become friends. Some send Christmas cards. Others invite me to their children's graduation ceremonies.

There is an exception to the idyllic picture I've just painted - my criminal clients. After thirty years of representing muggers, thieves, rapists and murderers, I can count on one hand those I'd consider as a friend or who I'd intentionally introduce to my wife. Simply stated, if someone has chosen as a means of livelihood burglarizing the homes of law-abiding citizens, I don't wish to socialize with such a felon and I'd prefer he not know where I live or what paintings hang on the interior walls of my residence.

Many attorneys whose practices are primarily focused upon criminal defense do not share my viewpoint, and openly wax poetic about the honor of single-handedly representing some downtrodden, luckless, ne'er-do-well against the might of the Commonwealth of Pennsylvania, with its countless legions of police, district attorneys, judges and jailors. But for the efforts of energetic defense counsel, so the theory goes, the rights secured by the Constitution would vanish overnight.

With such misgivings, why do I continue to take criminal cases? Because once in a while, it is possible to find a diamond hidden among the pieces of coal. It is possible to achieve that warm and fuzzy feeling, the indescribable rush that is generated when an innocent client actually is acquitted. Additionally, on rare occasions, I've become acquainted with a crook whose good qualities outweigh the bad, the unusual criminal whom I might actually consider a friend.

Toddy and Pierpont Bumpkins were brothers and house burglars. It would be inappropriate, almost presumptuous, to characterize them as "career criminals," since such a designation suggests that to one degree or another they were successful at their chosen craft. This was not the case. Every so often, they would conspire to engage in some daring criminal escapade by entering an unattended residence. Invariably, they'd get caught, then call me, and ultimately spend some time in jail.

I represented them at the beginning of their career when they entered Mrs. McGillicutty's bungalow. They had carefully planned the "caper" over a six-pack of beer. When she left for a long weekend, they snuck in through her basement window. Unfortunately, McGillicutty lived with seven cats. Only after entering the residence did Pierpont discover his severe allergy to felines, two of which insisted upon rubbing against his legs. He went into respiratory failure. Toddy called an ambulance, but couldn't adequately explain to the cops what he and Pierpont were doing there in the first place. Despite my best efforts, they ended up in jail.

With time off for good behavior, they were out on the street in less than two years. They decided to break into Thurgood Flanagan's rancher. Unfortunately, unbeknownst to the Bumpkins brothers, Flanagan's place was undergoing significant renovations, including replacement of a portion of the living room floor. Pierpont's flashlight battery went dead, and he fell through a gaping temporary construction hole into the basement. Toddy called an ambulance. When the cops arrived, he couldn't explain why Pierpont was stuck downstairs in a wheelbarrow full of cement.

"Can I sue for my injuries?" Pierpont asked me from a hospital bed in which he was handcuffed to the side rails. "Shouldn't the homeowner have installed warning barriers?"

Despite my best efforts, they were sent back to jail. With time off for good behavior, they were out on the street in less than three years. Two weeks later, I got a call from Toddy. They had just been arrested. I dropped everything and drove over to the lockup, because, if the truth be told, I actually liked these guys. Unlike most of the other criminals it had been my dubious distinction to represent, these idiots never lied about their exploits. They always admitted they were in the wrong and did their time without complaint or incident.

"What happened now?" I asked as we sat in the cramped prison interview room.

"This time the plan was foolproof," Toddy assured me.

"Foolproof," Pierpont echoed.

"We located this condo on the ritzy side of town and cased the outside. Nobody was home, so we pried the back kitchen window open and slithered in," Toddy explained. "We found a couple of watches and a pearl necklace in some drawers. That was enough, so we decided to make our getaway. But there was this big green parrot in the living room, perched on a bar in her wire cage. She watched every move we made."

"She never took her eyes off us," Pierpont joined in.

"Just as we were sliding out the kitchen window, the bird says 'Good-bye Pierpont' in this loud, distinct voice. It sounded almost human."

"It startled us, so we ran like hell," Pierpont explained.

"We didn't stop 'til we reached O'Dooleys's Bar over on Sixth Street," his brother added.

"We went in for a few beers," Pierpont noted, "to celebrate, 'cause this was the first time we hadn't been injured on the job."

"Well, there we were sipping on a brew when it hit me!" Toddy exclaimed.

"What hit you?" I asked.

"The bird. It knew Pierpont's first name. It must have overheard me calling to him and made a mental note to remember it."

"I never recall anyone's name," Pierpont interjected. "If I go to a party, I forget 'em as soon as the introductions are over. Obviously, this bird had total recall."

"We had to return to the scene of the crime," Toddy theorized, "so we could tell the bird a little fib. We wanted to convince the parrot that it was mistaken and that 'Pierpont' wasn't actually my brother's name. I intended to formally introduce him to the bird as 'Fernando.' Then, if the police interviewed the parrot, it wouldn't matter if she decided to squawk. She'd throw them off our trail by telling the cops some guy named Fernando had broken into the house."

"But as soon as we snuck in the window, the cops showed up. Something about a silent alarm," Pierpont a/k/a Fernando moaned.

I finished taking notes and told my clients I would review the arresting officer's file in preparation for the preliminary hearing. The next afternoon I went to police headquarters to study the official record. What immediately caught my attention was the name of the victim who owned both the burglarized condo and the telltale bird: Pierpont ... Pierpont Jones.

## Chapter Thirty-Five

### The Annual Exemption

It's not possible to predict whether a lawyer, upon ascending the bench, will transform into a good judge. Some jurists are "naturals," and understand that with such awesome powers comes an equal responsibility to temper their authority with compassion and patience. Real judges rarely find it necessary to flex their muscles.

The same observation is applicable to freshmen cadets newly graduated from the police academy. Most are dedicated to protecting and serving the public. Sometimes, however, a neophyte officer may exhibit overzealous behavior.

- - -

Amy Prendergast was my secretary's best friend. Both were members of a church prayer group. Amy was the young mother of two-year-old twin girls. She took her maternal duties seriously. Rare indeed was the moment when the babies weren't by her side. Today would be no exception; she brought the children with her to my office.

"Thanks for seeing me so quickly," she said as she took the matching pink bonnets off the twin identical heads and began searching through a large tote bag for the twins' juice cups.

"It's a pleasure to see you again," I assured the young mother. "Are the girls doing well?"

"Yes. Thanks for asking," Amy responded as she lovingly attended to the needs of her well-behaved offspring. She knew what color cup each child preferred, and she was able to produce additional age-appropriate toys as the toddlers sat poised and quiet. This was one lady who had her act together and was serious about motherhood. Many were the times a less observant, unprepared parent had appeared at my office, with but one child, only to permit the little tyrant to run about, touching everything in sight with grasping, lollipop-sticky fingers. But for the occasional scraping crayon noises, I would have forgotten Amy's little angels were in the room.

Amy was not the type to waste precious time. In less than 15 minutes, the twins would experience a Chernobyl-like meltdown, requiring an applesauce feeding followed by a duel poop change and a nap. She got right to the point.

"I was 'arrested' or as the cop called it 'cited' last week, and I don't think it's fair. He over-reacted."

"Arrested! You?"

"It's like this. I had driven over to the dry cleaner at the Highland Mall to pick up some shirts. As always, the twins were strapped in like astronauts in their safety seats. Do you have any idea how long it takes to suit them up and strap them in, just to drive 10 blocks? And of course the dog wanted to come, too. Well, as usual, the vibration and sound of the car engine put both of them to sleep in a minute, so I cell-phoned ahead and told the cleaner to be ready for a 30-second pickup.

"After I parked, I put the emergency flashers on and ran into the store. I kept the car running so the kids would have some AC. My van was locked and in plain view through the store's plate glass window. I wasn't going to wake two sleeping babies, unstrap them and drag them screaming into the cleaner.

"Thirty seconds. That's all. I grabbed the shirts, flew out the door and walked the 10 steps to the van. The kids never knew I left, and the dog was guarding them. But there was a new face in the crowd. A patrol car was parked behind me, and a tall blond cop about my age was peering through the windshield at the three occupants.

"'Lady,' he barks, 'do you know it's illegal to abandon children in a vehicle?' ABANDON? These kids haven't been out of my sight since the moment they left the womb.

At first I thought he was joking. He wasn't. 'You could be reported to the Division of Children's Service for endangering their welfare,'" he says.

"I told him I was 10 feet away for 30 seconds. He says, 'So you admit to the crime.' THE CRIME! Then he started writing up a citation."

The "criminal" rummaged through her purse and found the official, crumpled document. I unfolded it. Amy had been cited for leaving unattended minors in a motor vehicle.

"I'm not paying the stupid fine," she proclaimed. "I want a hearing, 'cause I'm not guilty."

- - -

A few days later, I had lunch at the club. Two familiar figures had just walked off the practice green, putters in hand, and had entered the patio dining area. They spotted me at the back table. I waived for them to join me.

Jim Stokely was the local magistrate in town. Tad Reynolds was an official court reporter, what we used to call a "stenographer" in the old days. They were good golfers and loved the game. Their enthusiasm was a mystery to me. Imagine hitting a ball and then having to chase after it!

"Every time I sneak away for a lousy hour, you guys are here whacking golf balls," I complained. "How do you do it?"

"I'm an elected official," Stokely explained. "Only the voters can fire me."

"Court's not in session this week," Reynolds added. "I'm free until Monday."

They both sat down and we ordered sandwiches. As usual, the conversation was lively and jovial, until Tad turned to the magistrate.

"Jimmy," Reynolds began, "I forgot to tell you what happened to my mother last week."

"Is she okay?"

"She was driving in town and this cop flags her down. He starts pointing at an expired state inspection sticker.

Well, you know Mom. She's kinda deaf and up to this very moment hasn't figured out why the cop stopped her. She was scared out of her mind. He ends up writing out a citation, rather than giving her the usual two-day courtesy warning notice."

"That's overkill!" Stokely observed.

"Excuse me," I interjected. "Was this cop tall and blond?"

"Yeah, that's how Mom described him, youngish," Tad confirmed. "Did the city just hire a new tough guy?"

"I think a client of mine may have had a recent run-in with the same officer," I noted.

The judge looked up from his sandwich as he addressed both of us. "Tell your mother and your client to plead 'not guilty,' " Stokely suggested. "I'll instruct my secretary to schedule your hearings at the same time. We'll get to the bottom of this."

Three weeks later, Tad and I showed up at Magistrate Stokely's office. We were ushered into his courtroom, where I introduced the two "criminals" to each other.

"This is Amy Prendergast, my client."

"This is my mother, Thelma Reynolds," Tad joined in.

"What did you say, Theodore?" Mom inquired as she adjusted her hearing aid.

At that moment, a tall blond cop entered the hearing room. He might have been 25 years old. I don't think I had ever been quite that young. He gazed upon the two defendants he had recently cited and nodded an unsmiling military nod, as he began to thumb through his official police files. "All rise," Jimmy's secretary called out as the magistrate, no longer carrying a golf putter and adorned in a flowing black robe, appeared at the side entrance. He strode with judicial poise to the elevated bench adorned with the seal of the commonwealth.

"Court is in session. You may be seated," he announced.

We all sat down.

"The first case before the court is the Commonwealth of Pennsylvania versus Thelma Reynolds," Magistrate Stokely called out. "How does the defendant plead?"

"What did he say?" Thelma whispered in the direction of her son.

"Very well. A plea of 'not guilty' is entered," His Honor observed. "Officer, present your case."

And he did. No one could accuse this freshman cop of being unprepared. He sketched the crime scene on a dry-erase board. He entered into evidence the statute pertaining to annual vehicular registrations. He testified that on the fateful day in question he had observed the defendant, Mrs. Reynolds, operating a motor vehicle upon the thoroughfares of the commonwealth, and the vehicle thusly operated did not possess a current inspection sticker. In closing, the officer advised the court that at no time did the defendant offer a plausible explanation for her blatant failure to abide by the law.

The learned judge soaked in all this vital information and then slowly lifted his scratched wooden gavel. He slammed it down on his desk. I was surprised it didn't splinter into a thousand pieces.

"Not guilty," he ruled, without asking Thelma if she had any exculpatory evidence to present. The cop's jaw dropped.

"Officer," the magistrate inquired, "how long have you been on the force?"

"Four weeks," came his shaken response.

"Were you out sick the day the police academy gave instruction on the annual exemption statute?"

"The what?"

"The statute that says every mother gets one exemption per year for any non-moving motor vehicle violation."

"They do? What's an exemption?"

"Well, there you are! That's why you wrote up these defective citations. You didn't know any better. See, Mrs. Reynolds is a mother. So is Mrs. Prendergast. So her case is dismissed, too. Now go over to the defense table and apologize to both of them."

The chastised peace officer did as instructed. From that day forward, this tall, blond public servant was a gentler, kinder protector of the law. Whenever he stopped a criminal, he always asked first if she was a mother.

# Chapter Thirty-Six

## The Engagement Ring

When is a contract legally binding?

The year was 1979 and love was in the air. Teresa and I decided to get married. The obligatory engagement ring would serve notice to the world of our intentions. It seemed to me that surprising my betrothed with a diamond ring, while quaint and chivalrous, missed the point. Marriage is a two-way street. A more practical approach mandated that Teresa choose the diamond she would wear the rest of her life. This would guarantee that she would be pleased with the gemstone, and it signified that I wanted her to have equal input in all our mutual decisions.

She could hardly contain herself. "When can we go to the jewelry store? When can we go to the jewelry store?" she repeated while jumping up and down.

"How about this Saturday?" I suggested.

"Two whole days from now?"

Two hours probably would have been too excruciatingly long, but she reluctantly agreed. Never had I seen her so excited.

"Binder's Jewelers advertises that it has the only certified gemologist on staff in the Lehigh Valley. He's an expert who will be able to explain the different cuts, quality and color of diamonds," I suggested.

That made sense to Teresa, and so on Saturday at nine a.m. sharp, we entered the jewelry store in search of just the right diamond that was predestined to grace her hand only, and no other.

There, under hidden quartz lights so intense they could have cooked a meatloaf, reposed silent row after row of dazzling diamonds. Some were cut in rectangular form, others similar to a pear, while yet another collection took the shape of tiny hearts. All seemed to cry out to Teresa, similar to homeless puppies at the dog pound.

When I buy something to wear, a pair of shoes or a shirt perhaps, I take a look, pay the salesperson and leave. Done and gone. Teresa apparently did not share the same time-sensitivity. Perhaps I should have brought a folding bed and a magazine.

She needed to study each diamond several times. Amazingly, this exercise in slow motion did not seem to bother Mr. Engler, the gemologist. He patiently answered each of her questions as if she were purchasing a new house or vehicle. Over the space of three hours, he discussed the concepts of clarity, color, cut and carat weight. He produced a magnifying gemscope and assisted her as she evaluated different imperfections and refractions. At long last she took a deep breath, turned to me and pointed at a brilliant diamond of modest size.

"That's the one," she solemnly pronounced. "Can we afford it?"

I swallowed hard. "You bet, Teresa."

Never had I seen anyone so giddy. She was happy, and so I had made a wise investment.

"Can I wear it now? Can I?" she begged Mr. Engler.

The jeweler explained that the ring had to be sized and the diamond fitted in a particular setting. He said he would be ready for us in a week, the longest week of Teresa's life.

"Good-bye, Diamond," Teresa sighed as she inched out the jewelry store door while staring over her shoulder in the direction of the rock that had become an important part of her life. "I'll see you next Saturday."

- - -

A week passed. Biblical plagues could not have kept Teresa from racing into the jewelry store at nine a.m. sharp. Mr. Engler appeared from behind a curtain separating his office from the showroom. He did not look well.

"Good morning," he solemnly offered, similar to the greeter dressed in black who first opens the door at a funeral parlor. Teresa didn't notice the gemologist's marked change in demeanor. She was busy scanning the display racks for *her* diamond. Engler decided to take the direct approach. He instinctively turned to me, since Teresa was preoccupied.

"I don't know how to tell you this ... " he began. "It's never happened in the 85 years we've been in business."

Teresa joined us at the counter near the gemscope examination area.

"I can't wait to see my new diamond ring," she enthused.

Apologetic Engler continued with his contrite explanation. "You see, it's like this. The diamond was sent to our fitting department in Easton, and while it was there, apparently a mistake occurred. A sales clerk put it on display and it was sold. The ring fit, so the customer left with it."

Teresa stopped breathing for a moment. She had a "stop all engines - Titanic - iceberg" look on her face.

"Someone is wearing *my* ring?" she inquired.

Then the tears began to flow. Lots of them. I had never seen one man cry so much. Engler was truly upset. And Teresa was, too. They engaged in an impromptu duet. He'd blow his nose, then she'd blow her nose, then he'd make those sucking noises as he gasped for air, and then she'd get the heaves, and the cycle would start all over.

Never had there been a gemological train wreck of this magnitude.

"*My* ... diamond ... ring ... is ... gone?"

Exhausted Engler could only shake his head up and down. "Gone!"

"But ... I ... never ... even ... got ... to ... wear ... it."

That last heartbreaking statement rendered poor Engler inconsolable. He buried his face in his second moist handkerchief.

I wondered if I should call for assistance. Did they keep oxygen on the premises?

"Of course ... (sob) ... (sob) ... it goes without saying ... you can pick out any other diamond, even if it costs a thousand dollars more. That's the least I can do."

Teresa stopped shaking. "Say that again, please."

"And ... (sob) ... the fitting would be free as well."

It was 1979. I could have purchased a new Volkswagen off the auto showroom floor for less than $3,000. Engler sure knew how to rectify a problem.

She stopped crying, so he stopped crying. I should have brought an army cot and a magazine. The two friends spent the rest of the morning looking at diamonds as they entered into a new contract.

# CHAPTER THIRTY-SEVEN

## The Foghorn

There are occasions when clients enter my law office and one can tell in an unspoken moment to what lifelong vocational pursuit the poor soul has dedicated his or her entire existence. The retired chalk-faced coal miners come to mind. They exhibit that unmistakable death rattle cough that emanates from deep within the recesses of what had once been their lungs.

I represented old Billy, a talented auto mechanic who actually repaired vehicles instead of just substituting new parts. He had amassed years of caked oil underneath his fingernails and petroleum stains had similarly woven themselves into the very fabric of his weathered hands. When he passed away, I attended his viewing and ultimately provided legal representation to his estate. His family hid his hands under the open coffin shroud to conceal the lingering vestiges of his chosen employment. Those discolored fingers should have been proudly displayed as silent tribute to an honest living extracted from stubborn pistons and broken timing belts.

And there was 97-year-old Vashka, the hunchback. His contorted frame suggested he had suffered with a deformed spine since birth. In truth, the retired maestro had played his beloved cello for the better part of a century, and over time his body had taken the shape of the instrument he constantly cradled.

The blast furnace steelworkers were the easiest to spot. To a man, they never merely spoke or engaged in polite conversation. They had been programmed to scream in such booming decibels that the veins in their necks constantly protruded. Trying to communicate above the din of hot steel manufacturing necessitated such behavior, and as might be expected, the bellowing unwittingly became a lifelong habit. Often, in order to be heard, the steelworker's entire family would scream at each other so that conversations were not one-sided.

The most unusual work-related acquired abnormality, however, was not displayed by a client visiting my office. That dubious distinction was reserved for two instructors I met during my first weeks at Coast Guard boot camp. It was 1984, and I was ordered to report to Yorktown, Virginia, for Reserve Enlisted Basic Indoctrination. Our class was composed of 50 volunteers who shipped in from across the country. We were strangers who quickly became close friends, since we shared a common desire to serve our country while saving lives on the open seas. A genuine camaraderie developed as we learned to march in cadence, engaged in swimming drills and calisthenics, shot various automatic weapons, and received instruction in Coast Guard etiquette, dress code, shipboard nomenclature and conduct.

One of the most interesting classes dealt with Coast Guard history and lore. The service wanted its newest recruits to be cognizant of the reasons for its traditions and to grasp the significance of the Coast Guard's roll as an integral part of the American military.

The morning's lecture focused upon the era of the lightship. Until that moment, I had never heard of such a floating aid to navigation and nautical safety. Lieutenant Grey addressed the new recruits. Grey epitomized the Coast Guard and the Coast Guard had fashioned every fiber of Grey. His spit-shined shoes, his collection of active-duty ribbons, his immaculate powder-blue shirt sporting a parallel military crease, his high and tight cropped haircut, and his flawless posture spoke silent volumes regarding his training and duty to country. His quiet confidence instilled a trust that guaranteed that his orders would be followed without hesitation. There was more information tucked away in his brain regarding Coast Guard history than might be found in the Library of Congress.

"Attention on deck!" the class monitor called out.

We collectively rose from our chairs and stood at silent, unbreathing attention as Grey made his entrance at the front of the classroom.

"Seats!"

We all sat down in unison.

"Good morning, class," Grey began.

"Good morning, Lieutenant," we all sang out.

"This morning we will study the essential roll that lightships played in protecting vessels at sea while enhancing the commerce of our great nation. Long before there were earth-orbiting satellite systems that are now utilized to pinpoint the location of a ship as it progresses upon the surface of the ocean, seafarers relied upon other less sophisticated aids to navigation to determine where they were situated. For about a hundred years, the Coast Guard was tasked with the staffing of lightships that lay stationary at anchor just off the U.S. coastline. As vessels from around the world entered our territorial waters en route to ports of call such as New York and Philadelphia, the lightships, equipped with their signal light beacons and foghorns, served as floating safety platforms confirming the location of the harbor entrance. During times of heavy fog or stormy seas, these lightships represented the first welcome contact with civilization a homebound sailor might have experienced in months.

"The lightships were manned by a crew of 'coasties' whose job it was to keep the signal mast light, initially powered by whale oil, aglow. Day and night, no matter what the weather condition or temperature, coast guardsmen climbed up the mast with buckets of whale oil and tended to the burning flame, similar to their counterparts serving in the coastal lighthouses.

"The lightships also sent out an audible signal day and night, to warn incoming ships of the approaching coastline. Initially the crew physically blew upon simple foghorns, but as technology became more sophisticated, electronic audible signals that could be heard for 20 nautical miles became common.

"Life on the lightships was dangerous. Sometimes the fog was so thick or the deterioration of weather so unpredictable that approaching ships would blindly steer toward the sound of the foghorn without actually seeing the light signal, only to cut right through the lightship itself. And the hours were tedious and long. The men who were assigned this duty often served 'round the clock for three-month intervals without relief."

The topic of this lecture fascinated me. I had no idea such stationary ships had existed to assure the safety of ocean commerce. What a strange life the coast guard crews inhabiting these floating hulks must have endured. Climbing up icy, swaying masts to replenish diminishing reserves of whale oil. Maintaining the incessant blasting audio signal. Keeping the ship painted and repaired. These poor souls were totally isolated. Back then there were no video games, heated cabins, DVDs, e-mail, television or telephones. Free time was spent carving etchings into whale bones. Bathing facilities consisted of a bucket and cold rainwater.

"Now class," Lt. Grey continued, "I have a special treat for you. The lightships may have been rendered obsolete and decommissioned decades ago, but two of the last retired coasties to serve as crew members are here today to share their personal insights regarding duty aboard the lightships."

Two ancient mariners shuffled into the lecture hall and stood before our astonished eyes. It was as if the world had stopped spinning for a moment and had regurgitated this pair of enlisted artifacts from some abandoned time machine. They might have been in their late eighties or nineties, yet each sailor appeared to be quite alert, almost robust. Neither wore glasses, and neither leaned on a cane, yet these hearty souls probably had enlisted in the Coast Guard prior to the onset of World War II. Before us stood real sailors, and it was a privilege just to be in the same room with them.

The weather-beaten duo turned to the rapt inductees. Retired Chief MacIntyre was the first to address the class.

"Top o' the morning, swabs. I served on the *Nantucket* out of New York Harbor. We had a crew of five, with a hand standing watch every six hours, while the others lay to the daily duties or caught a wink of shuteye. Back when I enlisted, there wasn't no automated foghorn, so when the weather closed in, you had to ring the big bell by hand and blow the foghorn every thirty seconds."

For a moment, I envisioned scenes from the hunchback of Notre Dame.

"That's right," Chief Mazewski chimed in. "There weren't no batteries or electrical apparatus on board until about 1940. So we had to do just about everything by hand."

It was becoming obvious that every 30 seconds, like clockwork, these two shipmates froze in their tracks, and stared into space, transfixed for exactly five seconds, after which they would, without any prompting, return to life.

They continued with their lecture for about half an hour, during which there were about 60 unannounced five-second, stop-action interludes. After a while, members of the class grew to expect the momentary pauses. During each of these short breaks, I could have sworn I heard a foghorn somewhere in the distance.

It was approaching 1100 hours, so we broke for lunch and marched over to the mess deck. The two ancient mariners sat at the next table. They were engaged in an animated conversation about the good old days. Every 30 seconds their discussion and munching of food would come to a simultaneous five-second halt, but they didn't seem to mind or notice.

# CHAPTER THIRTY-EIGHT

## The Unsatisfied Mortgage

Horace Huffnagal passed away a few months ago. Prior to his unexpected death, he operated a small title insurance company located on Union Street. During his last day on earth he worked nine to five as usual. Then he went home and died in his sleep without so much as a good-bye.

He lived alone. He had never missed work. When he failed to appear or phone the next morning, his secretary, Jennifer, became worried and called the cops. They found his body in the rear bedroom of his modest ranch home.

The coroner kept Horace on ice, waiting for someone to claim the body. Nobody did. For five days Horace simply reposed in the county morgue refrigeration unit.

Horace didn't have many friends. He preferred to keep to himself. His only social outlet was the Thursday evening quoit league at the YMCA. Two of his teammates, Oscar and Ferdie, heard about Horace's untimely death and stopped by the title company office to offer their condolences and to inquire about the time and location of the funeral. Jennifer, who appeared to be overwhelmed, didn't have a response. She was, nonetheless, grateful for the thoughtfulness expressed by these visitors.

"I don't know what to do," she lamented.

"What do you mean?" Oscar inquired.

"I'm so confused," Jennifer admitted. "See, Horace kept to himself. He never mentioned any family. I don't know if he had a last will. Who's in charge of things now? Clients keep calling to schedule real estate settlements."

"Can't you hold things here together for the time being?" Ferdie inquired.

"Not really," Jennifer sighed. "Horace intentionally ran a 'one horse' operation. I don't have the authority to sign company checks, I'm not bonded to conduct settlements, I'm not a notary, nor am I a recognized agent of the title company. That's the way Horace wanted it, total control. I'm just the secretary who answers the phone and types the letters."

"Maybe you should talk to a lawyer," Oscar suggested.

The next day, Jennifer stopped by my office. "Didn't you do some legal work for Horace, Horace Huffnagel?" she asked. "Didn't I send you a check for something last year?"

"Yes," I confirmed. "He was cited for going through a stop sign. I attended the hearing."

"That's right," Jennifer recalled.

"How is Horace?"

"He passed away last week. Listen, did he have a last will or something?"

"I'm sorry for your loss."

"Thanks. Did you draft his will?"

"No, he never requested one."

"Rats."

And with that pronouncement, poor Jennifer explained the unfortunate state of affairs. Horace had worked as a clerk at that title insurance office for about 20 years. Three years ago the former owner retired, so Horace bought the business and kept on the only other employee, Jennifer, the secretary. She knew very little about Horace, who apparently lived a modest and quiet life. No person or pet, not even a goldfish, resided with Horace. With the exception of the quoit league, he did not appear to socialize.

"What do we do now?" Jennifer begged. "Poor Horace is still in the morgue, and I don't have the authority or power to continue the operation of the title business."

The next morning I asked for an audience with the judge assigned to hear estate matters. Judge Carr patiently listed as I related the strange tale of Horace Huffnagel's passing.

"There's no family, no one's claimed the body?" His Honor asked.

"No, sir."

"How big is the estate?"

"I'm not sure, Judge. The decedent lived a conservative life in an unpretentious home working at a job that probably generated a modest income. He drove an eight-year-old car with 90,000 miles on it. My guess is he didn't own much other than the business, the house and the car."

"Well, things need to move on," His Honor noted. "Will you accept the appointment as administrator and legal counsel to the estate? You'll have two job titles, but you'll be paid only for one according to the usual fee schedule."

I agreed and set out to organize things. The first order of business was to finalize funeral arrangements. Most of the quoit team showed up at the service. I studied and researched the registry book signatures. No family members were present.

I made certain the ranch home and its contents were secured, that insurance was in place and that mail was routed to my office. The car was locked in the garage, and the neighbors were advised of my involvement. I envisioned that ultimately the house would be sold.

The primary issue was the continued operation of the title company. Jennifer agreed to stay on. We began the process of having her approved by the home office to conduct settlements. I retained a certified public accountant to perform an audit of all the business accounts to confirm that all ledgers, balance sheets, checking accounts and escrow fund balances were accurate.

I hired a detective to determine if there were any next of kin and to locate any property titled in the name of the decedent. Toward that same goal I sent a letter of inquiry to every local bank, stockbroker and financial advisor inquiring if there were any assets in the name of Huffnagel or maintained under his Social Security number.

Two weeks after the funeral service, things began to return to normal. Jennifer scheduled settlements and issued title insurance. A realtor agreed to list Huffnagel's house for sale, and I traded in the automobile at a used car lot. Detective Mattioli also had some news. There was an 18-

year-old nephew, Bertram Klumper, who appeared to be the only living relative. He resided in Lancaster, Pennsylvania, where he worked as a laborer on a mushroom farm.

That same week Jennifer had a surprise visit at the office from Paul and Gladys Terfinko, a retired couple. Three years prior, they had sold their home in Allentown to young newlywed buyers. The settlement had occurred at Horace's title company where Horace took care of everything. The Terfinkos had an outstanding $40,000 mortgage encumbering their home. The newlywed buyers paid $100,000 for the residence, so Horace issued a check to the mortgage company to pay off the mortgage and gave the Terfinkos a net check for about $60,000.

"We're about to buy a condo in Florida," Mr. Terfinko explained to Jennifer, "but when the condo people did a credit check, they said we still have an open mortgage on the Allentown home we sold. I know that can't be, since the mortgage was paid in full at settlement. Besides, I haven't made a payment on that mortgage in over three years, and the bank has never complained, so they must have been paid in full."

"Mr. Terfinko," Jennifer explained, "I'll get your credit report corrected immediately. This is very common. Often a bank is paid in full and yet it fails to mark the mortgage 'satisfied' at the courthouse. I see from your file that we paid that mortgage off three years ago. I'll write a follow-up letter demanding that the bank satisfy your mortgage."

"Okay," Mr. Terfinko agreed. "But do it soon. We can't buy our Florida condo until our credit report is corrected."

Two days later, I received a letter from the Lititz National Bank. It was in response to my inquiry to determine if Huffnagel maintained any assets there.

*Dear Mr. Fox:*

*Your inquiry regarding the Estate of Huffnagel has been received. We are saddened to hear of the decedent's passing. Please be advised that our institution maintains* savings account number A-371242 in the name of the deceased. The present balance is $1,027,812.67.

> Very truly yours,
> Fern McKenna
> Assistance Vice President

That was a lot of money, but not as much as I would soon learn was held in Huffnagal's name by the Beltzville Savings and Loan, and the Shomokin Merchants Bank. They each acknowledged separate accounts in excess of $2,000,000. Apparently the title insurance business had been good to Huffnagel.

The next day, I received a telephone inquiry from Bertram Klumper. He wondered if it was true what his friends were saying - that Bertram, as the only surviving relative, would ultimately receive most of the bounty from the estate.

"You appear to be the only heir and next of kin," I confirmed.

"Wow. Can I have my money now?"

"Not yet, Mr. Klumper. I'm waiting for the accountant's confirmation of all the assets."

"How much money will I get?"

"I won't know until the accounting is completed."

"Will it be more than $5,000?"

"Most likely."

"Wow. I'll call you in a week."

It was the next day's telephone call from CPA Stanley Wormcastle that proved to be one of those memorable conversations one does not easily forget. He had just completed his initial analysis of the decedent's business accounts.

"Are you sitting down," he began.

I found a chair.

"I think I know how Mr. Huffnagel reported an annual salary of only $40,000, yet was able to salt away five million bucks in less than three years without anyone being the wiser."

That statement carried with it the inference that dearly departed Horace Huffnagel might have engaged in something untoward.

"Your buddy Huffnagel had an interesting sideline. Every time someone using his title company paid off a long-term mortgage bearing a low interest rate, he kept the money and invested the funds in portfolios that generated a higher return. Then each month like clockwork he would send the usual mortgage payment to the bank. The bank was none the wiser, since it was getting paid on time. The debtors who thought their mortgages had been paid in full were none the wiser. They never received a late notice or a foreclosure letter from the bank. Meanwhile Huffnagel put the money in accounts earning more interest than the rate charged on the mortgage he should have satisfied. Over the years, he accumulated several million dollars and lived off the difference in the interest rates, which income he dutifully reported to the IRS, so they never became suspicious."

"But he should have been caught when someone ultimately learned that a mortgage had not been paid off," I protested.

"That was the beauty part," the CPA explained. "When someone complained to Huffnagel that a mortgage was still open, he just blamed the problem on the bank, claiming the bank had failed to send in the satisfaction papers to the courthouse. Then Huffnagel would reluctantly send the bank the payoff sum he had squirreled away, and the bank would nullify the mortgage."

"You mean to tell me none of the five million is his?" I stammered.

"He diverted funds from about 120 settlements. He was writing out about 120 mortgage payment checks a month."

The next week I sent letters to the three local banks holding the five million dollars. I advised them the funds were to be paid to the Estate of Huffnagel so I could pay off all the outstanding mortgages. The three banks expressed sadness at losing such a good client and his valuable accounts.

As for Bertram Klumper, he inherited the remainder of Huffnagel's entire estate, about $50,000. That was the net sum remaining after I sold the house and paid off Huffnagel's rather large first mortgage. The next time I go to the courthouse, I'll look to see if the bank sent in the mortgage satisfaction papers.

## Chapter Thirty-Nine

Enemies No More

The pilots I have known share certain common traits, such as a love of flying. I've never met an aviator who didn't maintain a detailed flight log chronicling every turn of the propeller or whir of the jet engine under his or her command. The keeping of such tachometer data is instinctive and unquestioned. It forms the basis for bragging rights; it leads to more sophisticated flight ratings; and it serves as an historic transcript of past adventures that may become, on occasion, the subject of embellishment.

The pilot's log usually includes the names of the others who inhabited the cockpit, the type of aircraft flown, the point of departure and destination, time en route and weather conditions encountered. A soldier possesses service medals as silent testimony of his past campaigns. Similarly, a pilot keeps his sacred flight log close to his chest.

- - -

Several local corporations maintain advertising exhibits at the Lehigh Valley International Airport in eastern Pennsylvania. Large illuminated glass display cases, some as big as a dining room, bear witness to home grown goods and services. Stranded passengers with time on their hands constitute a captive audience to these sophisticated testimonials, rented at significant cost by corporate sponsors.

But there's a smaller display case about the size of a vending machine. The forgotten exhibit, almost hidden from view in a corner of the lobby near an emergency exit, contains but one small worn and discolored leather-bound book. The volume was bequeathed to the airport when an old pilot took his last flight east. Few people ever stumble across this exhibit. Fewer still take the time to read the typed paragraph that pays tribute to a World War II pilot flight log and its owner. It contains the story of two enemies sworn decades ago to fight to the death.

- - -

I never flew with a better private pilot than Maurice Scheirer. Some fliers develop their talents with time, but a gifted few are born to soar as naturally as an eagle. Maurice possessed that instinctive talent. He was happiest when sitting in the left seat as pilot in command of any small single-engine aircraft. Similar to playing baseball, operating an airplane is a game of anticipation and inches. Maurice could see the invisible crosswinds. He could feel the runway rising to meet him. He knew without the benefit of aeronautical charts what vector to fly to locate even the most obscure uncharted grass landing strip. He could touch down on a sugar cube without employing the brake pedal. He and his flying machine were as one, like a jockey and his racehorse.

The secret to life is finding an activity that gives the participant greater joy with time. Maurice had found his passion: being airborne. One day we flew over to Blairstown, New Jersey, for the best apple pie made at any airport restaurant east of the Mississippi. We sat at a window booth so Maurice could watch the planes take off and land, an activity with which he never grew tired. Maurice took another bite of Blairstown Airport apple pie as he plotted with protractor in hand the course of our evening flight to Kutztown in search of Pennsylvania Dutch sausage with potato filling.

"Larry, the QBs are having a special meeting next month. I'd like you to come as my guest."

This offer was an honor not to be taken lightly. The Quiet Birdmen was an international organization of pilots, all of whom involuntarily looked skyward every time a plane flew overhead. Maurice fit right in. Many were the times I was invited as a guest to his home. When he heard the drone of an approaching airplane, he would politely excuse himself and run outside.

"Take your boots," his patient wife would call out if there was snow on the ground.

- - -

No one was admitted to one of the secret QB meetings other than by pre-approved invitation.

"Our speaker will be a guy who flew with the German Luftwaffe during World War II. He's going to talk about his participation in bombing raids over London."

It was chance of a lifetime to hear firsthand from an aging veteran his perspective on an important chapter in aviation history. Soon, perhaps quite soon, there would be no more survivors from one of the most significant wars in history, and then descriptions of the conflict would come only secondhand.

"I'd love to attend," I assured Maurice as we flew non-stop the 60 nautical miles for some authentic Pennsylvania Dutch cooking.

- - -

Quiet Birdmen. A most unusual group. The common bond uniting its membership was ostensibly the possession of a pilot's license, but as the sexist name implied, other criteria for admission awaited the uninitiated. There were no Birdladies. It was a fraternity of aviators who permitted only other males with substantial years of flying experience to join its noble ranks. Like any other secret society that guarded against unsolicited entry into its meetings, the group employed many unspoken sacred rituals and administered many complex tests to the aspiring entrant, sometimes over a period of years, to prove the pledge's loyalty to the organization. For a neophyte such as myself, it was similar to attending Catholic Mass for the first time.

That night, Maurice drove for two hours into the heart of the Pocono Mountains. This was no Rotary Club. He finally turned down a narrow gravel road that led to an isolated roadhouse. I felt as if I were participating in a scene from some gangster movie. Soon I'd either be a "made man," or found dead in a ditch.

Seventy or eighty cars were scattered across the rut-strewn parking lot of Trinkle's Tavern. The lot relied upon moonlight as its only illumination. There was nothing for miles around. Who in his right mind would stumble into this place for a drink?

"We're here," Maurice gleefully announced as he turned off the car engine.

We headed for the roadhouse door. Despite the lack of light, I noted that each car's back bumper had a small sticker with two silver letters affixed near the license plate - "Q B."

Maurice stepped up to the rough-hewn door of this place that had once served as a stagecoach stop. He knocked three times, paused, then knocked lightly twice again. Somebody on the other side peered through a viewing slit and unlocked the door. They both said something in Latin and exchanged a secret handshake. Maurice motioned for me to follow him. I was in, but was I up to the grade?

The lone bartender pushed a button and a hidden door leading to the cellar made a buzzing sound as it swung open. Maurice led the way downstairs where a multitude of voices intermingled.

"And now my fellow brothers," the exalted ruler proclaimed, "let us stand and face East, and remember those of our brethren who have taken their 'final flight'."

About a hundred men stood, most wearing tuxedos accentuated by a lone diamond QB lapel pin, and silently faced eastward.

Who was Trinkle? Was this really a tavern? Was it *his* tavern? Where were the other customers? Was Trinkle a QB too? Did he know what was occurring in his hidden basement? The exalted ruler interrupted my thoughts.

"You may be seated."

Four waiters appeared seemingly out of nowhere, served us a sumptuous five-course dinner, then vanished.

"And now for the moment we have all been waiting for. Our guest speaker, Helmut Schnabel, served as a lieutenant in the Luftwaffe during World War II and personally took part in bombing raids in and around London. He will now share his fascinating insights with us."

A distinguished, silver-haired senior citizen arose ramrod straight at the head table, saluted the exalted ruler, and advanced to the podium amidst robust and warm applause. The room full of aviators, some of them combatants during World War II, or veterans of Korea, Vietnam or the Middle East, heartily acknowledged the German flier as one of their own, even if he had once served across enemy lines.

Maurice sat to my left finishing what was left of his peach cobbler. To my right was an unassuming pleasant fellow. We had struck up a conversation between the second and third courses. Richard Shook displayed a hearty appetite for such an aged warrior. He, too, had flown during the last World War, as a member of the Army Air Corps back before there was such a thing as the U.S. Air Force. At eighteen, he had enlisted, and while still a teenager, found himself transported across the Atlantic and billeted in the small English town of Sussex, from which he flew escort cover for allied bombers. I was seated next to a real war hero.

"Ve ver assigned to a flight unit in Dusseldorf," the German guest speaker began, "vit tirty heavy bombers, und a support group to fend off de American gun ships. My squadron flew sorties from de May of 1941 trew de December of 1943. Ve focused on neutralizing de allied airstrips east of London."

"Forty-one to 43 ... east of London ... " my new friend sitting next to me mused out loud.

"At vun point, we dropped bombs 18 days in a row, despite some bad vetter. Sometimes de flak vas so heavy ve could have valked on it. Of course, all of dis activity is chronicled in my flight log." The German produced a tattered leather booklet from his vest pocket. He handled the volume as if it were the original Gutenberg Bible.

I noticed that Mr. Shook had begun to engage in a similar exercise. He too produced his own leather-bound logbook, which he tenderly held as if it were his only possession of value. His finger ran down a list of dates written longhand in faded ink. Then unannounced, he stood up as if by uncontrollable impulse and called out to the guest speaker:

"Sir, did you ever bomb Chelmsford?"

"Ver?"

"East of London? Did you bomb the airstrip at Chelmsford in June of '42?"

The Luftwaffe lieutenant gingerly paged through the diary written in his own hand. "Yah, June 14," he confirmed.

Mr. Shook stared at his logbook through the same eyes that at the tender age of 20 had recorded flights now almost forgotten.

"I'll be a son of a bitch," Shook interjected from the midst of the shocked audience. "You dropped a bomb on me and my squad! Blasted half of us out of our bunks. As soon as we could, we took off after you. But damnit. You were gone. See for yourself!"

Just about every QB jumped to his feet to converge upon the lieutenant and Shook, who were now comparing their historic notes. There was no doubt about it. Almost 60 years later, the mortal enemies had met again. I noted a clenched fist and a tightening of the jaw, as these two gladiators once again confronted each other.

Finally the two pilots smiled at each other and clasped hands. The members all broke into spontaneous applause.

- - -

I've represented Homer Twiggle at various times. He owns an apple tree. Some of the overhanging branches have occasionally permitted unwanted fruit to fall onto Fred Slobocki's yard. Periodically Fred may have commented about rotten apples falling onto his property. One summer afternoon Fred just couldn't take it anymore, so he picked up a wormy apple and threw it in the direction of the Twiggle residence. It shattered the living room window. Twiggle drove his car into the Slobocki side fence in retaliation. After that, Slobocki allegedly poisoned Twiggle's cat. Then came the mutual assault that brought both combatants to the Northampton County Prison to await a bail hearing.

They could have learned something of value at the QB meeting. Perhaps there ought to be a law that sworn enemies must refrain from any form of counterattack for approximately 60 years. Then they may compare notes and eat dinner.

# CHAPTER FORTY

## Calling Cards

*The Mark of Zorro* was on TV the other night. It's a classic "everyone has a sword and knows how to use it" movie starring Tyrone Power. What a name! If I had been born with a name like that, I'd probably have been a movie star, too.

The plot is rather complex, so please pay attention. Power returns to his native California where the Spanish are in charge. They're making things tough for the indigenous population of poor peasants. They are forever squeezing taxes out of the penniless farmers, and then these bullies drink everyone's wine and laugh out loud a lot. Power can't stand this inappropriate behavior, so he cuts a one-inch-wide strip of black fabric and fashions two eye slits. The minute he places this clever disguise over his face, no one can tell that he's still Tyrone Power.

His identity a secret, Power changes his name to Zorro and sets out to correct a multitude of social injustices. He locates a fast, jet-black horse with similar inclinations, and together they ride into the night, wreaking havoc upon the Spanish soldiers, most of whom appear to be confused or stupid. It is hard for them to track Zorro, because he and his ebony steed are dressed entirely in black, from the tip of the horse's tail to the slender mask covering Power's long, Hollywood-idol eyelashes.

Every so often, Zorro enters a Spanish barracks, holds all the soldiers at bay with his dazzling Errol Flynn-ish swordplay, kisses a lovesick maiden right on the lips without disclosing his identity, and escapes into the night. When it strikes his fancy, he tarries just long enough to carve a "Z" at the scene of his dramatic break-in. Sometimes he carves this letter on opponents' pants, sometimes on walls. Whenever he does this, there's an accompanying "swushing" sound, after which he jumps out of a convenient second-floor window, lands adroitly on his horse rather than upon the saddle horn, and vanishes. Power never actually clarifies what the "Z" stands for, but I think it's *The Mark of Zorro*.

I have never understood why individuals who feel the need to break and enter are often compelled to leave their individualistic mark behind as a calling card for the police. The Manson gang murderers scrawled bloody words on their victims' walls. Some criminals choose to mail the police periodic clues. If I were engaged in an unlawful act, I doubt that I'd make the job of the investigating officer any easier.

- - -

Adrien Crenshaw married his teenage bride, Julie, before either had reached the age of 20. Things were tough from the start and there was no improvement with time. There were no children. About two years after the wedding, Julie unilaterally decided to separate, moved into an apartment of her own and obtained an unlisted phone number. Somebody told Adrien his bride was seen talking to another man. This remark disturbed Adrien, so he drove over to his wife's apartment and began banging on the door. Julie made the mistake of opening it.

Adrien confronted Julie with his suspicions and refused to consider any explanations. He became enraged, grabbed an electric extension cord lying on the kitchen table, wrapped it around her neck and strangled her. The cops caught him two days later. His fingerprints matched those found at the scene of the crime.

I was assigned to represent the defendant, now accused of first-degree murder. He faced a possible death sentence. The district attorney was willing to let him plead guilty to a general charge of murder with an agreement that he receive a life sentence without the possibility of parole.

"No way, pal," Adrien responded through the prison bars separating us as I advised him of the D.A.'s rather lenient offer. "I've been talking to some of the other guys in here. They say I've got a good defense - that I acted in the heat of passion, and so her death wasn't permeated."

"Premeditated," I corrected.

"Yeah, whatever," Adrien snorted.

Adrien was being counseled by fellow prisoners, people who were in jail because their defenses had been found lacking by 12 neutral onlookers.

"Mr. Crenshaw," I interjected, "I don't think a jury will find that this homicide occurred in the heat of passion. On the contrary, you took the time to drive across town to your wife's apartment, you argued with her for more than ten minutes according to the neighbor downstairs, and only then did you kill her."

"She provoked me into it. I'll take my chances with a trial."

The client had spoken. I was his servant. I filed my omnibus motion for pre-trial discovery. I demanded to see every piece of evidence in the D.A.'s file. The D.A. complied and sent me a box full of documents, accompanied with a cover letter.

*Dear Counselor:*

*The enclosed material is remitted pursuant to your request. Should you wish to review autopsy photos, please schedule an appointment with the coroner's office. Such photos are not released to third parties for reasons of privacy.*

*Very truly yours,
District Attorney's Office*

I didn't need to see pictures of a dead person. He strangled her. She died. I advised the D.A. I wouldn't be viewing the gruesome evidence.

"You might want to reconsider," the chief prosecutor assigned to the case counseled me over the phone. "The pictures tell an interesting story."

I made an appointment to meet the coroner at the morgue. What a creepy place. No windows, two polished metal dissection tables and canisters for discarded body parts. This was no way to spend a Tuesday afternoon.

"How nice to see you," the coroner sang out as he extended a hand that had probably recently removed somebody's brain.

"How can you be in such a good mood?" I asked as I looked about.

"Simple, I'm not stretched out on one of these tables looking up at me."

He had a point. I followed him into his private quarters where he located a large file from which he produced several photographs. It was just another day at the office. He acted as if we were about to review snapshots of last year's summer picnic.

"You may find this of interest," came his understated observation.

I took a quick glance at the large black-and-white glossy photograph lying before me. There reposed the constricted face of a young lady, her eyes shut, her hair disheveled. Encircling her neck three times was an electrical extension cord that dug into her flesh. But it was something else that caught and held my attention. The ends of the cord had been fashioned into an intricate bow, similar to a bow tie. The assailant had taken the extra time and had expended the extra creative effort to fashion a special cynical calling card.

"Your client thought long and hard about what he was doing," the coroner theorized. "This wasn't a crime of uncontrollable passion."

The jury agreed. They took less than three hours to deliberate. They returned with a unanimous verdict: guilty of first-degree murder. They recommended the death sentence.

That decorative yet unnecessary bow tie had sent my client to the gallows.

If ever I meet Zorro, I'm going to suggest he refrain from carving "Zs" at the scene of the crime. As his defense attorney will undoubtedly agree, the less evidence, the better.

## CHAPTER FORTY-ONE

### Irving Wiggleman

*July 18, 1888 - Stutgart, Germany*

Young, newly widowed Helga Munhausen is invited by her neighbor, Inga Von Stutzen, to take a walk down to the rose garden in the town square. It will do her good to get out and about after her husband's recent funeral. She takes her fifteen-year-old son, Arnold, with her. While passing the livery stable, Helga steps on a sharp nail. She dies from tetanus three days later.

*September 3, 1888 - Stutgart, Germany*

Newly orphaned Arnold Munhausen is told that the streets in America are paved with gold. He hasn't eaten a nourishing meal in a week. He believes what he is told and sells the remaining family furniture to buy passage in steerage on a trans-Atlantic steamship. It will take him nearly three weeks to reach New York City. During the passage, he contracts pneumonia and almost dies.

*September 29, 1888 - New York City*

Arnold is released from Ellis Island and learns for the first time that very few streets are paved, and none is paved with gold. He gets a job in the German section of Brooklyn packing sausage skins with meat filling. He works 10 hours a day six days a week and is paid 18 cents an hour. He lives with five other sausage packers in the cramped basement room of a tenement building. He has no Social Security benefits, health insurance or pension plan, nor does he receive any bilingual preferential treatment. He struggles to learn English.

### *February 11, 1899 - New York City*

Twenty-six-year-old Arnold's hard work pays off. He is named assistant manager of the entire sausage production department. He is now earning 32 cents an hour plus production bonuses. He can afford his own room above street level. He still walks everywhere because he can't afford the trolley, but on Sundays he is now accompanied by his lady friend who works in a nearby blouse mill. Sometimes they talk of marriage.

### *August 8, 1907 - Eighty miles west of New York City*

Arnold and his bride decide to honeymoon in the nearby Pocono Mountains. The train takes them through Bethlehem, Pennsylvania. He notes that there isn't a German butcher shop despite the sizable Germanic population.
"Nice little town," he tells Lucy.
"Nice," Lucy agrees.

### *March 15, 1910 - Bethlehem, Pennsylvania*

Arnold calls upon the same spirit of adventure that induced him to leave Germany. He and Lucy take their baby boy, Herman, and use their life savings, all $800, as a down payment on a two-story, abandoned, narrow brick shop on the south side of Bethlehem. Arnold and Lucy, with a bit of luck and the grace of God, plan to open their own neighborhood meat market. Ice from the nearby Lehigh River is plentiful and cheap. The local ice house keeps the precious commodity in good supply right through the summer and fall. They will live upstairs with little baby Herman.

*June 12, 1925 - Bethlehem, Pennsylvania*

Bethlehem Steel Corporation grows into an industrial giant, having provided the U.S. Government with the materials to wage a First World War. The company sprawls for seven miles along the Lehigh River, where canal barges loaded with coal and iron ore maneuver for space. Arnold's tiny $4^{th}$ Street meat market is dwarfed on three sides by one of the corporation's new parking lots. Some employees now drive cars made of steel rather than rely upon horsepower or the trolley.

Herman is fifteen, and after school he helps pack sausages with his father and mother.

*August 18, 1940 - Bethlehem, Pennsylvania*

The canal barges have made their owner, Asa Packer, wealthy. He has endowed Lehigh University, and it has become an academic powerhouse on the other side of the river bearing its name.

*May 12, 1966 - Bethlehem, Pennsylvania*

Fifty-six-year-old Herman Munhausen carries on the family meat market business as the sole proprietor at the same location - $4^{th}$ Street on the south side of Bethlehem. His parents have passed on to their final reward. Herman, a bachelor, still lives on the second floor as he has since his infancy.

His meat display racks boast every type and style of meat. He also has a small selection of various cheeses and bread. As a result, he often prepares fresh sandwiches to order. He always adds a pickle and a small plastic container of mayonnaise. He caters to a modest but steady neighborhood clientele.

*September 8, 1966 - Bethlehem, Pennsylvania*

Hosaki Gutamora, an 18-year-old freshman foreign exchange student from Japan studying at Lehigh University, enters the Munhausen Meat Market. He points at a roll of meat and some bread and asks in broken English for a sandwich. He pays Herman $1.25, politely bows and leaves.

"Them Japs bombed Pearl Harbor. Now they study here free as you please," Herman complains to Mrs. Ronaldo, a customer.

"I'll take a half-pound of corned beef, if it's on sale," she responds.

*February 12, 1969 - Bethlehem, Pennsylvania*

Herman and my father chance to meet at Allentown Symphony Hall during a concert. They discover they have a mutual interest in classical string music. They agree to play violin duets together every Sunday night at Dad's house.

*May 30, 1969 - Manhattan, New York City*

The Board of Directors of Bethlehem Steel Corporation foresees significant profits as a result of the Vietnam War. It votes to undertake plans to significantly expand its Bethlehem Corporate headquarters. A site feasibility study is undertaken of southside Bethlehem locations. The parking lots surrounding the Munhausen Meat Market appear to be well-suited for the proposed 40-story skyscraper, if the outdated meat market building is razed.

*September 18, 1970 - Bethlehem, Pennsylvania*

Sophomore Lehigh University foreign exchange student Hosaki Gutamora appears at Herman's meat market. He no longer speaks in halting English. "Ham and cheese on rye," he requests. "Hold the mayo."

The following Sunday, Herman plays violin duets with my father, who has worked at Bethlehem Steel for 37 years. Dad has never known any other employer.

*April 7, 1971 - Bethlehem, Pennsylvania*

The first of several letters from Bethlehem Steel Corporation is delivered to the meat market.

*Dear Mr. Munhausen:*

*Bethlehem Steel Corporation wishes to acquire the real estate upon which your meat market is located. The corporation is prepared to pay in excess of the current appraised value. Kindly advise if you would be inclined to enter into an agreement of sale.*

*Real Estate Acquisitions Department*

Herman throws the letter in the trash. That Sunday he plays violins with Dad. During the second movement snack break, he mentions the letter.

"I heard they want to build the new headquarters on the parking lots surrounding your meat market," Dad responds.

"It ain't for sale," Herman proclaims. "I've lived and worked there my entire life."

*July 3, 1971 - Bethlehem, Pennsylvania*

A real estate acquisitions representative from Bethlehem Steel drops by the meat market. Herman is slicing ham for the approaching lunch rush.

"I'm Mr. Whitehorn," the well-dressed man announces over the meat counter.

"What can I do for you?" Herman inquires.

"I'd like to discuss the purchase of your building by Bethlehem Steel Corporation."

"It ain't for sale."

"Mr. Munhausen, we'd like to construct a new office building at this location. We're prepared to pay five times the appraised value of $40,000. That's $200,000 cash, Mr. Munhausen. You could open up a chain of meat markets with that amount of money."

"It ain't for sale," Herman repeats as he stands at the exact location envisioned by the architects as the front reception area of the proposed skyscraper.

*November 18, 1971 - Vineland, New Jersey, the home of Irving and Stella Wiggleman*

"I can't believe how handsome you look in that tux. You haven't gained a pound in 10 years," Stella gushes.

"The compliment is appreciated, dear, but it won't help. Why the Feldmans had to have Sammy's bar mitzvah in Pottsville is beyond me. Where the hell is Pottsville anyway? I've got no time for such nonsense. It kills the entire weekend," the sole owner of 48 Wiggleman's super gigantic luxury grocery stores laments.

"He's your cousin's son, honey, and you're going," Stella replies. "Pottsville is somewhere in Pennsylvania, I think."

*November 19, 1971 - Bethlehem, Pennsylvania, inside the Wiggleman Mercedes touring car.*

"I'm telling you, this is not Pottsville. The sign says 'Bethlehem.' You've got us lost again. Now we'll be late for the bar mitzvah," Stella cries.

"I should maybe ask that gas station guy over there where we are," Irving confesses. "You know something, Stella?"

"What?"

"This is a nice-looking town. Maybe we should build a Wiggleman's around here."

*February 8, 1972 - Bethlehem, Pennsylvania*

A second certified letter from Bethlehem Steel Corporation is delivered to the meat market.

*Dear Mr. Munhausen:*

*Bethlehem Steel Corporation is desirous of purchasing your $4^{th}$ Street real estate. The corporation is prepared to pay $500,000.00 for immediate acquisition. Please advise if you will enter into an agreement of sale reflecting your voluntary vacation of the premises no later than May 30 of this year. Our 24-hour direct dial telephone number as noted above is at your disposal.*

*Real Estate Acquisitions Department*

*February 12, 1972 - Bethlehem, Pennsylvania*

Herman and my dad finish a Mozart duet. It's time for their evening snack. Herman unwraps a large paper bag and produces six different neatly packaged mounds of cold cuts. There is also a clear bag of pickles floating in dill juice.

"What a feast," Dad notes.

"It's nothing," Herman responds. "Just some stuff left over from the lunch rush ... Listen, Fox, I got a question for you. You're a smart guy and my good friend."

Dad nods his head as he takes another bite of pimento loaf.

"Bethlehem Steel just made me another offer. I'm holding up construction of their proposed office. They'll give me half a million to move. Would you take that?"

Pimento loaf morsels shoot across the room as Dad starts to choke. It takes a moment for him to properly recover.

"$500,000 in American money!"

"That's right. Would you take it?"

"In a heartbeat!" Dad responds between heavy breaths. "You could retire to the French Riviera and just live off the interest."

Herman doesn't appear to be convinced. "I dunno. The 'Steel' has got more money than God, and they can't build without me. Maybe I should hold out for a cool million."

*March 2, 1972 - Tokyo, Japan*

Hosaki Gutamora accepts a job in the research department of Kioto Steel. He will investigate ways to produce steel at half the price incurred by other manufacturers in the world market.

*March 5, 1972 - Washington, D.C. - The Pentagon Office of Munitions Procurement*

Four-star General Reinhold Gottlieb puts the finishing touches on his weekly Vietnam strategy armament report. For the first time in memory, he does not requisition any high-grade steel or armored plate.

*March 12, 1972 - Vineland, New Jersey*

Irving Wiggleman sets out for Bethlehem, Pennsylvania, and doesn't get lost. He drives by a 300-acre cow pasture just outside the city limits. Old farmer Goshenhoppen is trying to lug one more bag of corn meal into the barn. Irving stops his Mercedes and on sheer impulse walks up to the struggling farmer.

"You want to sell this place?"

*April 2, 1972 - Manhattan, New York City*

The Board of Directors of Bethlehem Steel Corporation meets to review quarterly profit spreadsheets. For the first time in a century there does not appear to be a profit.

"That's strange," the Vice-President of Finance offers.

"It's the damned war. They're stopping it," the Assistant Vice-President of Finance explains.

"And the Japanese. They're dumping steel here at lower prices," the Second Assistant Vice-President of Finance chimes in. "We may not be able to pay a quarterly stock dividend."

"Will that affect our personal bonuses?" the concerned Assistant Vice-President inquires.

*August 14, 1972 - Outskirts of Bethlehem, Pennsylvania*

Irving Wiggleman carries the same silver shovel he has used 48 times before and turns the first earth in the former pasture. The festive crowd cheers as the caterers begin to serve 60 different types of Wiggleman's upscale meats and cheeses to the onlookers attending the ceremony.

*November 8, 1972 - Bethlehem, Pennsylvania*

Business continues to decline at the Munhausen Meat Market. Although Herman has no assistant vice-president of finance to conduct an analysis, it is clear nonetheless that once again there will be no profit this month. He reluctantly searches for the certified letter. After all, half a million is better than nothing. He calls the 24-hour hotline. The automated voice refers him to the Federal Bankruptcy Court.

*This afternoon - Bethlehem, Pennsylvania*

Two seven-year-olds walk to the Washington Elementary School. They pass a derelict, narrow brick building surrounded on three sides by a forgotten broken asphalt parking lot. Weeds grow up through the cracks. People drive by on the way to Wiggleman's, where the ham salad's on sale.

# Chapter Forty-Two

## I'll Be Right There

There was a time when I was one of the most sought-after criminal defense attorneys for miles and miles around. And with good reason. When some guy, friendless and incarcerated, called for help, I'd race over to the prison. I stood as the only ray of hope during the prisoner's desperate time of need.

My reputation as a defender of the downtrodden continued until someone repainted the wall above the third toilet in the prison bathroom. Then the volume and frequency of calls took a significant downturn. The words "for a really cheap lawyer, call ... " were still legible, since they were carved into the surface with a contraband nail file, but one of my phone number's seven digits had been obliterated, and so some shoe repair shop near Mertztown with a similar number became the recipient of most of my calls.

When some poor wretch got thrown in prison, he was usually permitted only one phone call. I knew that if I were contacted, I was at that moment in time the most important person in that inmate's life, a responsibility I did not take lightly. And so it was with Iggy Klotz. When his plea for assistance came, I dropped everything and ran over to the prison.

"What's the charge?" I asked my newest client as we sat together in his cramped cell.

"Burglary."

"When were you arrested?"

"Last week."

"Last week! Why did you wait so long to call me?"

"They only allow one call a week, pal. When I got there, it was late and I was hungry. So I ordered pizza to go."

- - -

Harvey Gillsap was a conscientious and energetic attorney. He and I had agreed to serve as co-counsel in a complex trial scheduled in a month, so each week we met to prepare our exhibits and outline our trial testimony. It was my turn to go to his office. I didn't recognize the lady answering his phones. Harvey ushered me into his office. He didn't look happy.

"My secretary underwent emergency surgery on Tuesday. I've had to hire a temp. Marg has been here 18 years. You can't imagine what it's been like since she left. The stand-in is trying her best, but she isn't Marg."

"Will Marg be okay?"

"I think so, but she may be laid up a month. Until then, things around here could be ... "

A knock at the door interrupted Harvey's thoughts. He turned to me. "She hasn't mastered the intercom yet ... Come in, Mrs. Filch."

The temp stuck her head through the door. "Pardon me, Mr. Gillsap. The man on the phone says he's calling from prison and can make only one call. He says he's about to be extradited to Arizona, and so he needs to see you today at the prison."

Harvey apologized to me as he reached for the phone.

"Yes ... Yes ... I see ... Am I the first attorney you've called ... The hearing is this afternoon? ... Okay, I'll be there ... We can talk about that when I see you ... No, don't say anything else - you never know who might be listening in." Harvey hung up the phone.

"Looks like our meeting may be cut short," I theorized.

"It sounds serious," Harvey explained. "The guy says he's never been to Arizona in his life, and some sheriff out there has him mixed up with somebody else. There's an outstanding warrant."

"What's the charge?" I asked.

"I don't know. I didn't want him to say anything incriminating over the prison phone." Harvey activated his intercom button. "Mrs. Filch, would you come in for a moment?"

The door opened, followed by the temp's nervous face. "Yes, Mr. Gillsap?"

"The man who just called - what was his name?"

"Name?"

"Yes, what was the name of the inmate who called from prison?"

"I don't know. Didn't you just speak with him?"

"What prison did he call from?"

"Prison?"

"Was it federal, state or local?"

"Are there different prisons, Mr. Gillsap?"

Harvey thanked Filch for her help as she gently closed the door.

"I sure miss Marg," Gillsap lamented. "I sure miss Marg."

## CHAPTER FORTY-THREE

The Monogrammed Towel

*May 17, 1974 at approximately 9:00 p.m.*

Some burglar breaks into the McGlochlin house while they are on vacation. The felon gains entry by smashing a rear kitchen-door window. This wrongdoer must not have given much thought to his criminal enterprise, as evidenced by the fact that blood in ever-increasing quantities is ultimately found by the police at the site of the broken window, with a trickle and then a trail of red leading from the kitchen, into the dining room, through the living room, and ending in the downstairs bath.

The intruder may have grabbed a towel near the shower stall to wrap around his wounds before pilfering some silverware and a few pieces of jewelry. It appears the criminal left in a hurry.

*May 17, 1974, 10:14 p.m.*

Randy Simonetta arrives unannounced at Bethlehem's St. Luke's Hospital emergency ward admissions desk. He must wait for about 10 minutes before he can be treated. He has sustained a severe laceration of the interior right arm, a deep cut traveling from just below his thumb to his elbow joint. Shards of window glass are embedded in the wound. He asks the receptionist for something to wrap around his arm while he waits. Ultimately, 55 stitches are required to close the wound, which arouses the suspicions of the attending physician, Dr. Clarence Mortimer. He calls the police, who respond quickly and confront the patient, who has just received a pint of blood to replenish the large quantity he recently lost. Despite various inquiries by the officers, Simonetta declines to offer an explanation as to how he was injured. One of the investigating officers, Sergeant Barry Miller, approaches Dr. Mortimer to gain further insight into the silent patient's mysterious loss of blood.

"Tell me, Doc, when you saw this guy tonight, did he have anything wrapped around his arm to slow the hemorrhaging?"

"A hospital towel," the physician recalls. "But somebody probably attended to him when he first showed up."

"Did any other patient appear here this evening with a deep cut of the arm aggravated by embedded shards of glass?"

"No," the physician confirms.

The zealous officer locates a pair of latex gloves and begins to rummage through the medical waste can in the admissions area. It doesn't take Miller long to locate a fancy towel, since it is the only one reposing among the usual refuse of newspapers and vending machine soda cans. He gingerly inspects his new-found prize before depositing it into an evidence bag. The large, powder-blue towel, highlighted with a gold fringe, is composed of hand-spun Egyptian cotton. It is an expensive, personalized bathroom accessary, as further confirmed by the presence of the hand-sewn monogram comprising three initials stitched into the fabric near the gold border: *PHM.*

*May 18, 1974, 7:00 p.m.*

Paul H. McGlochlin contacts the police to report that upon his return from vacation, he discovered that his home had been entered and certain personal property is missing.

"Did your loss include a powder-blue monogrammed bath towel?" Detective Longenbach inquires.

*May 19, 1974, 8:00 a.m.*

The police arrest unemployed 20-year-old Simonetta at his parents' home where he is recuperating from his unfortunate wound.

"Whaddaya takin' me in for?" he asks as they slap handcuffs around his bandaged arm. "I didn't do nothin'."

Randy fails to make bail, so that evening as he sits in the Northampton County Prison he fills out an application for a free public defender attorney.

- - -

I received notice of my newest assignment the next morning. It was the summer of 1974, and the world was an uncomplicated place. I just didn't know it at the time. No terrorists lurking in the shadows, no airport paranoia, no e-mail, no fax machines, no DNA evidence. I rang the bell at the prison door and 10 minutes later I was sitting face to face with Simonetta in his claustrophobic cell. No pat-down search, no sterile prison interview room, no video surveillance and no nervous guards with earphone headsets. Just Simonetta, a toilet, a bed and iron bars. He chose the toilet, so I sat on the bed.

Back then I actually made money at the practice of law. Having no secretary, no cell phone, no office and no overhead helped quite a bit. I got paid $50 for every guilty plea I attended and $150 for every jury trial - win, lose, or draw. In a good week, I could gross $300 and keep most of it. Nowadays I generate fees substantial enough that my CPA has convinced me to employ a bookkeeper to monitor the accounts, but at the end of the week I usually learn that I went a little deeper into the red. The CPA calls it the "positive retention of negative cash flow."

I took a look at my newest client. An army dog tag hung around his 18-inch neck. He hadn't shaved in a week. He looked quite content. Prison seemed to agree with him.

"You gonna ask me some lawyer questions, or just watch me sit on this here turlit?"

That inquiry helped me to collect my thoughts.

"You bet," I assured this gorilla-shaped linebacker. "Now let's see here ... " I mused as I flipped through the file, "... the police report reflects that a bloody towel bearing the three initials of the owner of the burglarized household was found in the emergency admissions room waste basket."

"What's your point, counselor?" inquisitive Simonetta asked. "Does that report claim that someone saw me walk in with the towel or toss it in the garbage?"

"No ... it doesn't."

"Then some other burglar probably brought that towel to the hospital. When I was treated, I was wearing a white hospital towel that they gave me."

"The report says they found glass shards in your arm similar to the glass from the broken window."

"So what? It just so happens there's a broken window at my house, too. I tripped and my arm went through it a day or so before I was arrested. The cops didn't give me a chance to show them."

Perhaps Simonetta wasn't quite as dumb as his first impression suggested.

"The fact is several people showed up at the hospital while I was there, and if memory serves, most of them were bleeding. That's probably why they was there."

It was hard to argue with Simonetta's logic.

"You tell the D.A. I want a jury trial. I ain't pleading to nothin'."

Three months later Simonetta and I sat shoulder to shoulder at the defense table in courtroom number three as we faced 12 jurors and Judge Grifo. Overeager Assistant District Attorney Feinstein was prepared to proceed. He called the arresting officer as his first witness. Sergeant Miller testified that he found a bloody towel in a waste can next to where Simonetta had been sitting. Mr. McGlochlin advised the jury that the towel was his and that it was stolen from his house. Dr. Mortimer described the defendant's wounds and opined that the injury was consistent with lacerations received from a glass window. The doctor noted that he removed glass window shards from Simonetta's arm.

Feinstein wasn't done. He decided to put the icing on the cake. He called Dr. Daniel Stubbs to the witness stand.

"Who's he?" I whispered to Simonetta.

"Beats me," my client-brute responded, "but he looks sorta familiar."

"Please state your name," spunky Feinstein began.

"Daniel Stubbs, M.D.," the 60-something, bifocal-bedecked, distinguished gentleman responded.

"Your profession?"

"Northampton County prison physician."

Simonetta came to life as he tugged at my sleeve. "Now I recall. That guy gave me a physical when they locked me up. Tuberculosis test, drug screen, blood pressure, the works."

"Doctor, are you acquainted with the defendant?" Spunky continued.

"Yes, I gave him an admissions physical at the prison."

"Objection, your honor," I called out as I rose to my feet. "The fact that my client was incarcerated is prejudicial."

"Sustained," Judge Grifo agreed as he turned to the jury. "Ladies and gentlemen, you are directed to disregard the fact that the defendant may have been incarcerated. That is not an indication of guilt."

That instruction gave me a warm and fuzzy feeling, and I'm sure the jury complied. If I noticed an elephant standing in the public library reading room and someone told me to ignore the three-ton mammal, I'd have no problem erasing the image from my mind. Elephant? What elephant?

Spunky was on a roll. "Now, Doctor, did part of your physical include a blood test?"

"Yes, I drew the defendant's blood."

"Doctor, did you at my request analyze the blood found on the victim's towel, the towel stolen from his house and retrieved at the hospital?"

"Yes."

"Did you also at my request analyze the blood found at the scene of the burglary?"

"Yes."

"Did you reach any specific conclusion?"

"Yes, the defendant's blood type is B-negative. The blood on the towel is B-negative. The blood at the crime scene is B-negative."

The only person sitting with me was Simonetta, so I had a good idea who might be tugging again at my sleeve.

"Fox!"

"What?"

"My blood type is A-positive!"

I looked Simonetta in the eye. "Says who?"

"Me, the U.S. Army, and this here dog tag hangin' around my neck."

"Is it possible you really aren't the burglar after all!" I blurted out in hushed amazement. Was this clown actually innocent and unjustly imprisoned for the last three months? Did everyone around here, including me, owe this guy an apology for presuming that he was guilty?

"I wouldn't go that far," honest Simonetta replied. "But I'd venture to guess that the good Dr. Stubbs sitting over there on the witness stand screwed up the blood-type identification testing procedure. I mean, think about it. If he were competent, do you think he'd be content day after day treating bums like me in the prison?"

I was beginning to experience some fondness for Simonetta. After all, he didn't kill people or sell drugs to kids. He just broke into empty houses and stole towels and silverware.

The judge interrupted my thoughts. "Mr. Fox, the hour is late. You may cross-examine this witness tomorrow morning. We'll resume trial at nine a.m. Court stands in recess."

Everyone went home except Simonetta, who was led back to prison. I had work to do. I located Philip Schlechter, a phlebotomist, and drove him over to the prison for a late-night extraction of some more of Simonetta's blood. Sure enough, this test concluded that Simonetta had A-positive corpuscles cruising through his veins. Schlechter took the stand the next morning and confirmed that the U.S. Army and Simonetta's dog tags were correct. That constant, annoying smile began to abandon Feinstein's pudgy face as the jury took on a collective appearance of confusion.

Unfortunately for Feinstein, he couldn't re-test the original blood samples to determine if Dr. Stubbs had made a mistake, since Feinstein knew he would be precluded from submitting rebuttal evidence that served only to impeach his own witness. He was stuck with the testimony he had initially entered on the record.

By mid-afternoon the jury retired to commence their deliberations. Legal counsel may not leave the courthouse during deliberations, since the jury may request further instructions or the judge may need to consult with counsel. For two days I sat in the law library pursuing legal research as the jury churned over the contradictory evidence.

- - -

As I have written these stories, I have maintained the philosophy that in the practice of law the end result is insignificant and that the reader need not concern himself or herself with the outcome. What is important is the road traveled and the elephants in the library that had to be ignored. It doesn't really matter whether Simonetta was found guilty or innocent. After all, the fancy towel was already ruined and Mr. McGlochlin didn't want it back.

But just this once I'm going to bend slightly, so that those of you who just *must* know may learn of Simonetta's fate. This trial actually did take place, the blood test was mis-identified, the jury did engage in deliberations for two days, and finally did return with an unanimous verdict. You may telephone the Northampton County Clerk of Criminal Courts Office at 610-559-3097 and ask for the official docket entry at number 277 May Term of 1974. If you are patient the clerk will locate the formal verdict slip and read it to you.